OP

11 $\frac{00}{-}$

CHURCH AND STATE
IN ENGLISH EDUCATION

Church and State in English Education

1870 TO THE PRESENT DAY

BY

MARJORIE CRUICKSHANK

WITH A FOREWORD BY

THE RT. HON. R. A. BUTLER, C.H., M.P.

LONDON
MACMILLAN & CO LTD
NEW YORK · ST MARTIN'S PRESS
1963

MACMILLAN AND COMPANY LIMITED
St Martin's Street London WC 2
also Bombay Calcutta Madras Melbourne

THE MACMILLAN COMPANY OF CANADA LIMITED
Toronto

ST MARTIN'S PRESS INC
New York

PRINTED IN GREAT BRITAIN

TO

D. W. J. C.

Foreword

————— ❊ —————

I<small>T</small> is fortunate that Mrs Cruickshank extended her original studies of the dual system in modern dress to cover the story of Church and State in our Education system. The result is a well-balanced historical survey ranging from the day when education received a grant of £20,000 from public funds to the present time when taxpayer and ratepayer carry a burden of hundreds of millions of pounds and appear to ask for more.

All the main bills or abortive measures are covered. Balfour's settlement of 1902, based on the plans of the forceful Morant, stands scrutiny well, lasting as it did over the Fisher period and up to 1936 and 1944. The author brings out the similarity between the Birrell Bill of 1906 and my 'White Memorandum' of the early 1940's. It is entertaining to note that Birrell was accused of starting a new creed, 'Birreligion'. William Temple to whom the 1944 plan owed so much asked me if I was starting a State religion based on the agreed syllabuses. This is not the only cord which binds together the various understandings or attempts to reach agreement between Church and State. In each case the student of history or human nature will be fascinated to follow the complexity of the puzzle and the passionate irreconcilability of opposite forces.

In each case where agreement was reached, or nearly reached, the protagonist, whether Forster, Balfour, Birrell, Oliver Stanley, or the faithful team who served me and Church Edc, recognised one key, that is the secular determination not to permit denominational teaching in State schools. This is stressed in a letter from Morant to the then Duke of Devonshire. It was when William Temple 'kissed Cowper-Temple' that my settlement was found.

Instead of the 'facilities' for the Church schools of Birrell's Bill my friends and I invented Controlled and Aided Schools. We have been rewarded by the great effort made by Anglicans and Roman Catholics alike to build their own schools in larger numbers than we expected, so large and so expensive in fact that the grant has had to be raised to 75%.

This excellent and objective study leaves one in some doubt whether the Scottish system will ever be adopted south of the Border. But the glowing embers of 1870 and 1902 had so much died in force by my time that almost any development can be envisaged in future years provided that religion is 'caught and not taught' in denominational schools and that council schools conduct their teaching on the non-denominational syllabus.

It is with confidence and pleasure that I now entrust the Reader to be guided through the maze by the clarity and skill of the Author.

R. A. Butler.

Preface

————— ❊ —————

THIS book is the outcome of invitations by the Rt. Hon. R. A. Butler first to write the history of the religious settlement of the 1944 Education Act and then to extend my field of research to the origin and development of the dual system. I should like to express my very deep gratitude to Mr Butler who has given me most valuable information and advice and who has obtained for me access to source materials. I am further indebted to him for his kindness in writing the Foreword to this book.

I should also like to thank Sir John Maud, formerly Permanent Secretary to the Ministry of Education, for permission to use appropriate archives in the preparation of my earlier theses, 'The Reform of the Dual System in England and Wales, 1941–1944' (University of London, M.A. 1950), and 'The History of the Dual System in England and Wales, 1870–1944' (University of Leeds, Ph.D. 1955) which contain more detailed and fully documented accounts. For the later chapters of the present work it has only been possible to refer the reader to published records.

I am grateful to those who have given me access to the source materials in their care, to the Rev. H. A. S. Pink, formerly Secretary of the National Society, to Mr R. A. G. O'Brien, formerly Secretary of the Catholic Education Council, to Mr E. R. Hamilton, formerly Principal of Borough Road Training College, to Dr E. W. Baker, formerly Secretary of the Methodist Education Committee and to officials of the Education Offices of Birmingham, Leeds, London and Manchester. I should also like to thank Miss P. M. Downie, Chief Librarian of the Ministry of Education, for her helpful co-operation.

I am very appreciative of the assistance given to me in the early stages of my research by Mr A. C. F. Beales of King's College, University of London. I also consider myself fortunate that I had talks some years ago with both the late Dr Scott Lidgett and the late Bishop Brown of Pella, who were able to draw on their recollections of past educational controversies and negotiations.

I am grateful to the University of Leeds for providing me with the opportunity and facilities for research. Among my former colleagues at Leeds I should like to thank Mr W. E. Tate and Dr L. Connell for their critical perusal of my typescript and for their advice.

In a very special sense I am indebted to my husband who has read my text many times and in many forms. While disclaiming any knowledge of history or any acquaintance with the niceties of English style, he has brought his scientific mind to bear upon my work by insisting on orderliness, clarity and simplicity. Needless to say, I hold myself entirely responsible for faults which remain.

Contents

———— ❋ ————

Abbreviations

———— ❉ ————

B.M.	British Museum
C.E.C.	Catholic Education Council
Minutes	Minutes of the Committee of Council
N.S.	National Society
Parl. Deb.	Parliamentary Debates
P.P.	Parliamentary Papers
P.R.O.	Public Record Office
Reports	Reports of the Committee of Council, of the Education Department, of the Board of Education and of the Ministry of Education

Introduction

———— ❉ ————

*A national system of education is the outcome of national
history.*

M. E. SADLER

To foreign observers and indeed to laymen of our own country
the educational system of England and Wales presents a bewilder-
ing picture of illogicalities and inconsistencies. Its ragged and
untidy shape can be explained only in terms of the past. Unlike
continental systems it has never been planned and conceived as a
whole; rather it has evolved gradually over a period of a century
and a half, influenced by private endeavour and group action, and
adapted by adjustment and compromise to embrace a variety of
opinions. Responsive to changing national needs and to public
demand it has emerged with all the complexities and diversities
which we see today, a peculiar combination of freedom and
authority, individual initiative and collective control.

Perhaps no single feature of the present system is more difficult
to grasp and comprehend than the place in it of the denominational school. In our own hedonistic age, when the emphasis is on
the things of this world, no more than a small minority of the
nation profess and practise a religious faith. Yet there is in the
State organisation of education a dual system; there are two sorts
of schools, those owned by the public authorities and those owned
by the churches, the latter teaching the faith and doctrine of
particular denominations.

The roots of the dual system lie deep in the past. Indeed, to
understand their origin we must go back to the middle ages when
the Church, as the great matrix of Christendom founded and
nourished educational institutions of all kinds, when schools were
an essential part of ecclesiastical organisation combining religious
and secular teaching as one. In the words of Newman, 'Not a man
in Europe who talks bravely against the Church but owes it to
the Church that he can talk at all.' It was this control of education

which the Church of England claimed in the nineteenth century when, inspired by the desire to save souls, she built large numbers of elementary schools for the instruction of the children of the poor. So numerous and so widespread were the foundations of the Established Church (and to a lesser extent of other denominations) that, when at last the State intervened in education in 1870, it was impracticable to dispossess those already in the field and start afresh. The new national system was therefore organised as a partnership between the denominations on the one hand and the new public authorities on the other. But the very terms of partnership, by placing them at financial disadvantage, bore harshly on the denominations and condemned them to fight a losing battle with wealthier rivals. Before the end of the nineteenth century and during the early decades of the twentieth century the churches surrendered numbers of their schools, yet the denominational system survived in considerable strength and by its survival confounded those who had longed for its complete submergence within the public system. Through the years of hardship and strain the vitality of the denominational principle had been enduring and unmistakable. As Mr R. A. Butler has said, speaking of the 1944 settlement, 'no single step would have made the education service simpler or tidier than to transfer voluntary schools to the ownership and total control of the State or local education authorities. But simplicity and tidiness are not the relevant criteria and few steps would have been more stupid.'[1]

Denominational endeavour, one of the main strands visible throughout the nineteenth and twentieth centuries, has been inextricably woven into the present system. A second strand discernible throughout the pattern of events has been the influence of Nonconformity. In the early years of the nineteenth century, Nonconformists joined in the pioneer work of education but, in contrast to the practice of the Established Church, they confined religious instruction in their schools to simple Bible teaching. Rivalry between the two religious groups bred feelings of suspicion and distrust which persisted long after the Nonconformists had merged their own schools into the public system and lingered far into the twentieth century. With their bitter memories of the past, Nonconformists have resented denominationalist claims on the public purse and have looked forward to

[1] University of London Institute of Education, *Jubilee Lectures*, 1952, 46.

the day when all schools should be controlled entirely by elected bodies, but they have always insisted that undenominational religious instruction should be available for all children and it is this which is their great positive contribution to the present-day public system.

Secularist opinion has represented a third strand in the history of English education. In greater or lesser strength there have always been those who have urged a complete break with the past. Left-wingers in politics, they have, in their enthusiasm for educational progress, sought to cut the tangled skein of religious control and start afresh; the Radicals of the nineteenth century deplored the dual system from its very foundation, the Socialists and Trade Unionists of the twentieth century have fulminated against the delays and frustrations which dual control has imposed. Nevertheless, despite the logic of their views and despite the pressures they have brought to bear, they have never rallied the country as a whole and have never decisively influenced practical politics.

The fierce rivalries of the day were reflected in the dual system of 1870. In the circumstances a simple solution to the educational problem was judged impossible and what emerged was a compromise between the two extremes, between those who wanted the Church to control education and those who wanted a completely secular system. On grounds of economy also the settlement was in tune with the times, for it was designed to secure literacy 'on the cheap' and by using existing agencies to keep public expenditure as low as possible. The dual system was therefore a product of an age which, still unconvinced of the need for education, desired only the most meagre form of popular instruction. Rising standards of education inevitably compelled adjustments in the financial terms of 1870, but the successive settlements, while modifying the details, have continued to place denominational schools at a disadvantage. To twentieth-century reformers any revision of the dual system has posed a major political problem for, although the old passion and fury have largely subsided, they have left 'submerged rocks' which the unwary and the incautious have ignored at their peril. The real tragedy is that with so many attempts at legislation wrecked and abandoned, educational progress has been retarded and hopes of advance frustrated.

The layman may doubt whether the dual system, wasteful as it is in time and money, is worth preserving. He may regard with envy more logical solutions adopted in other democratic countries; on the one hand, the purely secular education of the United States where denominational enterprise is restricted to private schools, or, on the other hand, the complete financing of denominational schools at public expense as in Scotland or the Netherlands. But the historical background in England and Wales has been unique. For there has never been, as in the United States, strict separation of Church and State. Nor is there a close parallel with the situations in Scotland or in the Netherlands, where settlements have been between Catholics on the one hand and a single coherent body of Protestants on the other. Elsewhere, as in France and Belgium, the issue of Government subsidies to religious schools has brought even more rancour and political strife. The problem of the part which denominational schools play in a national system of education is common to all countries. The solution depends on history as well as on contemporary opinion.

———————— ❈ ————————

Chapter 1

The State and Elementary Education before 1870

Throughout the middle ages education was under the complete control of the Church. In the sixteenth century the main groups of Reformers of this island, Anglican and Presbyterian, assumed a like control, claiming in accordance with the principle of 'cuius regio, eius religio' that Church and State were one. Indeed, in Scotland, where the Presbyterians worked out a logical system of education, the Kirk had undisputed authority over educational foundations of all kinds. There 'new presbyter was but old priest writ large' and parish schools were an integral part of ecclesiastical discipline. In England, however, the coherence and comprehensiveness of the Scottish provision were lacking and, though the right to teach was restricted to sound Anglicans and, in theory at least, the conduct of schools was placed under episcopal control and regulated by visitation injunctions, the Established Church in fact never moulded a national system of education. In the seventeenth century, political and religious cleavage split the nation in two and it was this deep rift between Church and Dissent persisting into the nineteenth century which embittered national life and brought educational strife in the new industrial age. On the question of religious teaching men differed profoundly, and the Anglican claim to control the schools became a paramount issue in the conflict between the Establishment and Nonconformity.

In the early years of the eighteenth century, religion and philanthropy had been the impelling motives in the foundation of a network of charity schools which were geared to the needs of a stable society. By the latter part of the century, however, growing industrialisation with its concentration of population in factory towns was transforming the old pattern of English life. The mass of factory workers were ignorant and uncivilised and their children were growing up without education, secular or religious. The great work of the churches and chapels during these years, the foundation of Sunday schools, was essentially a rescue operation to get the children off the streets and to inculcate in them some sense of decency and order. Indeed, in the history of Nonconformity the Sunday school movement has a special significance, for it was the only attempt the dissenting churches ever made to secure large-scale provision for popular education under their own control. Sunday schools fitted in very well with the climate of the age and were popular with employers and employees alike, but their teaching of the secular subjects was of the most meagre kind. Day schools alone could provide efficient instruction and with the introduction at the end of the century of a novel method of teaching, the monitorial system, the attractive prospect was opened up of mass education at a minimum cost. The pioneer school, established by a Quaker, Joseph Lancaster, in Borough Road, Southwark, drew considerable support, but it also roused antagonism from Anglicans who were opposed to the non-sectarian character of Lancaster's teaching and they prevailed upon Dr Andrew Bell, an Anglican clergyman, who had earlier used the monitorial system in Madras, to organise Anglican schools upon similar lines in this country. Partisans rallying round the two men organised rival societies: the British and Foreign School Society, established originally as the Royal Lancasterian Society in 1808, was supported by members of the dissenting congregations and by a number of Liberal Churchmen; the National Society for Promoting the Education of the Poor in the Principles of the Established Church, founded in 1811, had the backing of the great body of Anglicans. The two Societies, representing the fundamental cleavage in religious opinion, were to dominate English elementary education for the greater part of the nineteenth century. Both Societies had the same objective, the salvation of souls and the permeation of all instruction by religion, but whereas the British and Foreign School Society, with one conception of religion, advocated simple Bible teaching, the National Society, inspired by a different ideal, insisted on the teaching of the doctrines and liturgy of the Established Church. These conflicting principles led to a bitter and prolonged controversy in which each group accused the other of the most wicked intentions. The fanaticism and intolerance of the age were reflected in the vehemence of the struggle, which served, however, a useful purpose in stimulating the rival societies to greater efforts. Very soon the greater resources of the National Society enabled it to draw ahead of its rival. Indeed, one of the most conspicuous features of the period was the zeal of the parochial clergy whose efforts were so fruitful that by the early 1830's there were in existence a large number of parish schools, including some 3,500 connected with the National Society.[1]

Not surprisingly attempts to secure State intervention were baulked for many years by religious antagonisms and it was not until 1833, the year following the First Reform Act, that the State made its first gesture towards education, a subsidy of £20,000 towards the cost of building schools attached to the two voluntary Societies. As yet, there was no suggestion of authority or control over the schools themselves, but six years later, in 1839, the Whig Government launched their plans for State control: the creation of a Committee of Privy Councillors responsible for the distribution of Parliamentary grants, the establishment of a system of inspection of all schools participating in the grants, and, lastly, the foundation of a nonsectarian State normal school for the training of teachers.[2] The new State policy came at the very climax of the Anglican revival and it was the supporters of the new Oxford movement, the Tractarians, who were fiercest in their denunciation. So intense was the opposition by the Church as a whole to the proposed State normal school that on this issue the Government surrendered. It was highly significant, however, that it retained and put into force the plan for a central Committee, which in the course of time was to grow and develop into a major department of State. On the question of Government Inspectorship, there was a long and bitter struggle until in 1840 the Committee of Council, guided by its Secretary, Dr Kay (later to become Sir James Kay-Shuttleworth), offered satisfactory terms: the extension of inspection to religious as well as secular instruction and the right of the Archbishops to nominate members of the Inspectorate.[3] The concordat, which embodied these terms, was a skilful compromise between the claims of Church and State. In the general reckoning, however, the State had strengthened and consolidated its powers, for it had established two fundamental

---

[1] *Report of National Society*, 1832, 10–11.   [2] *Parl. Deb.*, 3rd Ser., vol. xiv, col. 273.
[3] *Minutes*, P.P. 1845 [22] I, 3–4.

principles, the right to promote the extension and improvement of elementary education, and the right to inspect its secular efficiency. By 1840, therefore, it had entered into a more active partnership with the churches. Its first step in 1833 had been cautious and hesitant; its policy at the end of the decade was positive and definite.

Dissenters had welcomed the Government scheme for non-sectarian education and had contested the claims of the Establishment at every step. Naturally, they were more kindly disposed than the Anglicans to the whole principle of State action; it was the State which, in the past, had removed many of their legal disabilities and it was to the State and, in particular, to the Whigs, that they looked for the abolition of Church rates and for the establishment of a national system of education. On the Tories' return to power in 1841, therefore, the Dissenters were naturally apprehensive, and their suspicions were confirmed by the publication in the Spring of 1843 of Graham's Factory Bill, which proposed to vest control of the new factory schools in representatives of the Church of England. Throughout the country Dissenters rose in protest and even the Wesleyans, members of the largest and most conservative of the Nonconformist churches, were now so thoroughly roused by fear of Tractarianism that they too swelled the opposition. Despite Graham's efforts to amend the offending clauses, the Dissenters' wrath continued unabated and the Bill had to be withdrawn. It was, in fact, a very slight educational measure — Richard Cobden calculated that it would provide for only 60,000 children — yet, for the Nonconformists, the principles involved were vital since it was an attack on their own ground, an insidious attempt to undermine their influence in the manufacturing districts. After 1843, therefore, many of them ceased to look to Parliament for help and support. Instead they adopted the principle of Voluntaryism, of the non-interference of the State in education, and determined to build schools entirely from their own resources.

There were, in fact, now three important groups prepared to press their views on education and working strenuously to achieve their ends: the members of the Established Church, the dissenting Voluntaryists and the Radicals who wanted a secular State system. Between these extreme groups there were various gradations and shades of opinion.

The Church of England as a body was devoted to its schools but some of its members were more vigorous than others in asserting the Church's right to determine educational policy. In recent years doctrinal differences had split the Church in two; on the one side stood the Evangelicals and Broad Churchmen; on the other, the Tractarians. The National Society itself was one of the main centres of conflict. Clergy of both sections were dedicated to their schools, subscribing generously from their small stipends and serving in the capacity of treasurers, secretaries, managers and teachers. Indeed, they were unstinting in the sacrifices they made. The clergyman, in the words of a later report, 'begs from his neighbours, he begs from the landowners; if he fails to persuade them to take their fair share of the burden, he begs from his friends and even from strangers; at last he submits most meritoriously and most generously, to bear not only his own proportion of the expenses, but also that which ought to be borne by others.'[1] The great difference between the parties was on the issue of State intervention. While the Evangelicals wanted co-operation with the State, the Tractarians, led by Archdeacons Denison and Manning, stood for exclusive clerical control over the schools. They were the 'medieval party' of the Church, denying to the State any role in education save that of paymaster and, as the dominant group in the National Society, they were prepared to resist any attempt by the State to restrict their independence. Yet, though the Tractarians were deeply resentful of State interference, they were not unwilling to accept State aid. Their objection was to the conditions attached to such aid, particularly to the right of inspection. (As one High Church clergyman put it, he 'would never permit an emissary of Lord John Russell, or any other Turkish Bashaw, to enter his school'.) Accordingly, their efforts were concentrated on modifying these conditions and in defending the schools from the encroaching powers of the State.

Dissenting extremists pursued a more logical policy than the High Church party. As Voluntaryists they repudiated not merely State direction but State aid as well and, according to the principle of 'ourselves alone', they prepared to build and support schools entirely from private resources. The movement was enthusiastically supported by Congregationalists and Baptists. Within two and a half years the Congregationalists alone, under the leadership

[1] *Newcastle Commission*, P.P. 1861 [2794-1] xxi, 78.

of Samuel Morley, had collected £100,000 and had established 147 schools.[1] Three years later they founded their own training college at Homerton, near Cambridge. The educational standpoint of the Voluntaryists was simple and straightforward. They assumed two premises: firstly, that education must be religious or it would be worthless and, secondly, that the State must not meddle with religion. They concluded, therefore, that the education of the people was not the function of the State. Yet they had reached this conclusion belatedly; in fact, the greatest weakness of their argument was that, as supporters of the British schools, many of them had co-operated with the State for a period of ten years. There was no doubt that their present opposition to State aid was political as well as religious in origin. It was part of the individualistic philosophy of the Manchester School, part of the popular doctrine of *laissez-faire*, that any interference with private enterprise or individual undertaking tended to stultify, to deaden and to destroy. They had adapted the principle of free trade in food and in commerce; they now extended that doctrine to education.

Dissenters, however, were a heterogeneous body and on education, as on many issues, they were divided and subdivided into different groups. In addition to the Voluntaryists, there were many who still adhered to the British and Foreign School Society; others, members of the powerful Wesleyan Methodist Church, were also organising their own schools on a voluntary basis and were not averse to State aid. By 1843 the Wesleyans had 290 day schools financed entirely out of their own resources[2] though it was not until four years later that they decided to co-operate with the State and accept public aid. Their objective was the building of a great network of schools; in the words of their Education Committee's Report of 1847, 'No chapel will be complete in all the great practical objects for which chapels are, or ought to be, intended, unless there be found in immediate connection with it an efficient day school.'[3] Wesleyan policy was midway between that of the two existing Societies: unlike the National Society, the Wesleyan body found no difficulty in accepting a Conscience Clause[4] and admitting children of other denominations in its

---

[1] *Congregational Year Book,* 1846, 48.
[2] *Report of Wesleyan Education Committee,* 1843, Appendix, 'Summary of Schools'.
[3] *Ibid.,* 1847, 22–3.   [4] See p. 10.

schools; unlike the British and Foreign School Society it insisted on imparting denominational instruction. All three religious associations were now assisted and supervised by the State, but they were supervised only by Inspectors whose appointments they had themselves approved.

The Radicals stood apart as a minority group advocating a national system of secular education controlled and directed by the State. J. A. Roebuck, M.P. for Sheffield, had long championed the Radical solution in Parliament; the Chartists had adopted it in their programme of social reform. In the late 1840's the movement was to gain important recruits, men who like Cobden were not so much opposed to religious instruction inside the school as repelled by religious wrangling outside. Despairing of educational progress so long as energies were absorbed in sectarian strife they adopted the secular solution in the hope that it might prove a short cut to educational advance. They were able to claim support of politically conscious members of the working class who longed in vain for the denominations to abandon their differences and who, while the controversy waxed hotter and more furious, lamented that their little ones were being forgotten. In an age of deep spiritual concern, however, opposition to the secular solution was overwhelming. Despite their differences, denominationalists were united in their belief that religious and secular education were inseparable, united also in their faith in the philanthropic and personal value of voluntary work and in their distrust of the bureaucratic powers of the State.

★   ★   ★   ★   ★

The lessons of 1839 and 1843 made future Governments very cautious in dealing with educational problems. In the words of Lord Ashley, later the Earl of Shaftesbury, 'united education is an impossibility. The Dissenters and the Church have each laid down limits they will not pass, and there is no power that can either force, persuade or delude them.'[1] Nevertheless, working within these limits the State was determined to secure the efficiency of secular instruction and, when the Whigs came to power again in 1846, they immediately sought to improve educational standards by raising the qualifications of the teachers and, in particular, by

[1] Parker, *Sir Robert Peel* (1899) II, 561–2.

replacing the old monitorial teaching by a more efficient pupil-teacher system. They proposed, therefore, to contribute towards teachers' salaries and accordingly, in the Minutes of Council of 1846, they regulated the qualifications of teachers and the position of pupil-teachers and monitors. The Dissenters were immediately up in arms and even members of the British and Foreign School Society were reluctant to accept this new measure of State interference. Once again all parties, Churchmen, Dissenters and secularists, flung themselves into the political conflict. Naturally, Anglicans found no difficulty in accepting additional aid. Dissenters, on the other hand, denounced the proposals as a further attempt to subject them to clerical and bureaucratic influences and the Voluntaryists, in particular, were so alarmed that they organised themselves into a distinct political group and put forward a number of independent candidates at the 1847 election.

In the course of the debate Lord John Russell had hinted that the new regulations[1] might be extended to apply to Roman Catholic schools, and in 1847 the Catholic Poor School Committee was formed as the official body to receive Parliamentary grants. Roman Catholics were in an exceptional position. The Irish famine of 1845–6 had started a great influx of Irish immigrants, who swarmed in their thousands into the industrial areas. There, huddled together in conditions of abject poverty, they sought to earn a living as unskilled labourers. By 1849 there were said to be 80,000 Irish in Manchester and 100,000 in Liverpool.[2] The whole problem of educational destitution was aggravated enormously and the English Catholics found themselves faced with the impossible task of providing schools for the children of their Irish co-religionists. In other religious communities the rich had some natural connection with the poor, either as landowners or as factory masters. The English Catholics, on the other hand, were called upon to provide education for the children of thousands who were not the natural growth of their own poor and whose poverty was not counterbalanced by any abundance in their own riches. The Irish immigration had a most potent effect on the English imagination; it revived old suspicions of Roman Catholicism as a force alien in spirit and disloyal to the traditional English way of life. This sinister, irrational fear of Popery,

---

[1] Dated August and December 1846, P.P. 1847 [787] II, 10.
[2] *Parl. Deb.*, 3rd Ser., vol. xci, col. 1212.

persisted through the century and still further aggravated educational controversy. By 1850 some 500 Roman Catholic schools had been built,[1] but the poorest areas, unable to raise the necessary voluntary contributions, remained without schools for many years. Wherever Roman Catholic schools were established they catered for a more depressed section of the populace than did the British, the Wesleyan or even the National schools. No schools save the Ragged schools, which had been founded specially for the waifs and strays of the great towns and cities, were touching a similar class of children.[2]

The middle years of the century brought new conflict between Church and State when the Committee of Council took steps to limit clerical control of the schools. Already in 1839–40 the Committee had published specimen Management Clauses,[3] designed to increase lay influence but these had been put forward merely as suggestions and there had been no question of compulsory adoption. However, in 1847 there was a radical change of policy when the Committee insisted on the insertion of one or other of these clauses in the trust deeds of grant aided schools. The compulsory imposition, which was agreed to without much difficulty by both Wesleyans and Roman Catholics,[4] roused a storm of protest from Anglicans. Again it was the Tractarians led by Denison and Manning, who denounced the new State policy and urged the members of the National Society to preserve clerical control, even if, in the last resort, they had to repudiate State assistance altogether. However, the Committee stuck to its guns. It was true that certain minor alterations in the Management Clauses were made at the request of the National Society,[5] but these were far from satisfying the extremists. Denison was bitterly disappointed and denounced State interference. 'I will fight till I die for the Catholic Church of England. I will not move one finger for a Church which negotiates with the House of Commons, or any of its creatures, about the means of discharging the trust committed to her by God.'[6] In fact the National Society never

[1] Report of Catholic Poor School Committee, 1849, Appendix N.
[2] Kay-Shuttleworth, Public Education, 145.
[3] Minutes, P.P. 1847 [787] 25–33.
[4] The question was never one of dispute with the Wesleyans. A compromise was finally arranged with the Catholic Poor School Committee. Report of the Catholic Poor School Committee, 1850, Appendix K.
[5] Minutes, P.P. 1849 [1090] 29–34.   [6] Denison, Fifty Years at East Brent, 26.

agreed to the Management Clauses which were imposed without its consent.[1]

In the 'fifties the Conscience Clause caused a new flare up in the controversy between Church and State. The Committee of Council now insisted on the insertion in trust deeds of a clause which would enable parents of other creeds to secure for their children entire exemption from all religious teaching. Under pressure from the Tractarians the National Society made a firm stand; it declared that, though individual requests might be granted as favours, the general principle could not be conceded as a right.[2] The dispute dragged on for many years with Archdeacon Denison once again rallying the opposition. He had for a time withdrawn from the National Society as a protest against what he considered its weak and vacillating policy, but in the 'sixties he was back again, the very soul of resistance to public intervention, urging Churchmen to greater effort in order that they might dispense with Government aid altogether. In one important respect the Conscience Clause dispute differed from the earlier struggle between Church and State. For the first time the Dissenters were directly and intimately involved; for the first time, therefore, the Church found herself in conflict with a powerful combination. Final defeat was inevitable. Perhaps nothing in the educational controversies of the nineteenth century did more to inflame denominational bitterness than the Anglican refusal to concede rights of conscience, for it bred deep resentment and distrust which were to rankle in dissenting hearts for many years to come. Herein lay the problem of the single-school area, where there was only one school and that a Church school. The Dissenters were never reconciled to the Anglican monopoly of the village schools, and right into the twentieth century they had good cause to regard it as the most humiliating of their injustices.

During the years 1847–57 all attempts at educational legislation had failed. There had, however, been a steady expansion of the State's activity. In 1847 the State was spending £100,000 on education, in 1857, £500,000.[3] In 1847 it had spent public money only on school buildings; ten years later it was contributing towards teachers' salaries, towards the provision of apparatus and,

[1] Burgess, *Enterprise in Education*, 156–7.
[2] *Report of National Society*, 1860, Appendix XI.
[3] Summaries of Statistics. *Minutes*, P.P. 1847 [787], P.P. 1857 [2237].

by means of capitation grants, towards the annual income of the schools. Nevertheless, it was clear that under the existing arrangement the religious bodies could not provide and maintain the number of schools necessary for a national system. Accordingly, in 1858, a Royal Commission under the chairmanship of the Duke of Newcastle was established to inquire into the state of popular education and to consider the necessary steps to be taken 'for the extension of sound and cheap elementary instruction to all classes of the people'. The Commissioners, in their report published in 1861, estimated that of a child population of $2\frac{1}{2}$ millions only $1\frac{1}{2}$ millions were at school and that only half of these were at inspected schools.[1] They agreed that the voluntary system was the only acceptable system and that the secular system had won no wide support in the country. Though the Minority still clung to Voluntaryist doctrines, the Majority advocated the extension of the existing system by the distribution of two sorts of grant, one from State taxes depending on average attendance and one from county rates depending on results of examination in the 'three R's'.[2] Rate aid, however, would have introduced the religious dispute into local politics and so the Vice-President of the Council, Robert Lowe, rejected the proposal but in his Code of 1861 he adopted the suggestion of payment by results. Despite opposition from members of all denominations, who regarded the Code as a deliberate policy of secularisation, it was, with only slight modifications, in force from 1862. Though tragic in many respects, in its stunting of the curriculum and its degradation of the teaching profession, the experiment was not wholly disastrous. Between 1863 and 1869 over 1,000 new schools were opened and 300,000 more children were in attendance, with greater regularity and for longer periods than formerly.[3] Nevertheless, there remained formidable gaps in the supply of schools and there were vast areas of educational destitution in the industrial towns where large numbers of children had never set foot in school at all. For example, according to one of the Liverpool magistrates, there were in 1869 from 25,000 to 30,000 children wandering about on the streets of that city, 'learning habits of vagrancy, mendicancy and crime.'[4]

[1] Newcastle Commission, op. cit., 278.   [2] Ibid., 301–8.
[3] Reports, P.P. 1863 [3171], P.P. 1870 [C. 406] Statistics of Inspections.
[4] Parl. Deb., 3rd Ser., vol. cxciv, col. 1194.

During the 'sixties the principle of educating the poor had come to be generally accepted, even if only for reasons of political expediency. The task, however, was completely beyond the resources of the voluntary societies and, despite the opposition of the National Society, rate aid in some form became inevitable. The thorough-going secularist solution was never popular and with the decline of Radicalism its possibility had receded into the background. Instead, various compromises were suggested. In 1867 a Manchester organisation, the Education Aid Society, sponsored legislation for permissive rate aid to voluntary schools,[1] and in the following year Robert Lowe advocated the establishment of local rate aid schools supplementary to existing voluntary effort.[2] Neither scheme was adopted, but both were to influence future legislation. Meanwhile the Nonconformists were reconsidering their educational policy, for Voluntaryism had proved a practical failure. Already a section of the Dissenters had adopted the principle of the separation of secular and religious instruction; now the great body of Voluntaryists shifted their position and, under the leadership of Rev. R. W. Dale of Birmingham, looked to the State to provide a national system of education.[3] By the closing years of the decade secularists and Voluntaryists had a good deal in common. Both were in favour of a State supported system but, while one party maintained that religious instruction should be excluded from the school curriculum, the other held that it should remain but it should be given independently of State payment and control.

Thirty years had passed since the first measure of State intervention in 1839. The intervening period had been one of continued progress. Twenty-four million pounds had been spent on elementary education from all sources and over $1\frac{3}{4}$ million school places had been provided, but it was significant that out of the total sum, no less than fifteen million pounds had been raised from local contributions, from voluntary subscriptions and endowments and from school pence.[4] Throughout the period the initiative had been taken by denominationalists who had organised their schools on the principle that religious and secular education were

---

[1] Bill introduced 5th April, 1867. *Parl. Deb.,* 3rd Ser., vol. clxxxvi, col. 1168.

[2] *The Times,* 25.1.68. Speech at Education Conference at Liverpool.

[3] Dale, *Life of R. W. Dale,* 158.

[4] Figures quoted by Earl de Grey, 25th July, 1870. *Parl. Deb.,* 3rd Ser., vol. cciii, col. 822.

inseparable. They had sought to cater for the children of the poor, for the offspring of those flooding into the industrial towns, but neither their resources nor their energies, great though they were, were equal to the task and the dregs of the child population remained largely untouched. The voluntary system was not for the poor, not for the urchins who swarmed in the streets of the great towns and cities, not for the unfortunates who were early absorbed in the mines and factories. For these, the children of the under-privileged, the State alone could provide. Yet the acceptance of the idea of education as the responsibility of the State had been long hindered by conflicts between religious and secular education, between the religious parties and the State. The problem was to find a common basis so that all parties could work side by side.

———————— ❋ ————————

Chapter 2

The Establishment of the
Dual System

By the end of the 'sixties the political climate was exceptionally favourable to educational advance. The death in 1865 of Lord Palmerston had completed the emancipation of the Liberal Party and Gladstone, the new leader, was eager for reform. On the opposite front bench Disraeli, who had spent long years educating his party to Tory democracy, had in 1867 succeeded in enfranchising the urban proletariat. Politically the Second Reform Act was a party bid for public support; educationally, it was, in Robert Lowe's words, a direct challenge 'to compel our future masters to learn their letters'.[1]

It was an age of fierce sectarian rivalry. Throughout the 'sixties until the final victory in 1868, the energies of Dissenters were absorbed in the struggle against Church rates. Thereafter, their objective was Disestablishment. It was to them anathema that the law of the land should recognise 'one man, and one man only, as the authorised religious teacher of the parish' and should regard all others as 'interlopers, trespassers, poachers on his spiritual preserve'.[2] Never had Dissent been so consciously and militantly political as at this time. The Second Reform Act, by enfranchising the ranks from which Nonconformists were drawn, greatly strengthened their power and influence and in fighting for their rights against a privileged State Church they became automatically the champions of the under-privileged working class. It was the inspiration of Nonconformist piety as well as the goad of economic injustice which had produced many of the working class leaders, men of burning sincerity who had learnt the art of oratory in their local chapels. The natural alliance of Dissent therefore was with

---

[1] *Parl. Deb.*, 3rd Ser., vol. clxxviii, col. 1549.
[2] *Ibid.*, 3rd Ser., vol. cxcix, cols. 1974–5.

the party of reform, with the Liberals, who, opposed to privilege in Church and State, aimed at sweeping away the obsolete survivals of an oligarchic past. Thus the Liberal Party drew much of its fire and fervour from Nonconformity while Dissent enjoyed a degree of power reminiscent of Commonwealth days. The Tory Party was, of course, traditionally Anglican; indeed, some Churchmen wistfully recalled the period when Church and State, at least in theory, had been coterminous. As members of a privileged State Church they inevitably stood for the *status quo*; in the industrial age their hostility to Chartism and to other reform movements had so alienated them from the mass of the people that Dr Hook, from his observations as Vicar of Leeds in the 1840's, could describe the Church as an 'object of detestation to the working classes'.[1] The Liberal emphasis, therefore, was on innovation and the rights of the individual; the Tory reverence was for tradition and for an hierarchical organisation in Church and State.

In November 1868, the newly enfranchised working class cast their vote and the first Liberal (as distinct from Whig) Government was formed with Gladstone as Prime Minister. One of the striking features of the election was the success of urban Radicalism: Henry Richard was returned by Merthyr Tydvil, George Anderson by Glasgow, Edward Miall by Bradford and A. J. Mundella by Sheffield. Other prominent Radicals included Sir Charles Dilke, William Harcourt, G. O. Trevelyan, Henry Fawcett and George Dixon. More liberal than the Liberals they were constantly spurring the main party on to swifter reform. But the Liberal Party as a whole had drawn support from many sections of the community and represented not only Nonconformists but also Broad Churchmen and Free Thinkers; indeed, it included every shade of political opinion from aristocratic Whiggery to extreme Radicalism. In the end the Cabinet which Gladstone selected was strongly aristocratic in character and sympathy. The Prime Minister was himself a curious political mixture, combining a profound veneration for the past with a passionate desire for political and social reform; his ministers, for the most part, came from the great Whig families. There was a Hyde, a Leveson Gower, a Wodehouse, a Robinson, a Campbell and a Cavendish. In fact, John Bright was the solitary representative of Radicalism, and even he was a Radical of the old school

[1] Stranks, *Dean Hook* (1954) 75.

who had little sympathy with the growing collectivism of the great industrial centres. However, Radical supporters were cheered by the appointment of W. E. Forster as Vice-President of the Committee of Council, while the early attack on the Established Church in Ireland put them in good heart.

It was the Radicals of Birmingham who provided in 1869 the powerful organisation for a national agitation, the National Education League, which immediately launched a widespread campaign for a universal system of education, free, compulsory and unsectarian, supported by rate aid and subject to public management. Politically the League was frankly partisan. There was however, no attempt to confine it to Dissenters and members included not only Anglicans, like the first chairman, George Dixon, who were prepared to accept the unsectarian principle but even agnostics and atheists. Naturally, however, the League drew the bulk of its members from the dissenting churches. Congregationalists included the Rev. R. W. Dale and Samuel Morley, and Unitarians, Dr Crosskey, Jesse Collings, George Dawson and Joseph Chamberlain. By means of its numerous branch committees and its close associations with the trades unions the organisation operated on a large scale. Even in the early stages, however, there was some conflict on the interpretation of the word unsectarian. At the first general meeting of the League in October 1869, the chairman explained the meaning as 'the exclusion of catechisms, creeds or tenets peculiar to any particular sect'.[1] Some of the members, however, would have preferred the emphasis to have been on secular teaching so that religious teaching could be excluded altogether or left to voluntary agencies, while others wanted Bible reading 'without note or comment'. In the country as a whole there was a good deal of confusion between the terms 'unsectarian' and 'secular' and at the Parliamentary level this formed the subject of correspondence between the Radical members, Dilke and Harcourt.[2] Dilke's desire for a secular solution was vigorously resisted by Harcourt. 'Neither in the House of Commons nor in the country can we beat denominationalism by secularism', he wrote. 'If we attempt to meet the flood by a direct dyke it will simply be over our heads and we shall go to the bottom. We must break the force of the wave by a side

---

[1] *Report of First General Meeting*, 12th and 13th October.
[2] Gardiner, *Life of Sir William Harcourt*, 215 et seq.

slope.' Unsectarianism would, he thought, form a convenient 'side slope', a line of defence behind which a strong party could be rallied.

Conservatives and Churchmen were considerably alarmed at the League's activity. They retaliated by founding in Manchester a rival organisation, the National Education Union, with the avowed objective of securing the extension and development of the existing system. By the autumn of 1869 the Union was in action. Meetings held in the great northern centres rallied support from various denominations, from the Roman Catholics and Methodists[1] as well as from the great body of Anglicans. Indeed, one of the stalwarts of the Education Union was Edward Baines, editor of the *Leeds Mercury*, who as a prominent Congregationalist had been one of the leaders of the Voluntaryist movement. Though Baines had abandoned his opposition to State aid, he continued to support the voluntary principle and was one of the most vigorous representatives of the Union interest in Westminster. League and Union had a common aim, universal elementary instruction. Their divergence was on the question of ways and means and, in particular, on the role of the denominational schools for, while the League looked forward to their absorption in a national unsectarian system, the Union sought to make them the staple provision of the future. The result was a bitter conflict which was both religious and political in its expression.

To what extent was there educational destitution in the country? The figures of the official Blue Books speak for themselves; only half the parishes in England and Wales had schools earning Privy Council grants, and of the children in those schools three-quarters were below the age of ten.[2] In fact, fewer than a third of the total number of children between six and twelve were in regular attendance at inspected schools. The greatest lag in school provision was in the expanding industrial towns of the north and midlands and in 1869 a Government enquiry into the education of the poor in Birmingham, Leeds, Liverpool and Manchester revealed that fewer than one-fifth of the children were effectively

---

[1] Both Thomas Allies, the secretary of the Catholic Poor School Committee, and Dr James Rigg, principal of Westminster College, spoke at the inaugural meeting on 3rd November, 1869. *First Annual Report of National Education Union*, 57–64, 83–9.

[2] Forster's Statement, *Parl. Deb.*, 3rd Ser., vol. cxcix, col. 440.

c

reached by State aided schools.[1] Joshua Fitch, Her Majesty's Inspector, reporting on conditions in Birmingham and Leeds gave some illuminating details. He commented, for example, on the haphazard siting of the denominational schools which left large areas unprovided for.[2] He criticised Anglicans for their use of the parish as a unit of educational administration since the close proximity of parishes often brought schools too near to each other, and since the wealthiest parishes were rarely the areas of greatest need. Moreover, he recorded that 'zeal and enthusiasm' were variable qualities, sometimes absent in those parishes where they were most required.[3] Thus the weakness of the existing system was due to parochial (as well as to sectarian) jealousies and to the lack of a central authority able to co-ordinate effort over a wide area. As for the Nonconformists, he found that their contribution to education bore no relation to their numerical strength. Such dissenting schools as there were tended to be not in the poorest areas but in the centre of the trading classes, so that again there was no attempt to distribute schools over a general area or to plan school provision on a district basis. In Leeds, a great centre of Nonconformity, Fitch reported that, with the exception of the Wesleyans and Unitarians, he had been unable 'to find a single Nonconformist congregation which is doing anything to help forward primary education'.[4] The reason was, of course, because Leeds had formerly been the stronghold of Voluntaryists who, as time went on, had found themselves unable to compete with the State aided schools. Now, thoroughly disheartened with the existing state of affairs, they looked forward to a time when the State should take complete responsibility.

Of the 8,000 State aided schools in England and Wales 6,000 were National schools and 1,500 British and Wesleyan schools. In urban areas it was the children of the respectable poor, of the tradesman and artisan class who were to be found in the National and dissenting schools; only the few Ragged and Roman Catholic schools took the poorest children.[5] The Roman Catholics had their own peculiar problems in the field of education. They were

---

[1] *Return, confined to the Municipal Boroughs of Birmingham, Leeds, Liverpool and Manchester*, P.P. 1870 [91] liv, 74 and 107.
[2] *Ibid.*, 71.   [3] *Ibid.*, 21.   [4] *Ibid.*, 87.
[5] In Birmingham, for example, 13 per cent of children in Church schools paid fees of 4d. or more, 18 per cent in British schools, but only 3 per cent in R.C. schools. *Ibid.*, 91.

a small, and, for the most part, an alien minority; but, with the largest section of their community, the Irish immigrants, concentrated almost entirely in the great cities, they formed no inconsiderable portion of the urban population of the country and Gladstone himself estimated their educational destitution to be between a tenth and a sixth of the whole.[1] In Leeds, for example, the plight of some 20,000 Irish, many of them 'from the wildest parts of Connaught', was vividly described by Fitch,[2] who reported that 'the worst and least civilised of the population has not yet been reached by any educational measures whatever, although the Catholic clergy have probably dug deepest'. Roman Catholic schools had to be financed very differently from the schools of other denominations for unlike the Anglicans, who could rely a good deal on subscriptions and endowments, and unlike the Nonconformists, who could charge high fees, the Roman Catholics had few resources save the pence of the poor, collected by regular house to house visitation. It was a considerable achievement that they had some 350 State aided schools though these were often hard pressed to meet the Government requirement that funds raised locally should be equivalent to the Government grant.

In addition to the State aided schools there were large numbers of private schools. In the city of Birmingham, for example, they were three times as numerous as the inspected schools.[3] Their popularity was due very largely to ignorance and to the false pride of parents who thought that because the fees of the private schools were higher than those of inspected schools they were buying a superior type of education. Local dame schools were also patronised by parents who objected to sending their children to sectarian schools; they were patronised by many more who were indifferent and who had no intention of sending their children anywhere with regularity. And always, of course, there were the feebly benevolent parents who plaintively protested that 'the dame must live'. The private adventure schools were very often poor joyless places run by pathetic old women or spiritless and disheartened men who had failed in other walks of life. Perhaps some attempt was made to teach the boys the three R's, whilst the girls spent most of their time knitting. One visitor to a dame school noted with some astonishment that the girls were at work on strange garments, 'coarse stockings whose distorted proportions

[1] *Parl. Deb.*, 3rd Ser., vol. ccii, col. 277.　[2] *Return, op. cit.*, 89.　[3] *Ibid.*, 33.

might fit a club-footed person or possibly an elephant.'[1] Last in the list of school provision were the Ragged schools, 'refuges from the miseries and temptations of the streets', as Fitch described them.[2] Entirely dependent on voluntary support, Ragged schools were an expression of the philanthropic zeal of the age and owed their expansion in the 1840's to the efforts of Shaftesbury. By the middle of the century London had 110 Ragged schools[3] and most of the populous centres had one or more catering for the lowest of the low, the offspring of beggars, paupers and criminals, children from 'the mire and gutter'. In Shaftesbury's words, 'the children were in a filthy and miserable state. We washed and fed and civilised them.'[4]

Stark poverty lay behind the brutalised conditions of the times. Often individual improvidence and fecklessness were to blame; but frequently the poverty was a result of trade depression which struck the deserving and the undeserving alike. In such conditions parents were frequently too ignorant and degraded to avail themselves of education even when it was offered free of charge.[5] There were many thousands of children who had never been to school at all. In the rural districts they provided a fund of juvenile labour, but in the cities they were urchins of the streets. At the best they might profitably occupy themselves running errands or selling newspapers, at the worst they degenerated into thieves and gamblers.

Everywhere the defects of existing denominational organisation were only too apparent: duplication of schools by rival sects and duplication of inspection. Nor had State grants been distributed to best advantage. In the words of Forster, 'in helping those only who help themselves or who can get others to help them we have left unhelped those who most need help.'[6] Clearly, existing provision was totally inadequate and educational reorganisation would have to be one of the most urgent tasks of the new Liberal Government. Already social and industrial developments had undermined a good deal of the old prejudice against educating the

---

[1] *Report*, P.P. 1870 [C 406] 146.   [2] *Return, op. cit.*, 58.

[3] Kay Shuttleworth, *op. cit.*, 145.

[4] From his speech at the Annual Meeting of the National Education Union 1873. *Fourth Annual Report of National Education Union*, xvii.

[5] Manchester Education Aid Society had (between 1864 and 1869) issued 35,000 tickets for free education which were never used. *Parl. Deb.*, 3rd Ser., vol. cxciv, col. 1200.

[6] *Ibid.*, 3rd Ser., vol. cxcix, cols. 442–3.

children of the poor. There were some who felt that an education rate would save the prison rate and the pauper rate. Others, concerned with the challenge of foreign industries, looked to education to raise the efficiency of labour. Above all, the recent rise of Prussia, the nation of schoolmasters, was an object lesson to those who remained doubtful. There was, in the words of T. H. Huxley, 'a chorus of voices, almost distressing in their harmony, raised in favour of the doctrine that education is the great panacea for human troubles, and that, if the country is not shortly to go to the dogs, everybody must be educated.'[1] The need for elementary education was generally admitted; the real clash of opinion was on the religious issue. And yet there was plenty of evidence to suggest that the majority of parents cared little about the type of religious training their children received. The Newcastle Commissioners, for example, had reported that 'their (the parents') selection of a school, in so far as it is affected by the character of instruction, seems rather to be determined more by the efficiency with which such things tend to the advancement in life of the children who are taught in it and by its general tone and discipline'.[2] This was also the experience of Her Majesty's Inspectors, who found children of Church parents attending British Schools and children of Nonconformist parents attending Church schools.[3] There was undoubtedly discrimination in the case of individuals, but it was magnified by sectarian enthusiasts. Lord Shaftesbury, with his forty years' experience in the educational field, declared in 1870 that he had never come across a case of religious discrimination.[4] Nevertheless, it would be quite delusive to dismiss the dispute as a 'clerical' difficulty. In an age of spiritual and intellectual concern the supreme questions, the nature of God and the function of the Church, exercised profoundly the minds and imaginations of thoughtful men and women. Many reflecting, serious-minded Victorians were intimately involved in the fundamental differences of interpretation and deeply stirred by the religious conflicts of the time. To them, education was not for this world; it was for the salvation of souls, a preparation for immortality, and therefore education which was

[1] *Lectures and Lay Sermons* ('Address to the South London Working Men's College' January 1868), 1938, 55.
[2] *Newcastle Commission, op. cit.*, 34.
[3] *Report*, P.P. 1870 [C 406] 89, 94, 264, 316.
[4] *Report of Meeting of National Education Union*, 8th April, 1870.

bereft of religion or suspect in its form of religious teaching was fraught with the peril of eternal damnation.

*   *   *   *   *

The new Vice-President of the Committee of Council, William Edward Forster, was able to regard the educational scene with cool detachment. A Quaker by birth he had left the Society of Friends on his marriage, in 1850, to Dr Arnold's daughter. Henceforth, though he had much in common with Dissenters, he remained aloof from denominational life. Forster was frankly of the opinion that the religious issue had been greatly overrated and, as he told his constituents in Bradford, he hoped to 'canter over' a difficulty which he believed existed in the minds of the talkers and not in the minds of the educators or parents. In his preliminary thoughts on the problem he expressed his aim as being 'to obtain complete and efficient school provision . . . (with) the least possible expenditure of public money and the least possible injury to existing efficient schools'.[1] As a member of Gladstone's Government he had to take account of the prevailing passion for economy which required that educational progress should be 'on the cheap'; as a practical politician he could not ignore the work of the religious communities which had been actively encouraged by the State for almost forty years. Of the schemes which had already attracted attention Forster rejected completely the proposals of both the League and the Union. Of the latter he wrote, 'I cannot but think that it has been proved that educational volunteers will not supply national education, and that any attempt to bribe them to perform an impossible task would be most costly to the State.' As for the plan of the Education League, it would not only 'entail upon the country an enormous expense (but) — a far more dangerous loss than that of money — (it) would drive out of the field most of those who care for education and oblige the Government to make use solely of official or municipal agency'. It seemed to Forster that Robert Lowe's plan for the compulsory provision of rate aided schools 'if and where necessary' offered the best chance of success. He was hopeful of gaining support all round, 'if, on the one hand, we acknowledge and make use of present educational effort, and, on

[1] Reid, *Life of the Rt. Hon. W. E. Forster*, I, 463 *et seq.*

the other hand, admit the duty of the central government to supplement these efforts by means of local agency.' Accordingly, he proposed that, after allowing a period of grace to the voluntary bodies, responsibility for filling the gaps in school provision should rest with the localities which might, if they wished, assist voluntary schools from the rates.

Of the other members of the Cabinet whose views were significant, Gladstone himself was not intimately involved. He described his own responsibility as 'that of concurrence rather than of authorship'.[1] His views differed from Forster's but, immersed as he was in the Irish question, he did not press them. Some eighteen years later he wrote, 'If we had been dealing with a *tabula rasa*, I should have preferred the provisions of the Scottish Education Act, which gives the local school board a free discretion with regard to denominational education.' But the entire situation was different in Scotland where for many generations the ancient parochial system had supplied educational needs, and where new authorities were merely to take over the work of the old heritors' meetings, and the rates were to replace the land taxes. In his reply to Forster's proposals he asked, 'Why not adopt frankly the principle that the State or the local community should provide the secular teaching and either leave the option to the rate payers to go beyond this *sine qua non*, . . . or else simply leave the parties themselves to find Bible and other religious education from voluntary sources.'[2]

In the end the Government Bill, as published on 17th February, 1870, followed closely on the lines of Forster's proposals and steered midway between conflicting difficulties. As Forster pointed out, the Government had considered the lessons of the past as well as the needs of the present and had come to the conclusion that the time was not ripe for any one system. Their object was to cover the entire country with good schools, to 'fill up the gaps' but, in so doing, to give a fair field to the various forms of endeavour, in Forster's words, 'not to destroy the existing system in introducing a new one'.[3] Each locality was to estimate the extent of its educational destitution and a year of grace was to be allowed to the voluntary bodies to give them the opportunity of meeting the deficiency. Thereafter, in areas where

[1] *The Nineteenth Century,* vol. 24, 453.   [2] Morley, *Life of Gladstone,* II, 300.
[3] *Parl. Deb.,* 3rd Ser., vol. cxcix, col. 439.

educational destitution remained, school boards were to be appointed by town councils in municipal boroughs and by vestry meetings in parishes outside boroughs. A good deal was to be left to the discretion of the local school boards; they could make contributions from the education rate towards the maintenance of voluntary schools and they could provide such religious instruction, sectarian or otherwise, as seemed good to them. It was, therefore, open to the school boards to make any or all their schools secular, undenominational or denominational.

Forster had rejected completely the secularist programme but he was at pains to forestall the objections of the secularist element in the country. 'Why', he asked, 'do we not prescribe that there shall be no religious teaching? If we did so, out of the religious difficulty we should come to an irreligious difficulty. We want . . . to do that which the majority of parents of this country really wish; and we have no doubt whatever that an enormous majority of the parents of this country prefer that there should be a Christian training for their children.'[1] The exclusion of religious teaching would mean the exclusion of the Bible from schools, and, Forster asked, 'would it not be a monstrous thing that the book which, after all, is the foundation of the religion we profess, should be the only book that was not allowed to be used in our schools?'[2] Secular efficiency was to remain a condition of Government grants, but for reasons of practical convenience the old method of denominational inspection was to be abolished. Inspection of religious instruction was now to cease and all types of schools were to be examined by Inspectors appointed on an area basis. Finally, acceptance of the Conscience Clause was included in the conditions of Government grant. In future any parent who applied in writing could have his child withdrawn from religious instruction.

The Bill was very much a product of the Victorian mind which had come to accept State action as inevitable, but had done so cautiously and reluctantly. It was designed to give scope to two great bodies of educational thought, that which stood for a universal system of State education and regarded voluntary schools as a temporary necessity, and that which placed its faith in the voluntary system and sought to confine State intervention to the smallest possible limits. Neither of the contending parties

<hr/>

[1] *Ibid.*, 3rd Ser., vol. cxcix, col. 457.   [2] *Ibid.*, 3rd Ser., vol. cxcix, col. 458.

had got what they wanted and the Radicals in particular expressed their astonishment and alarm at the main features of the Bill which they defined as permissive school boards, permissive compulsion and permissive supremacy of the strongest sect. On the very morning following the publication of the Bill *The Times* contained a full-page advertisement of the National Education League which was speedily mobilising its resources. It was during these momentous days that there first came into prominence Joseph Chamberlain, 'a crude provincial, a dissenter, a purveyor of screws,'[1] who soon became one of the great leaders of the Radical cause. As head of an official deputation on 9th March, he denounced the timidity of the Government measure and especially the permissive sectarianism of the Bill. It was, he insisted, the Government's duty to decide on vital matters of principle instead of leaving them to become the subject of annual dispute in each locality.

Meanwhile the Nonconformists were organising themselves for action in close liaison with the Education League.[2] The headquarters of their association, the Central Nonconformist Committee, was in Birmingham and its secretaries, Dr Dale and Dr Crosskey, were both prominent members of the League. Nonconformists, however, were not of one mind on the education issue and even within the individual sects there was division of opinion. At one extreme of Nonconformity stood the Methodists who were united on the need for Bible teaching in all schools. Their great problem was whether to devote their energies to their own school system or to the new national system; one section led by the principal of Westminster College, Dr James Rigg, urged the need of maintaining and even extending the number of Methodist schools,[3] other Methodists preferred to throw in their lot with the Education League. Officially, the Wesleyan Education Committee gave qualified approval to the Bill,[4] but among the rank and file there was a good deal of resentment against a measure which would throw the parishes more than ever into the hands of the squire and parson and also would compel the minority to contribute towards the expenses of the Anglican schools.

[1] Garvin, *Life of Joseph Chamberlain*, I, 108 (from which the material for the rest of the paragraph is taken).

[2] Dale, *History of Congregationalism*, 675–6.

[3] Rigg, *History and Present position of Primary Education*, 1870, 34.

[4] *Report of Wesleyan Education Committee*, 1870, 15.

On the evidence of Rigg himself,[1] it is clear that the Methodists were influential in securing various modifications in the original Bill. In May 1870, an official deputation of the Methodist Church suggested to Forster certain adjustments in the Bill: the immediate cessation of building grants to denominational schools, the election of school boards directly by ratepayers, the exclusion of Church catechisms from board schools and the making of the Conscience Clause as effective as possible.[2] In fact all the Methodist proposals were later incorporated in the form of Government amendments. The significance of Methodism was not that it had, except in the matter of building grants, suggested anything new, but that it represented the most convenient mid-way point between extreme secularism on the one hand and extreme denominationalism on the other.

Among the great body of Nonconformists there was a good deal of confusion on the religious issue. One of the resolutions which Forster received was couched very strangely. 'Education', it said, 'must be free, unsectarian and secular in rate supported schools.'[3] But, as well as general bewilderment, there was division on grounds of principle. A large section of the Congregationalists, led by Edward Miall, sought to exclude religious instruction altogether. 'Secular education', he wrote in the *Nonconformist*, 'is a condition of true denominational instruction. It restricts the schoolmaster to his proper work, but leaves the minister of each church full freedom and offers them every facility for giving strict denominational instruction to the children of their own communion.'[4] Other Congregationalists, however, felt like Samuel Morley that a secular system would 'wither up all that was fresh and vital in our religious communities',[5] and, similarly, the powerful Baptist preacher, C. H. Spurgeon, carried many of his brethren with him when he declared for Bible teaching.[6]

While Forster's Bill did not go far enough in the way of public school provision for Nonconformists and secularists, for Anglicans and Roman Catholics it went too far. Members of the National

---

[1] Rigg's account of the meeting of the Wesleyan deputation with Gladstone, 25th May, 1870, was given in *The Spectator*, 26.4.06. Rigg also had conversations with Forster which he referred to in 1891. *Report of a Special Methodist Education Meeting*, 27th and 28th January, 1891.

[2] Published in the *Methodist Recorder*, 13.6.70.

[3] Quoted by Forster, *Parl. Deb.*, 3rd Ser., vol. cxcix, col. 1936.

[4] 15.6.70.   [5] *Parl. Deb.*, 3rd Ser., vol. ccii, col. 543.

[6] Spurgeon's declaration reported in the *Methodist Recorder*, 17.6.70.

Society were highly critical of certain features. They were very suspicious of the provision regulating the transfer of denominational schools to the new school boards and keenly resentful of the imposition of the Conscience Clause.[1] In the Commons, though Anglican speakers were prepared to give their general support to the Bill, they were clearly apprehensive of the dangers of school board competition and quoted the words which Gladstone himself had used in 1856, 'The day you sanction compulsory rating for the purpose of education you sign the death warrant of voluntary exertions.'[2] Roman Catholics, for their part, objected chiefly to the large discretionary powers which were to be given to the new school boards for, though they had every confidence in the fair and impartial conduct of the Privy Council, they had good reason to fear discrimination by unfriendly local authorities.[3]

In the second reading discussion concentrated on what Mundella called 'the miserable religious squabble'.[4] The actual conditions of educational destitution were scarcely mentioned. Robert Lowe in picturesque language likened members to a noble herd of cattle who preferred to neglect the rich meadow pastures in order to quarrel about a bed of nettles in the corner.[5] *The Times* stressing the same phenomenon, described the children to be educated as 'the flotsam and jetsam on the tide of life'. 'No sooner does the State put its hand to the work', it said, 'than every party feels a sudden interest in these new foundlings and demands that they shall be treated in its own way.'[6] Mundella was among the few who sought to divert attention from the religious controversy to the educational needs of the country, referring by contrast to the standards and range of subjects taught in the German states.[7] Lyon Playfair, too, was similarly devastating in his comments, 'What we call "education" in the inspected schools of England, is the mere seed used in other countries; but with us that seed, as soon as it has sprouted, withers and dries up, and never grows into a crop for the feeding of the nation.'[8]

Radical members were most vocal in the House and in their

---

[1] The *Monthly Paper,* June 1870. Report of the Annual General Meeting.
[2] *Parl. Deb.,* 3rd Ser., vol. cxcix, col. 473.
[3] *Minutes of meeting of Catholic Poor School Committee,* 18.6.70. C.E.C.
[4] *Parl. Deb.,* 3rd Ser., vol. cc, col. 239.   [5] *Ibid.,* 3rd Ser., vol. cxcix, col. 2060.
[6] 23.6.70.   [7] *Parl. Deb.,* 3rd Ser., vol. cc, cols. 241–2.
[8] *Parl. Deb.,* 3rd Ser., vol. ccii, col. 563. Lyon Playfair was formerly Secretary of the Science and Art Department.

fury they accused the Government of bad faith, of favouring their foes at the expense of their friends. The proposal to give a year of grace to the denominations called forth their wrath and indignation. As one of them declared, 'If . . . nothing is done, then the year is wasted, if under the dread of a school board and rates, a denominational system is set up — is forced and struggles into existence — then the year is worse than wasted — it is misused.'[1] They could see little good in the proposed Conscience Clause, for country labourers would not be capable of making written application and would, in any case, be too much in awe of the squire and parson to try to do so.[2] Similarly they denounced the undemocratic method of election of the school boards[3] and the lack of provision for compulsory and free education.[4] But their chief target of fire was the permissive sectarianism of the Bill for their fear was that in many country areas board schools would become Church schools in all but name; an Established Church was bad enough, but 'an Established Church in every school would be incomparably worse'. For three nights discussion centred on Dixon's amendment, 'that no Measure for the elementary education of the people will afford a satisfactory or permanent settlement which leaves the question of religious instruction in schools supported by public funds and rates to be determined by local authorities.'[5] All the leading Radicals spoke in the debate. Harcourt, for example, picturesquely described the sort of conflict which would arise at school board elections, 'Blue and yellow placards will invite the voter to support "Jones and the Thirty-nine articles" or "Smith and No Creed", "Robinson, and down with the Bishops". There will be a great deal of religious discussion and a good deal more of religious beer.'[6] The weight of Radical opposition to the Bill was formidable but the Radicals themselves were far from agreement on constructive proposals. The purely secular solution had few supporters. Indeed, forthright and determined though individual secularists were, they never openly stood apart as a body by themselves, but fought the Bill under cover of a larger following which repudiated sectarian education. When an amendment in favour of secular schools was put to the vote, it was overwhelmingly defeated.

[1] *Ibid.*, 3rd Ser., vol. cxcix, col. 1969.   [2] *Ibid.*, 3rd Ser., vol. cxcix, col. 1973.
[3] *Ibid.*, 3rd Ser., vol. cxcix, col. 479.   [4] *Ibid.*, 3rd Ser., vol. cc, cols. 238, 291.
[5] 14th, 15th and 18th March. Amendment proposed, *Parl. Deb.*, 3rd Ser., vol. cxcix, col. 1919.   [6] *Ibid.*, 3rd Ser., vol. cc, cols. 220–1.

Religious wrangling in Parliament had given a foretaste of the civil and parochial strife which would arise under a system of permissive sectarianism. Moreover, local bodies had made no secret of their reluctance to assume responsibility for making a choice.[1] The Government, therefore, was compelled to reconsider the principles on which the Bill had been based. The scheme it had propounded, the teaching of everyone's religion at public expense, was an attempt at a logical solution of the religious problem, but there was one other logical solution, the teaching of no one's religion at public expense, the establishment, that is, of a secular system which should either exclude religious teaching altogether or leave it to private effort. It was this second solution which the Prime Minister favoured and which apparently had considerable Cabinet backing.[2] However, there was yet a further possibility, namely to restrict board school teaching to undenominational religion, a compromise which would arouse little enthusiasm, but would cause less violent opposition than either of the two logical solutions. Neither Gladstone nor Forster was enamoured of this suggestion. Both admitted frankly their preference for the original principle of the Bill but, in the end, both felt compelled to accept the undenominational compromise.

On 14th June the Cabinet decided on vital changes in the Bill[3] and two days later Gladstone took the lead by explaining the new proposals to a Committee of the House. In the first place the religious issue was now to be decided at the national level. The complexities of the situation had, as the Prime Minister emphasised, confronted the Government with a dilemma: on the one hand, the general public demanded a religious education, on the other hand, the Nonconformists threatened to organise a rate-payers' war against the payment of rates to denominational schools. The remedy therefore was two-fold, to sever completely the link between denominational schools and school boards, and to permit only undenominational instruction in schools erected by local agency. The precise form of the new settlement was subsequently embodied in the Cowper-Temple amendment,[4] a private amendment accepted by the Government. This was the origin of

[1] Ibid., 3rd Ser., vol. ccii, col. 1249. The Manchester City Council and various Metropolitan Vestries had been consulted.

[2] Dr Temple, Bishop of London, later made reference to these Cabinet discussions. The School Board Chronicle, 13.9.94.

[3] Morley, Life of Gladstone, II, 303.   [4] Ibid., 3rd Ser., vol. ccii, col. 275.

the famous Cowper-Temple Clause which prohibited in rate aided schools the use of any 'catechisms or religious formularies distinctive of any particular denomination'. The clause was entirely negative. Local boards were permitted, but not compelled, to give undenominational religious instruction in their schools; they could, therefore, if they so desired, run their schools as secular institutions.

The Government proposal was severely criticised. The *Guardian* referred to it as 'an irrational concession to an irrational prejudice'.[1] There was some doubt as to what was meant by 'formulary'. 'Was a prayer a formulary, was a creed or a hymn?' asked Sir Stafford Northcote.[2] Why, in any case, were the consciences of ratepayers treated so tenderly when the consciences of taxpayers were ignored? Robert Lowe had already pointed out the dangers, 'You try to distinguish between dogma and precept but after all, what is dogma and what is precept?'[3] Government speakers themselves were very vague about the meaning of the term 'undenominational Christianity'. 'We do not know what, in the language of the law, undenominational and unsectarian instruction mean,' Gladstone told the House. 'But we know perfectly well that practical judgment and the spirit of Christianity, combined with common sense, may succeed and does succeed in the vast number of cases.' He was convinced that the plan was 'one which is perfectly practicable, which to a very large proportion of the community would be highly acceptable, and which, to all those to whom it was not absolutely acceptable, would yet be much less unacceptable than any other that could be adopted'.[4]

The Government recognised that if the denominational schools were to be deprived of the chance of rate aid they must be given additional State aid. Indeed, the conditions regulating rate aid would have been thoroughly unsatisfactory to the denominations and would have brought a dangerous sense of insecurity and unsettlement. Instead of the precarious asset of rate aid, therefore, the Government now proposed that church schools should receive a larger Exchequer grant amounting to 50 per cent of maintenance.[5] At the same time all building grants were to be abolished and the year of grace, the time allowed to the denominations to fill the gaps, was to be curtailed to six months.[6]

[1] 22.6.70.
[2] *Parl. Deb.*, 3rd Ser., vol. ccii, col. 1241.
[3] *Ibid.*, 3rd Ser., vol. cxcix, col. 2062.
[4] *Ibid.*, 3rd Ser., vol. ccii, col. 276.
[5] *Ibid.*, 3rd Ser., vol. ccii, col. 280.
[6] *Ibid.*, 3rd Ser., vol. ccii, col. 272.

Radical objections were fully met on two points. In the first place the original Conscience Clause was replaced by a more effective Time-table Clause;[1] Section 7 of the Bill now prescribed that religious instruction and observance were to be 'at the beginning or at the end, or at the beginning and the end of the school meeting, in accordance with a time-table exhibited in the school'. In the second place the method of election of school boards was revised. It was Sir Charles Dilke who, speaking on behalf of the Radicals and Nonconformists at the Committee stage on 1st July, had moved that the school boards should be elected directly by ratepayers instead of by town councils and vestries.[2] Dilke's motion had failed by a margin of only five votes and the lesson of the division was not lost on the Government. The point was that the vestries with their ecclesiastical associations were disliked by Nonconformists. As a correspondent to the *Pall Mall Gazette* wrote, 'If Forster had ever attended a vestry meeting in "our parish" he would never have desired to shift the responsibility of great educational reforms from the Government to the vestry. The clergyman and two or three of the largest farmers do just as they please. Indeed it is seldom that any one else attends. . . .'[3] Now, by an amendment to the Bill, school boards were to be elected directly by ratepayers.[4]

In their revision the Government had tried to preserve the balance between the two conflicting groups. Both denominationalists and secularists had gains and losses to record. Both groups, therefore, remained dissatisfied. In Parliament the denominationalists protested vigorously against the exclusion of their schools from rate aid and condemned the undenominational teaching which was to be given in the new board schools. Disraeli, for example, saw sinister possibilities in the Cowper-Temple Clause and prophesied that the schoolmasters, in future responsible for interpreting the Scriptures, would become 'a new sacerdotal class'.[5] In the closing stages of the debate he again returned to the attack. 'You will have', he said, 'the formulary of Bradford, the articles of Manchester, you will have the creed of Leeds or Liverpool.'[6] Nor were the Radicals in any sense pacified. They could see no security in the Cowper-Temple Clause, and

[1] *Ibid.,* 3rd Ser., vol. ccii, col. 281.   [2] *Ibid.,* 3rd Ser., vol. ccii, col. 1398.
[3] 22.2.70.   [4] *Parl. Deb.,* 3rd Ser., vol. ccii, col. 1476.
[5] *Parl. Deb.,* 3rd Ser., vol. ccii, col. 289.   [6] *Ibid.,* 3rd Ser., vol. ccii, col. 1261.

they denounced the proposal to increase subsidies to church schools as 'political simony', a scheme deliberately designed to perpetuate denominational schools which in the normal course of things would gradually merge into the public school system.[1] Indeed, G. O. Trevelyan felt so strongly on the issue that he later resigned his position in the Government.[2] He was, he said, astounded that the Liberals, after their crusading election in favour of religious equality and after their repudiation of denominational ascendency in Ireland, should now proceed to lavish public money on sectarian schools.[3] The Government, however, stuck to its guns. Gladstone took up the challenge, 'If we treat these voluntary schools as institutions either to be proscribed, or at the best only to be tolerated, limited, hemmed in, permitted to exist merely because they do exist . . . on what principles can we justify such a policy? On none that I know of, but that secular instruction becomes tainted by being brought into the neighbourhood of specified religious teaching.'[4] Nevertheless, the Prime Minister emphasised that whatever was given in Government grants to voluntary schools, should be given only for secular results,[5] and he gave a specific assurance that under no circumstances should the public grant be allowed to cover, together with school pence, the entire cost of maintenance. There must always remain 'a void which must be filled up by free private contributions and without which, failing other sources of assistance, these schools would no longer deserve the character of voluntary'.[6]

During the later stages of debate Gladstone accepted an amendment in favour of cumulative voting at school board elections,[7] a device which would enable due weight to be given to the interests of minority groups. Each ratepayer was to have as many votes as there were members of the board so that he could either 'plump' his votes in favour of one candidate, or distribute them among various candidates. In Parliament as well as in the country as a whole the Radicals kept up vigorous and unremitting efforts. Miall, in the concluding stages of the debates, charged the Government with betraying their Nonconformist supporters, who had been 'the very heart and hands' of the Liberal Party. '"Once bit,

---

[1] *Ibid.*, 3rd Ser., vol. ccii, col. 647.
[2] Trevelyan, *Sir George Otto Trevelyan*, 91. He was Civil Lord of the Admiralty.
[3] *Parl. Deb.*, 3rd Ser., vol. cciii, col. 76.   [4] *Ibid.*, 3rd Ser., vol. ccii, cols. 941–2.
[5] *Ibid.*, 3rd Ser., vol. ccii, cols. 937–8.   [6] *Ibid.*, 3rd Ser., vol. ccii, col. 938.
[7] Incorporated in Clause 29.

twice shy" ', he exclaimed.[1] Gladstone was stirred to great wrath. 'I hope my honourable friend will not continue that support given to the Government one moment longer than he deems it consistent with his sense of duty and right. For God's sake, sir, let him withdraw it the moment he thinks it better, for the cause he has at heart, that he should do so.'[2] At last on 9th August 1870, the Education Bill reached the Statute Book. Twenty-eight days had been spent in debating a measure which, in the end, was carried only with the aid of the Conservative Opposition. Inevitably, the religious compromise was a disappointment to members both of the Education League and of the Education Union. The halfhearted assertion of State power disappointed the hopes of those who wanted a national system of public elementary schools under local control; the creation of rate aided local agencies roused the fears of those who stood for the denominational principle in education. Undoubtedly the establishment of the dual system in English education was the most significant of all the decisions taken in 1870. In the future there were to be two types of school, different not only in the spirit of their religious teaching, but different also in their control and management. The gulf was enormous; and the tragic consequence was that churches and school boards, instead of being partners in the work of education, were to be rivals and competitors. No one was anxious to claim responsibility for the new settlement. Forster had publicly stated his preference for the original scheme.[3] Gladstone was similarly evasive, 'it was in no sense my choice or that of the Government', he wrote. 'Our first proposition was by far the best. But it received no active support even from the Church, the National Society or the Opposition.'[4]

What in general reckoning were the losses and gains? For those who had sustained and supported denominational schools through the years there was only one provision, the increase of the Government capitation grant, which directly favoured them. All other provisions served to discourage voluntary effort: building grants were stopped after six months; the Conscience Clause and Timetable Clause were enacted; inspection of denominational instruction was abolished, as were rewards for religious teaching. Most serious of all was the establishment of a rival system of education

---

[1] *Ibid.,* 3rd Ser., vol. cciii, cols. 741–3.   [2] *Ibid.,* 3rd Ser., vol. cciii, col. 745.
[3] *Ibid.,* 3rd Ser., vol. ccii, col. 593.   [4] Morley, *op. cit.,* II, 306.

D

which was to be financed largely at the public expense. Neverthe-less, though their monopoly was challenged, the voluntary schools were not uprooted; they were intended to form part of the national provision and to that end were given a reasonable chance of existence.

Anglican losses were gains for the Nonconformists. Most significant from their point of view was the establishment of a system of undenominational schools run by democratically elected local boards. Among the Nonconformists Samuel Morley gave wholehearted approval to the measure. 'It would have been unjust, even if it had been possible, to force upon England a Bill in all respects carrying out mere Nonconformist views', he said.[1] Few Nonconformists however had Morley's breadth of vision, and few foresaw the evolutionary value of the Bill. Alone among their leaders Auberon Herbert, Member of Parliament, prophesied that the great principles of the Bill, the principles of rate aid, of com-pulsion and of free schools, would never be lost sight of again.[2] In their indignation the majority could take only a narrow view, denouncing the new capitation grants to sectarian schools as an infringement of the rights of conscience and an obstacle to the establishment of a national system of education.[3] So deeply con-cerned were they for their own rights of conscience that they ignored the rights of others and showed complete indifference to the fate of the children in denominational schools. Of all the sects the Methodists had the best cause for satisfaction, for modifications in the original Bill had followed implicitly the lines of their pro-posals. In the future their own schools would benefit from in-creased grants, while the new board schools would be run on the undenominational principle. Methodists apart, Nonconformists as a whole were harshly critical of the settlement of 1870 but they found it impossible to unite on a constructive policy for, while the majority insisted on undenominational religious teaching, the smaller and more logical section demanded universal board schools where secular instruction alone should be given. Politically the Nonconformist defection sapped the Liberal Party of its main strength and support. Both the Education League and the Central Nonconformist Committee extended the range of their political

---

[1] From address to constituents after the Bill was passed. Hodder, *Life of Samuel Morley*, 255–6.
[2] *Parl. Deb.*, 3rd Ser., vol. cxcix, col. 2051.   [3] *Parl. Deb.*, 3rd Ser., vol. ccii, col. 647.

activities and campaigned ceaselessly against the Liberals. John Morley in his editorials in The *Fortnightly Review* denounced the Liberal leaders. 'Mr Disraeli had the satisfaction of dishing the Whigs who were his enemies', he wrote, 'Mr Gladstone, on the other hand, dished the Dissenters who were his friends.'[1] Miall's threat of desertion was no idle one: it took deadly effect on the dissolution of 1874 when the Nonconformist revolt turned a Liberal majority of 110 into a Tory majority of 66.

The Dissenters were not alone in their abuse of the new settlement. At the other extreme the *Church Times* reacted violently, 'Truly the Church has come to a pretty pass', it declared, 'Feed my lambs? Yes, upon the husks which a Liberal Government, egged on by political Dissenters, leaves after sifting out all the grains of dogma.'[2] Many Anglicans were filled with foreboding for the future. Lord Shaftesbury, for example, foreseeing the fate of his beloved Ragged schools wrote sorrowfully, 'The godless, non-Bible system is at hand; . . . Everything for the flesh and nothing for the soul; everything for time, and nothing for eternity.'[3] Naturally Churchmen were keen to build as many schools as possible in the reduced period of grace which was left to them; every new school that could be built before the school boards entered the field would, they felt, be a 'brand snatched from the burning'.[4] They were also encouraged to deprive the Act of its sting by securing strong Church membership on the new school boards.

The new Time-table Conscience Clause was bitterly resented. In the words of the Bishop of Gloucester and Bristol, 'Religion must be the essence of all education, and if it is driven into a corner, if it is placed, so to speak, on the out-skirts of secular teaching, what must be the impression made both on the children and the teacher?'[5] The National Society was extremely reluctant to accept the new form of Conscience Clause and it was only after some prolonged negotiations that the Society finally yielded.[6] Despite the misgivings within their community, however, a great body of Anglicans were prepared to accept the Act as a challenge. In the words of the *Guardian*, it would 'give us all we need, "fair

---

[1] The *Fortnightly Review*, 'The Struggle for National Education', vol. 14. New Ser., 149.
[2] 12.8.70.   [3] Hodder, *Life and work of the Seventh Earl of Shaftesbury*, III, 260.
[4] The *Record*, 17.6.70.   [5] *Parl. Deb.*, 3rd Ser., vol. ccii, col. 1170.
[6] A concordat was negotiated by Earl de Grey. Wolf, *Life of De Grey*, I, 235.

play and no favour." It is our own fault if we do not make use of the fair play, and prove ourselves superior to the need of favour.'[1]

Little had been heard of the views of Roman Catholics during the Parliamentary debates. Their position was unique. It was that of a minority religious group insisting that its children should be educated in a fully denominational atmosphere. Above all Roman Catholics stressed the right of parents to have children educated in schools of their choice. As Manning, now the Roman Catholic Archbishop of Westminster, wrote to Gladstone, 'They (the children) are as we make them, and they make society. The formation of men is the work you have given to the school boards. God gave it to the parents. . . . Let us all start fair in this race. Let every sect, even the Huxleyites, have their grant if they fulfil the conditions.'[2] Forster admitted the justice of the plea. 'We can and should meet their case' he wrote, but confessed, 'I cannot but think this would have been easier to do if we had framed the Bill in accordance with my original Memorandum and had made allowance for exceptional localities desiring either purely secular or distinctive schools.'[3]

The Act of 1870 is a landmark in the history of religious education in England. Before that date the State had insisted on the union of religious and secular instruction and had made this union a condition of all grants. No school had been entitled to support unless it was connected with one of the religious societies; and, although the amount and quality of the religious teaching might differ in schools run by the various organisations, grants had been given only on condition of supplying what each considered fitting instruction. After 1870 State responsibility was confined to the secular sphere; school managers might, if they wished, arrange for religious instruction, but such instruction would no longer be examined or rewarded by State grants. In the Act itself all references to religious instruction were restrictive, board schools were to exclude catechisms and formularies from their teaching, denominational schools were to confine their religious instruction to the beginning and/or end of the school session and, where parents objected, no attendance at religious worship or instruction was required. The year 1870 is thus the great dividing line. Before that date the central Government had had a positive regard for the teaching of religion and had in fact

---

[1] 13.7.70.   [2] Morley, *op. cit.*, II, 308.   [3] Reid, *op. cit.*, I, 503.

insisted that there was no education without religion; now and for three-quarters of a century it assumed a negative attitude and confined its interests to the sphere of secular instruction.

Forster's measure marks the end of an era in English education, the end of a period of State supervision and the beginning of a period of State participation. Faced with the religious antagonisms of the age, as well as the necessity of providing a system of education with the least possible expenditure of public money, he adopted the typically English expedient of compromise by retaining the old system and grafting on it a new. His settlement, therefore, reflected the spirit of the age in which religious strife made the establishment of a single system impracticable and in which the prevailing passion for economy required that educational progress should be 'on the cheap'. In Scotland, however, where the situation was less involved it was possible to apply a simpler solution and in 1872 the Education Act for Scotland incorporated the very principle of permissive sectarianism which in England had been rejected. The educational structures in the two countries, therefore, developed very differently; in Scotland where there was no Cowper-Temple Clause it was possible in the early twentieth century to merge the two types of school into a single comprehensive whole; in England, on the other hand where the principle of undenominational instruction became thoroughly embedded in the public system, dual control remained and is still an integral part of the organisation of English education today.

Chapter 3

————————————— ❈ —————————————

The School Board Era, 1870–1902

Under the Act of 1870 the provision of a school board in the Metropolis was made mandatory; councils of boroughs or rate-payers in parishes might petition for school boards as soon as they pleased. In London and in those great provincial centres where there was enthusiasm to start the new system elections were held in the autumn of 1870. The first board was actually established in Liverpool where, by a remarkable feat the opposing parties had managed to reach a preliminary agreement on its composition. In the other great centres, London, Manchester, Birmingham, Sheffield, Bradford and Leeds, there was a trial of strength between Liberal (or Radical) Dissenters, pledged to unsectarian teaching, and Tory Churchmen, concerned to safeguard the interests of their own schools. As in the Parliamentary debates, religion was the dominant issue of the election, with the 'Pro-gressives' on the one hand and the 'Moderates' on the other abusing each other mercilessly. Naturally, the London election of 29th November was watched everywhere with great interest. In the event the Progressives secured a majority, but on the elected Board both parties were represented by some of the distinguished men and women of the time including Lord Lawrence of India (who became chairman of the Board), Professor T. H. Huxley, members of Parliament like Lord Sandon, W. H. Smith, Charles Reed and Samuel Morley, three College principals, Dr Rigg of Westminster, Canon Cromwell of St Mark's and Dr Barry of King's College, and Emily Davies and Elizabeth Garrett, women pioneers in public and professional life.

In Birmingham, headquarters of the League, and Radical stronghold though it was, the Church party was victorious. The Radicals, who had fought the election on the slogan 'The Bible without note or comment', had not been prepared for the dangers and eccentricities of the cumulative vote. They had put up candidates for all fifteen seats whereas their opponents, by more skilful strategy, ran only eight candidates and urged their supporters to 'plump' their votes. The result was that all the Anglican 'eight' were elected while the one Roman Catholic candidate came top of the poll. Altogether it was a bitter blow to members of the League and a lesson they were not to forget. Less surprising were the results in Nonconformist Leeds where the Progressives were victorious, and in Manchester, the Anglican stronghold, where the denominationalists were returned with a strong majority.

The new boards had first to survey their areas and, by means of a census of the child population and of existing school provision, estimate the extent of educational destitution. Everywhere the result of voluntary effort was found to be patchy, unorganised and of varying quality. Everywhere it was discovered that apart from the Ragged schools and Roman Catholic schools the poorest children were completely ignored.[1] London had 120,000 who were unprovided for, Leeds 20,000 and Birmingham 16,000. In all the great cities there were, growing up in complete neglect, large armies of children belonging to the 'submerged tenth' of the population, to the casual and unskilled labourers, or, worse still, to the unemployed and largely unemployable. Often they were the offspring of the sick, the crippled and the mentally incapable, the spawn of the vagabonds, beggars and thieves who swarmed in the festering slums of the Victorian underworld. Professor Huxley, who had worked for many years in the poorest part of London, declared that the surroundings of the savages of New Guinea were more conducive to leading a decent, human existence, than the conditions of many of the inhabitants of the East End. Indeed, even within a stone's throw of the Houses of Parliament were courts and alleys of indescribable squalor and wretchedness, 'moral plague spots,' as Dickens called them. It was for children bred and brought up in such surroundings that schools had to be built, schools which must civilise as well as instruct.

The preliminary work of surveying and planning occupied most of the first triennial period. Even the energetic and progressive School Boards of London and Leeds did not open their first new schools until the summer of 1873,[2] though they were

---

[1] For example, *Report*, P.P. 1873 [C.-812] 25.

[2] The first London board school was erected in Whitechapel, July 1873. *Minutes of Proceedings of the London School Board*, 3, 612. The first Leeds board school was erected in Bewerley Street, July 1873. *Report of the Leeds School Board*, 1873, 10.

already organising education on a considerable scale in transferred and temporary buildings. Before the second triennial election the London Board had taken over some fifty voluntary schools and had gathered another 50,000 children into makeshift buildings,[1] while the Leeds Board, which in the scale of its work came second to London, had organised fifty-five school departments with more than 12,000 children on their rolls.[2]

For many years the problem of irregular attendance caused constant anxiety. It was one thing to pass byelaws in favour of compulsory attendance but it was quite another to make them effective. Her Majesty's Inspectors were constantly deploring the fluctuation in school populations; of a school in Marylebone, for example, one Inspector wrote, 'the labours of the schoolmaster upon the incessant stream of fresh scholars are for the most part written in water. He is like a man trying to teach a kaleidoscope in which the atoms are not only continually taking some new shape, but are themselves continually changing.'[3] The problem was complex. It was not merely a question of getting the poorest children into the schools, it was also a question of making such provision that respectable parents would not take offence at their own children mingling with those who were both dirty and depraved.

Meanwhile Anglicans and Roman Catholics had reacted vigorously to the challenge of the 1870 Act and within the six months of grace allowed them they had made every effort to provide the much needed accommodation. Even before the passing of the Bill, in June 1870, Roman Catholics had founded an Education Crisis Fund which, within a few weeks, had collected £28,000.[4] By April 1871, the National Society had promised over 1,400 grants in response to local contributions estimated at £850,000.[5] Altogether, within six years some £5,000,000 was subscribed voluntarily.[6] Denominationalists[7] were also keen to secure election to the school boards. Indeed, many of them, men who valued good education and knew something about it, were

---

[1] *Minutes of Proceedings of the London School Board,* 3, 1140–1.

[2] *Report of the Leeds School Board,* 1873, 6.

[3] *Report,* P.P. 1874 [C.–1019–1] 29.

[4] *Report of Catholic Poor School Committee,* 1870, Appendix iii.

[5] *Report of National Society,* 1871, 11–12.

[6] By 1876, 1,726 applications for Building Grants had been approved. *Report,* P.P. 1876 [C.–1513–1] x.

[7] The term is used here and in succeeding pages in the special sense of supporters of denominational schools.

well qualified to assist in the new work. There were, however, other reasons why the denominationalists were anxious to secure denominational representation, for the Act of 1870 had left a good deal to the discretion of the school boards, which could fix the amount of fees, make attendance compulsory and determine, within the limits of the Cowper-Temple Clause, the extent of religious instruction. In many ways it was within their power to show a genuine concern for the interests of existing schools or by sheer ruthlessness to drive them out of business. Naturally, denominationalists were anxious to safeguard their own schools, built and maintained through the years at great sacrifice, but some of them were out for much more and wanted to confine the activities of the school boards to the poorest children, the ragamuffins and arabs of the street, while they themselves catered for the children of the deserving poor. As candidates at the school board elections their slogan was 'economy and efficiency'; as school board members their principal concern was to restrain the Progressives in the expenditure of public money. They were therefore constantly opposed to innovations and improvements, the introduction of experimental methods, the appointment of specialist teachers and the extension of the curriculum. Members of the Education League denounced these tactics. They charged the denominationalists with building far more schools than they could afford to equip or organise, simply in order to keep the school boards out, and they accused them of sitting on the school boards merely to safeguard their own vested interests. In Chamberlain's words, the Church party was trying everywhere 'to stunt the programme of the board school system, to prevent the erection of new schools and the provision of sufficient accommodation, to prevent the reduction of the cost of education to the parents and to prevent the expenditure necessary to secure the efficiency of the schools'.[1]

In the early period of school board history the subject of greatest controversy was Section 25 of the Act. The significance of the clause, which permitted school boards to pay the fees of indigent children attending denominational schools, had previously escaped the Nonconformists. But it was not long before they awoke to the danger that it might provide a new source of income

[1] Speech delivered on 23rd March, 1876, and printed by the National Education League.

for Anglican and Roman Catholic schools. The result was a nationwide conflict with the League and the Liberals on the one side and the Union and the denominationalists on the other. Yet, as John Morley noted, it was 'the smallest ditch in which two great political armies ever engaged in civil war'.[1] In fact, the clause was to be in operation only six years and during that period the total payments came to only £18,000.[2] It was, however, the principle of the twenty-fifth clause to which the Nonconformists objected; like Hampden's twenty shillings, it was to them symbolic of greater issues.

Throughout the country the controversy absorbed a prodigious amount of school board time and energy. The London debates were exceptionally bitter and prolonged. Dr Rigg was among those who championed the clause, Professor Huxley, most forthright of the opposition leaders. Finally the London Board decided on a compromise resolution to the effect that it would remit or pay fees only in exceptional circumstances.[3] Of the great northern boards Liverpool and Manchester accepted the clause. Indeed, the Manchester Board interpreted it so generously that in four years it spent £9,000, about half of the total expenditure in the country under the clause, and even appointed a special inspector to supervise the denominational schools receiving aid.[4] Manchester's neighbour, Salford, came in for a good deal of criticism since it ran no schools of its own in the early years but simply paid for the education of some 10 per cent of the children attending denominational schools.[5] Some school boards took the opposite view and, while passing byelaws which would remit the fees of poor children attending their own schools, refused to allow the payment of fees in denominational schools. Others investigated the possibility of establishing free schools. The great storm centre, however, was Birmingham where, during the first triennial period, there was each year a clash between the Conservative School Board, which sanctioned payments under the clause, and the Radical Town Council, which refused to levy a rate to cover the expenditure. Each year the tension mounted until in 1873 the

---

[1] Morley, *op. cit.*, II, 309.
[2] *Reports*, P.P. 1875 [C.–1265–I] xxx, P.P. 1876 [C.–1513–1] xxi, P.P. 1877 [C.–1780–1] xxvi.
[3] *Minutes of Proceedings of the London School Board*, 1, 324.
[4] *Report of Proceedings of the School Board of Manchester*, 3, 106.
[5] *Report*, P.P. 1873 [C.–812] 55.

School Board applied for a *mandamus* and won its case before the court of Queen's Bench.[1] Even then the *mandamus* could not be enforced; feeling was so strong that distraints would have been necessary on an unparalleled scale. In 1876, during the debates on Lord Sandon's Bill, which aimed at making education compulsory, the Government accepted from a Roman Catholic member, Lord Robert Montague, an amendment transferring responsibility for payment of fees in denominational schools to the Poor Law Guardians.[2] Henceforth there were to be two authorities dealing with the problem of necessitous children: the school boards, which would continue to remit the fees of children attending their schools, and the Guardians, who were to be responsible for the fees of poor children attending denominational schools. The device satisfied neither party. Radicals pointed out that grants, optional under the old Section 25, would now become compulsory;[3] denominationalists, on the other hand, complained of unfair discrimination: application to the Poor Law authority was associated with the stigma of pauperism and parents would naturally prefer to present their case to the school boards rather than undergo the more searching inquisition of the Guardians.[4]

The 25th Clause was only one of the topics of religious controversy in the school boards. There was also the problem of deciding the form and amount of religious instruction in the new public schools since the Act itself was vague and permissive and left a good deal of scope to the individual boards. Again it was the London Board which gave the lead by resolving, after considerable discussion, that the Bible should be read and that there should be given 'such explanation and such instruction therefrom in the principles of morality and religion as are suited to the capacities of the children'.[5] There was a proviso to the effect that the Board might under special circumstances exempt particular schools from the operation of the resolution,[6] but an amendment to secure reading of the Douai version of the Bible by Roman Catholic children was defeated.[7]

---

[1] The *School Board Chronicle*, 17.5.73.
[2] *Parl. Deb.*, 3rd Ser., vol. ccxxx, col. 518.
[3] *Ibid.*, 3rd Ser., vol. ccxxxi, col. 527.
[4] *Minutes of the Standing Committee of the National Society*, 9.3.81. N.S.
[5] *Minutes of Proceedings of the London School Board*, 1, 86.
[6] Subsequently applied to Jewish Schools.
[7] *Minutes of Proceedings of the London School Board*, 1, 81.

Many of the provincial boards adopted the London compromise. Manchester and Birmingham, however, after the 1873 elections, came to represent the two extremes. In 1874 the Manchester Board replaced a very general scheme of instruction by an elaborate syllabus prepared by its new chairman, the Rev. J. Nunn, and even appointed a special inspector to examine the children in religious knowledge.[1] The Manchester syllabus was warmly praised by Anglican clergymen. Indeed, one of the Manchester diocesan inspectors was to tell the Cross Commission in 1887 that 'the amount of work to be done under it was more than we require in Church schools'.[2] Generally regarded by Anglicans as the best possible solution under the existing law, the syllabus was adopted by other boards which were sympathetic to the denominational interest.

In Birmingham the pattern of events was very different. At the time of the first School Board election the Radical slogan had been 'the Bible without note or comment'. The Radicals, however, had lost the election and during the next three years the minority 'six' were engaged in challenging every move on the part of the denominationalists. Even after a majority vote had decided that 'the Bible shall be read and taught daily' they had continued their campaign. Chamberlain, for example, on the occasion of the Board's appointment of the first teachers, had subjected the unfortunate candidates each in turn to a searching interrogation on such points as the teaching of the Trinity and the Atonement[3] in order to demonstrate from the variety of their interpretation the futility of trying to secure undenominational instruction. By the time the Radicals were returned to power at the second triennial election, the Education League had revised its policy on religious instruction and, instead of the old unsectarian compromise, now stood for secular education combined with facilities for giving religious instruction by voluntary agency.[4] The old policy of the League had never satisfied members like Dr Dale who had favoured the 'thorough' policy of secular instruction, and practical experience on the school boards had confirmed Dale and his supporters in their belief that the old position was untenable. In

---

[1] *Second General Report of the Manchester School Board,* 1876, 8.

[2] *Cross Commission, III,* P.P. 1887 [C.–5158] xxx, 48,075.

[3] The *School Board Chronicle,* 25.1.73.

[4] *Report of the Executive Committee of the National Education League, presented at the Fourth Annual Meeting,* 3rd November, 1872.

November 1872, they had won over the League so that henceforth, League policy was one of 'entire separation' of religious from secular instruction. Secular teaching must be given by teachers, paid by and responsible to public authority, religious instruction, if given at all, must be given by external and voluntary agency. Many prominent Nonconformists including Dr Rigg, the Rev. C. H. Spurgeon, Samuel Morley and Charles Reed, publicly denounced the new policy. Dr Dale, on the other hand, defended the League's decision, maintaining that Cowper-Temple instruction could never be strictly undenominational since it must always be interpreted according to one of the schools of theology. To him the teaching of common Christian principles seemed 'fatal to the reality of all religious faith'. He was convinced of the necessity of doctrinal teaching, but he was equally convinced that this was the function of the Church and of the Church alone.[1]

The new policy was adopted by the Birmingham School Board in 1873.[2] Already Dr Dale and his supporters had established the Birmingham Religious Education Society to provide voluntary religious teaching in the board schools. The experiment, however, was not a success for the Nonconformists found it difficult to find suitable volunteer teachers. Consequently, the Society was disbanded in 1879 and Bible reading 'without note or comment' was introduced in the Birmingham board schools.[3] The purely secular solution received little support in the country as a whole. According to the Parliamentary Returns for 1875 only 15 school boards in England and 26 in Wales had followed the example of Birmingham in divorcing secular and religious instruction, though some 140 school boards out of the total of 500 confined religious teaching to the barest minimum.[4] On the religious issue, the School Boards of Manchester and Birmingham, centres respectively of the Union and the League, represented the two extremes. Elsewhere there was a broad distinction between Nonconformist areas, where religious teaching was of the simplest, and Anglican regions where it was more specific and detailed.

---

[1] *Religious Teaching by School Boards.* Speech delivered on 19th November, 1872, and printed by the National Education League.

[2] *Minutes of the School Board for the Borough of Birmingham*, 2, 48.

[3] This was to be supplemented by lessons of Moral Instruction given twice weekly. *Minutes of the School Board for the Borough of Birmingham*, 3, 660–1.

[4] *Return, School Board Schools (Religious Observances)* P.P. 1875, lviii, 415.

In large-scale planning as well as in minor matters of administration school board practice varied enormously. Some boards were especially sympathetic towards existing schools. In Liverpool, where the relation between the Board and the denominations was of the friendliest, managers of the voluntary schools were given the first option of supplying any local deficiency of accommodation.[1] Indeed the Board was even prepared to allow reading from the Douai version of the Scriptures to selected groups in their own schools.[2] But in other areas, where the two agencies were constantly at war with each other, dramatic changes of policy were liable to follow reversal of party fortunes at the triennial elections. In Leeds, for example, where the Moderates gained control for the first time in 1879, the entire programme of the Progressive Party was swept aside,[3] a detailed and elaborate system of religious instruction was introduced and school expenses were drastically pruned. The effect was at once apparent in the examination results and for two years in succession Leeds was below the other great towns on the Education Department's grant list. On the return of the Liberals to power in 1882, however, there was an immediate reversal to earlier policy.

So far as the London Board was concerned, the years 1873 to 1876 were the stormiest in its entire history. The elections of 1873 had reinforced the denominationalist minority, and among the new members was Canon Gregory, who, as treasurer of the National Society, was the most militant of denominationalists. Immediately after the 1873 election the Moderates, led by Canon Gregory, Canon Cromwell and Dr Rigg, attacked the Board's building programme.[4] Week after week for a period of three years they challenged official estimates of necessary school places and in the end succeeded in curtailing the original plans. The Moderates were also responsible for a resolution introduced by Canon Gregory and later presented to the Government in the form of a petition 'praying for an increase in the annual grants to elementary schools on account of the increased cost of education.'[5] It was a patent attempt to ease the denominational burden by one who, though a member of the School Board, was to declare some years

[1] *Cross Commission, II*, P.P. 1887 [C.–5056] xxix, 32,357 *et seq.*   [2] *Ibid.*, 32,086.
[3] *Reports of the Leeds School Board,* 1882 and 1885.
[4] *Minutes of the Proceedings of the London School Board,* 4, 48.
[5] Petition dated 2nd February, 1876. *Minutes of the Proceedings of the London School Board,* 5, 57.

later that he had never yet set foot in a board school and fervently hoped that he would never do so.[1]

It is an interesting reflection that in their opposition to the religious settlement both the prototypes, Canon Gregory of London and Dr Dale of Birmingham had a good deal in common. Both viewed the problem logically, both recognised the supreme importance of religion and both deplored the lukewarmness of board school religion because of its divorce from religious doctrine. Thereafter they parted company, Canon Gregory believing that the schools should be permeated with religious influences, Dr Dale maintaining that religious teaching should be left to external agency. There was thus no conflict on whether or not children should be religiously educated, but simply when and where that education should be given.

Denominationalists had responded enthusiastically to the challenge of the 1870 Act. Within a decade their schools had increased from 8,000 to 14,000 and the number of children attending them had risen from 1,200,000 to 2,000,000.[2] The results of their efforts were comparable with those of the public system which by 1880 was responsible for between 3,000 and 4,000 schools catering for some 750,000 children. By 1883 Anglicans alone had raised £12¼ millions for the building and maintenance of Church schools compared with £15 millions raised during the preceding fifty-nine years of the National Society's history.[3] Nevertheless, the increase in voluntary school accommodation was not so spectacular as it appeared at first sight. It was due partly to the adhesion to the National Society of parochial schools which had previously been organised privately,[4] and partly to the patronage of local landowners who preferred to supplement existing effort rather than face the imposition of a compulsory education rate. In this way arose the strange phenomenon of railway companies, breweries, collieries and even race-course proprietors paying large sums in order to keep open, or even to start, denominational schools. Sometimes, too, in the villages, all the local landowners would agree to levy a voluntary rate in support of the existing school, simply in order to avoid the costly

---

[1] The *School Board Chronicle*, 15.11.79.   [2] See Appendix C.
[3] *Report of National Society*, 1883, 10.
[4] *Cross Commission, IV*, P.P. 1888 [C.–5485] xxxv, 253. There were between 500,000 to 600,000 school places in the schools transferred.

machinery of a school board. But once the threat of a school board had passed, interest flagged and there was complete indifference to the conduct and efficiency of the school.

As the years passed voluntary schools everywhere felt the keen blizzard of school board competition and before long many were fighting for their lives. Once the period of grace was over and the spirit of enthusiasm had died down it became increasingly hard to maintain the schools. The Government insisted, as a condition of grant, that local contributions in fees and subscriptions should equal the amount of Exchequer aid, but at a time when compulsory local rates were drying up the sources of voluntary help, the condition became increasingly difficult to fulfil. Every inch of the ground that the denominational system lost was gone for ever to the new public authorities. The key to the disparity was finance. Whereas the denominationalists had to pinch and scrape to keep their schools going, the school boards could finance their activities from the bottomless pocket of the rates. Forster had prophesied that the education rate would never exceed 3d.,[1] but already by 1875 some of the Yorkshire towns were levying rates of 6d. or more,[2] while by 1880 the London rate had risen to 5½d., and those for Leeds and Birmingham to 7½d. and 6½d. respectively.[3] The progressive school boards built lavishly, and adopted the latest in the way of planning and design so that their schools were lighter, loftier, better ventilated and more convenient in every way than the vast majority of voluntary schools. As one of the Inspectors put it, 'the better the schools are, the more attractive they are to the better class of parents.'[4] There was no question of the public system catering merely for the waifs and strays of society. Instead, the great school boards, firm and energetic in their purpose, pursued inexorably the policy of rating, building, extending, compelling and prosecuting. Denominationalists complained bitterly of the ruinous competition and compared their schools to the lean kine which pined and starved while the fat kine approached out of the river of plenty to devour them.

Inevitably there were transfers of voluntary schools to local boards, and the National Society became greatly alarmed at the rate of transfers of Anglican schools. Some were handed over simply because individual clergy cared little about them and were

---

[1] *Parl. Deb.*, 3rd Ser., vol. ccii, col. 638.   [2] *Report*, P.P. 1876 [C.–1513–1] 88.
[3] *Report*, P.P. 1881 [C.–2948–1] 38, 60, 62.   [4] *Report*, P.P. 1876 [C.–1513–1] 369.

only too glad to rid themselves of the burden of anxiety and expense; some were thrown over unnecessarily in moments of temporary despair. The National Society made great efforts to stem the rate of transfer and gave special assistance to poor schools, but even so its policy was only partially successful.[1] In 1876 the Conservative Government provided, by Lord Sandon's Act, a measure of relief: whereas under the 1870 Act schools had had to match the Government grant by money from other sources, now they could obtain up to 17s. 6d. for each child without qualification, and could obtain even more if they were themselves able to raise equal amounts. Welcome though it was, the extra financial aid was rapidly absorbed in an attempt to keep up with the school board standards, and within a short time the plight of the voluntary schools was worse than ever. In 1880 the average cost of each child attending a Church of England school was £1 14s. 10¼d., an increase of 5s. 2¾d. on the expenditure in 1873. Board schools, however, were spending £2 1s. 11¾d. on each child and the difference was continually increasing.[2] In the large urban areas, in particular, there was an obvious disparity between standards in the board schools and the voluntary schools. Progressive school boards were constantly experimenting and improving, their premises were more inviting, their appliances more generous, their courses more varied. They could afford, for example, to introduce kindergarten teaching on Froebelian lines, to employ specialist instructors in cookery, hygiene, science and Swedish drill, and to set up school museums and school libraries. Indeed, the larger northern boards were soon providing something more than elementary education for a proportion of their senior pupils by means of higher grade schools and were experimenting also with pupil-teacher centres. It was not surprising that even by the late 'seventies members of the Education League felt that their organisation had served its main purpose and could be disbanded.[3]

Churchmen, not unnaturally, condemned school board innovations as unnecessary extravagance and resisted every attempt of the Education Department to raise standards. In the hope of alleviating their burdens they petitioned Parliament for some

---

[1] *Minutes of Standing Committee of National Society*, 2.4.79. N.S.
[2] See Appendix C.
[3] *7th Annual Report of the National Education League*, November 1876.

E

measure of relief, for an increase in Exchequer grants, for exemption of school buildings from the rates, and for permission to appropriate rate contributions to schools of their choice. It was in the northern industrial towns, in precisely those areas where competition was most severe, that National schools in self-defence first began in the early 1880's to merge themselves into district federations, Church Day School Associations, modelled deliberately on the larger boards. They were able to improve the grant earning capacity of Church schools by the provision of centres for specialist instruction and by the employment of visiting organisers, ex-teachers of repute, who by their skill and mastery of the intricate Government Codes could give practical help to the individual schools.[1]

Though the Anglicans were seldom able to break fresh ground, they sometimes put up determined resistance before they yielded to a school board. In York, Nottingham, Willesden and Birkenhead, for example, a central organisation, the Church Extension Society, assisted local endeavour by sending in nuns, members of the Kilburn Sisterhood, either to open new schools or to take charge of existing schools. In York, when the British school failed in 1888, it was the Kilburn Sisters who took over and for a time kept out a school board by opening a new school.[2] The challenge of the Church Extension Society was greatly exaggerated by the opponents of the denominational schools who depicted the Kilburn Sisterhood as a most mysterious and sinister organisation disciplined by rack and thumbscrew![3]

In exceptional areas all the denominations agreed to combine to keep out a school board. The city of Winchester was a case in point where the eleven denominational schools of the city came under a composite Elementary Schools' Council. Voluntary rates and subscriptions were put into a common fund and disbursed to each of the schools by the Council.[4] In Birkenhead, too, the denominationalists united to keep out a school board and in 1882 organised the collection of a voluntary rate of 1s. in the £, which raised £17,500 and went towards new buildings and extensions for voluntary schools of all denominations. So successful were their efforts that average attendance more than doubled in

---

[1] *Cross Commission, III, op. cit.*, 46,583 *et seq.*
[2] The *School Board Chronicle*, 26.1.89.   [3] *Ibid.*, 2.6.88.
[4] J. G. Hodgins, *Report on Popular Education in England*, 1897–8. Toronto, 1899, 30.

the nine years between 1878 and 1887.[1] Winchester and Birken-head, however, were quite exceptional. The general picture in the towns was of denominational schools struggling to compete with rate aided schools, being compelled to charge higher fees and even so providing an inferior secular education.

In rural areas the picture was quite different. Here such school boards as existed were rarely progressive or efficient; indeed one Inspector, who was transferred from the West Riding to rural Kent, expressed his astonishment at the contrasts he found. He recalled 'the princely buildings of the West Riding schools and the willingness of the citizens to pay school rates of nearly 1/–'. In his new area he found a school board 'with a rate of less than 2d. in the pound, straining every nerve to save a pound here and a shilling there'.[2] In the country districts the voluntary schools frequently showed up to greatest advantage and Inspectors often made a point of mentioning the devotion and personal interest of the managers of many village Church schools, contrasting their attitude with the apathy or even hostility of school board members who left their teachers to grind on without a word of sympathy or encouragement.[3] On the whole the Established Church was able to retain control of the majority of village schools but the numerous difficulties, uncertainty of subscriptions and indifference of parents and children, put great strain on the rural clergy. It was true that sometimes the whole community levied a rate in support of the Church school, but this was merely to avoid the expense of a school board and costs were therefore kept as low as possible. There was little hope of improving educational standards of village schools and so increasing their grant earning capacity. Not infrequently an Inspector was faced with a dilemma in the examination of village schools. 'He must either refuse the grant and perhaps crush the schools or he must recommend the grant for work which he knows falls lamentably short of the standard laid down for him in the Code.'[4]

It was not surprising that there were members of the Church of England who doubted whether the effort involved in maintaining their schools was worth while. For example, the distinguished Dr Fraser, Bishop of Manchester, was convinced that the voluntary system was doomed and was prepared to transfer his schools to

---

[1] *Cross Commission, III, op. cit.,* 47,760 *et seq.*   [2] *Report,* P.P. 1888 [C.–5467–1] 379.
[3] *Report,* P.P. 1878 [C.–2048–1] 571.   [4] *Report,* P.P. 1887 [C.–5123a] 337.

public authority.[1] But, at the other extreme, board schools were regarded with horror and detestation by clerics like Canon Gregory who once declared that he would be afraid to die if he had given up one of his schools.[2] The fundamental distinction was on religious teaching. Whereas Evangelicals and Broad Churchmen regarded Cowper-Temple instruction as 'not quite complete', High Churchmen spurned it as 'worthless'. Nevertheless, even among the High Church clergy few were prepared to go to the lengths of the veteran Archdeacon Denison, who had never accepted the conditions of State aid, but had continued for almost half a century to run his own village school efficiently, without a grant, without a Conscience Clause and without the interference of Her Majesty's Inspectors.[3]

Roman Catholics, though few in number compared with the Anglicans, had a much more coherent policy. Their views were clear and definite; in the words of Thomas Allies, the devoted and able secretary of the Catholic Poor School Committee, they had 'a total objection to the principle that religion and education, either for the poor or for the rich, can be severed'.[4] As Manning explained, the State had rights of self protection, but it had no commission to teach and must always allow parents free choice of schools.[5] The Roman Catholic response to the challenge of the 1870 Act had been remarkable. In the decade 1870 to 1880 the community had more than doubled the number of its schools from 350 to 758 and it had carried through the greater part of its building programme without the help of Parliamentary grants.[6] Once built, the great problem was how to maintain the schools for fees had to be kept as low as possible. Indeed, of all types of schools, including the board schools, those associated with the Catholic Poor School Committee charged the lowest fees and had the largest number of free admissions. The balance, therefore, had to be contributed by voluntary subscriptions and, since there were few wealthy members of the community, the subscriptions had to come from the poor labouring classes. Weekly house to house

[1] *Report of British and Foreign School Society*, 1875, 2.

[2] Speech at the Church School Association Meeting at Southampton. The *School Board Chronicle*, 17.5.90.

[3] Denison, *op. cit.*, 371–2.   [4] *Cross Commission, I*, P.P. 1886 [C.–4863] xxv, 9,105.

[5] The *Weekly Register*, 31.10.85.

[6] Because many localities could not fulfil the condition that no debt upon the school fabric should remain after the grant had been paid.

collections became a regular feature of parish life, and working men were often waylaid on wages night in order that they might contribute coppers from the shillings they had earned. By supreme efforts annual contributions by 1880 had been increased to 7s. 4½d. for each child at school, but even this sum bore no comparison with the average rate-borne expenditure of 18s. 7d. per child in board schools.[1] Altogether, a combination of negligible endowments, low fees and early leaving brought the income of Roman Catholic schools well below that of all other types of school with the result that there was much pinching and scraping to make ends meet. Teachers' salaries were kept as low as possible,[2] equipment and apparatus was supplied sparingly and there was continual resistance to the raising of standards. The same spirit of devotion and sacrifice which had built and maintained the schools kept the teachers loyally at work in them. But as the years passed the higher salaries offered by the school boards were an increasing temptation and, to the dismay of the Poor School Committee, some teachers trained in Roman Catholic colleges began to seek service in board schools.[3]

Roman Catholics were no less anxious than Anglicans to secure representation of their interests on the school boards and in the larger towns the cumulative vote could usually be manipulated to return at least one member. Just how important it was to have the good will of the new local authority was illustrated by the famous episode of the Dan-y-craig school, Swansea. The case originated because the Swansea School Board in 1883 refused to allow the Roman Catholics of Dan-y-craig to build a school for their children insisting, instead, on its own prior right of supplying the deficiency. In defiance of the School Board, the voluntary school was built and for years existed without a grant. The quarrel assumed very large dimensions and the question was referred to legal counsel, to Parliament and, in 1886, to the Royal Commissioners before the school was finally admitted to grant aid in 1888.[4]

---

[1] See Appendix C.

[2] *Cross Commission, III, op. cit.,* 50,109. The headmaster of a Liverpool R.C. School, said that if he were teaching under the Liverpool School Board he would be earning £70 a year more. Under the London Board he would double his salary.

[3] *Cross Commission, I, op. cit.,* 8295–7. Allies said that about forty teachers trained in R.C. colleges had taken posts in board schools.

[4] *Cross Commission, IV, op. cit.,* 56–7.

In contrast to the Roman Catholics and to the great majority of Anglicans, the main body of Dissenters had, despite their initial disappointment in 1870, become enthusiastic supporters of the new public system. Some, of course, still disapproved of the Cowper-Temple compromise and urged, as did the secularists, the complete exclusion of religion from education, but many, including the supporters of the British and Foreign School Society and members of the Methodist Connexion, upheld the principle of undenominational teaching. Indeed, the British and Foreign School Society displayed no regrets at the prospect of handing over its schools and after ten years of school board activity the Society recorded with satisfaction, 'School boards are in reality British School Committees, some upon a gigantic scale, and with a few exceptions, the schools are British schools with another name.'[1] The parent body, therefore, advised local committees not to prolong the existence of schools which were in financial difficulties unless they were in areas where a school board could not be obtained or where the existing school board had a secular or denominational bias. Undoubtedly the feeling of the Society was that the battle for undenominational teaching had been fought and won and that the field could safely be left to the school boards. As early as 1871 the parent body had decided to concentrate its resources on the training of teachers in the belief that this was the best service it could render to education. In the words of the Annual Report of that year, 'They (the school boards) will soon be crying out to the country, "Here are the schools." . . . It will be well if your Committee could meet them with the response "and here are the teachers".'[2] The results of the new policy were soon evident for by 1884 it had six colleges training some 15 per cent of all intending teachers.[3] The decline in subscriptions, however, was a constant source of anxiety, for old patrons, who had given generously, belonged to a passing generation, and the Society, with no party cry and no startling development of policy, found it almost impossible to attract new subscribers. In fact, the great days of the British and Foreign School Society were over; the principles it had championed were firmly established and it was to confine itself to a narrower, though significant, sphere of activity.

---

[1] *Report of British and Foreign School Society*, 1881, 15.   [2] *Ibid.*, 1871, 43.
[3] *Ibid.*, 1884, Appendix.

Unlike the supporters of the British and Foreign School Society Methodists regarded the school boards with very mixed feelings. In 1870 the Methodist Connexion with its 700 schools was unique among the dissenting churches in having a vested interest in the existing system. It could have chosen to buttress the old denominational position or it could have used its influence to mould the new public system. In fact it did neither, since Methodists could not agree on a single policy and the long period of internal strife which followed paralysed Methodist educational activity both in the voluntary and in the public system. Gradually Methodists tended to be driven out of all save their urban schools where high fees excluded the lowest class of children. In the large Lancashire towns, for example, their schools charging fees of 7d. a week became highly selective and also highly efficient. The more prosperous and discriminating parents, not necessarily Methodists themselves, were attracted by the liberal curriculum and the character of the schools.[1] In the villages, however, Methodists, in common with other Dissenters, were bitterly resentful of the Anglican control of the schools. They viewed with alarm 'the Popish revival' in the Church of England for it seemed to them that the country clergy were now imbued with a new spirit of aggressiveness and audacity. Unfair inducements of all kinds were used in the defence of Anglicanism. The farmworker might be bullied by the threat of losing his cottage or his employment, the children might be perverted with buns, and the aged bribed with blankets. Even the rural board schools were not free from the sinister influences of clericalism.[2]

*   *   *   *   *

By the middle of the 1880's rivalry between voluntary schools and board schools had become acute. The new public system was expanding rapidly and between 1880 and 1885 the proportion of the school population attending board schools had increased from a quarter to a third. Financially the churches had no hope of keeping pace with the school boards. By 1885 the average expenditure from the rates for each board school child was 19s. 0¼d.

[1] *Cross Commission*, III, *op. cit.*, 45,874–5.

[2] In 1888 there were thirty-four school boards (all in rural areas) which allowed Church catechisms to be taught in their schools. *Cross Commission, Appendix*, P.P. 1888, [C.–5485–iv] 400.

per annum compared with 8s. 6½d. which voluntary contributions made available for each child in denominational schools.[1] Money made more money, poverty bred worse poverty. The wealthy boards, able to extend the range of subjects, to employ specialist teachers, school organisers and inspectors, were rewarded by larger grants, while the voluntary schools were continually stunted by their inability to provide the very teaching power and equipment which would have brought increasing returns. The issue of free education was to bring things to a head.

It was Chamberlain who precipitated matters in the election campaign of 1885 by declaring himself in favour of free schools. According to his Autumn Manifesto, grants, in lieu of fees, were to be paid to board schools,[2] but there was no mention of corresponding grants to denominational schools and churchmen were immediately up in arms. Cardinal Manning at once entered the political fray urging members of his communion to put two questions to their Parliamentary candidates. '(1) Will you do your utmost to place voluntary schools on an equal footing with board schools? (2) Will you do your utmost to obtain a Royal Commission to review the present state of education in England and Wales?' He concluded, 'As they answer "Yes" or "No", let us decide.'[3] The Cardinal's challenge evoked instant response. In the close political duel the Roman Catholic minority had a strategic importance and within a matter of days the Home Secretary, Sir Richard Cross, announced that his party, if re-elected, would appoint a Royal Commission to consider the increase of public subsidies to denominational schools.[4] The Irish vote was won, though the election itself in November 1885 was a stalemate, and the Conservative Ministry appointed a Royal Commission under the chairmanship of Cross (now Viscount Cross). Strongly denominational in composition, its members included Cardinal Manning, Canon Gregory, Dr Rigg, Dr Temple (the Bishop of London), and the Earl of Harrowby (formerly Lord Sandon). It was hardly surprising that the Liberals, when they came to power in February 1886, should evince little enthusiasm for what they regarded as a 'packed Commission'.

Over a period of many months the Commissioners conducted an exhaustive enquiry into the condition of elementary education

---

[1] See Appendix C.   [2] Garvin, *op. cit.*, II, 56 *et seq.*   [3] The *Tablet*, 24.10.85.
[4] Retrospective account in the *School Board Chronicle*, 23.6.88.

in England and Wales. Comparison of conditions and standards in board and voluntary schools were among the points of enquiry, topics which generated considerable heat and passion, and there were some lively moments when Commissioners and witnesses engaged in spirited exchanges. Despite differences of opinion it was evident that the school boards had done a remarkable job of work. The drive to secure regular attendance had succeeded and the schools were turning out children who were disciplined and drilled in the rudiments. The real clash came on the subject of financial aid to voluntary schools. In their evidence, denominationalists had spoken feelingly of their difficulties. They had referred to the arbitrary rating of their schools: in London, for example, where there were nine separate systems of rating, one school might be assessed at twice the rateable value of a similar school in a different district, and the position was even worse in the provinces.[1] Similarly, denominationalists complained of the conditions governing Privy Council grants; each year some schools were compelled to forfeit part of their grant because the amounts earned exceeded the sums they could raise locally by fees and subscriptions. Grants which were given with one hand were taken away with another and excellent schools in poor districts suffered from no other fault than that they were poor. Roman Catholic schools, in particular, were penalised by their poverty: a Liverpool headmaster quoted his losses from deduction as £49 in one year and £38 in another, sufficient, in fact, to pay for the employment of another assistant teacher who would have raised the general standards of the school.[2] The deduction was a penalty on effort and enterprise: as school work improved and grants were increased, so correspondingly larger deductions were made. As for the Merit Grant, introduced by Mundella's Code in 1882, its effect was, in the words of one of Her Majesty's Inspectors, 'to reward the rich and favoured schools and to punish the small poor schools.'[3]

There was overwhelming evidence of the superior provision which the larger school boards could make for their children and teachers. Spacious buildings, libraries, museums, school prizes and certificates, as well as larger and better qualified staffs appealed to parents and children; higher salaries and superannuation schemes attracted the cream of the teaching profession. It was hardly

[1] *Cross Commission, III, op. cit.,* 29,850 and 36,380–1.   [2] *Ibid.,* 45,242.
[3] *Cross Commission, II, op. cit.,* 37,255.

surprising, therefore, that in the London School Board area attendance in voluntary schools had declined by 60,000 in twelve years while in board schools it had gone up by 300,000.[1] From the evidence it was clear that school boards differed enormously in their attitude towards denominational schools. The Liverpool Board, for example, had always sought to co-operate with the voluntary schools and was now pressing for legislation to ease denominational burdens.[2] In complete contrast was the policy of the Birmingham Board which by large-scale remission of fees lured children away from neighbouring church schools.[3]

The Final Report of the Commissioners, published in the summer of 1888, reflected a distinct cleavage on the religious issue. There were in fact two reports, the Majority report carrying fifteen signatures and the Minority report with eight signatures. In effect there was substantial agreement on purely educational matters but complete divergence on religious matters. The Majority urged the removal of outstanding grievances which had been hampering the voluntary schools: the limitation of the Government grant, the rating of schools, appeal by indigent parents to the Guardians, and the prior right of school boards to provide new accommodation.[4] They maintained that the voluntary system was not merely a part but the foundation of the whole of national education, and as such was clearly entitled to claim support on equal terms with the public system. Since their concern, however, was to devise some means of assistance which would not at the same time dry up the sources of voluntary contributions their recommendations on rate aid were timid and cautious; local authorities were merely to be empowered to provide rate aid and in limited amounts calculated not to diminish voluntary effort.[5] Though Cardinal Manning signed the report he was plainly dissatisfied with the financial proposals and added his own reservation.[6] He was not explicit, but he clearly favoured a bolder approach to the entire problem and had already in 1882 asked for compulsory rate aid to denominational schools.[7]

---

[1] *Ibid.*, 29,851–3.   [2] *Ibid.*, 32,192.
[3] There were 10,000 children admitted without fees to Birmingham board schools. There were 3,000 vacant places in church schools. *Cross Commission, III, op. cit.*, 45,295.
[4] *Cross Commission, IV, op. cit.*, 188 *et seq.*   [5] *Ibid.*, 222.   [6] *Ibid.*, 224.
[7] Mundella's Code, which came into force in 1882, had roused Manning. He asked directly for rate aid in an article in *The Nineteenth Century*, vol. 12, 958 *et seq.* His detailed proposals were submitted in the form of a Parliamentary petition (2nd June, 1883).

The Minority eight, including among their number Dr Dale, Henry Richard and the Hon. E. Lyulph Stanley, were extremely critical of the general tone and arguments of the Majority report, which appeared to them 'too often to approach proposals for the improvement of education from the point of view of considering how such improvements may affect the interests of certain classes of schools rather than how far they are desirable'.[1] Rate aid in any form they considered quite impracticable and they concluded by reiterating the long-felt grievances against the existing system and urging the establishment throughout the country of 'schools of an undenominational character and under popular representative management'.[2] Between the two sides the gulf was complete and the two reports were clear evidence that time had done nothing to assuage the old antagonisms. What was certain was that the denominationalists were now divided among themselves for, while the Roman Catholic minority favoured a clean break with the past and the replacement of the old piecemeal grant system by one which was both logical and comprehensive, the great body of Anglicans shrank from the necessary control which such a policy must entail. The result in the Majority report was a half-hearted scheme which offered no prospect of long-term settlement.

Nevertheless the recommendations of the Majority report were sufficient to alarm the Nonconformists. In the past there had been a deep rift between those Nonconformists who wanted unsectarian teaching in schools and those who objected to any form of religious instruction. For years Nonconformity had been weakened by division on this crucial matter of policy. Now, as a direct consequence of the Majority report, both sides were prepared to sink their differences. The Baptist Union, for example, abandoned its old secular platform; the Congregationalists and Presbyterians showed a similar willingness to compromise. The result in November 1888 was a public proclamation of Nonconformist unity at the Exeter Hall Conference, where it was agreed that the question of undenominational or secular instruction should be left to local option and that both sections should combine in support of school boards.[3]

The Majority report led to a decisive change in Methodist policy. District meetings throughout the country repudiated its recommendations and among Methodist leaders Dr Hugh Price Hughes,

---

[1] *Cross Commission, IV, op. cit.*, 247.   [2] *Ibid.*, 387.   [3] *The Times*, 22.11.88.

editor of the new *Methodist Times*, condemned the proposals and expressed his horror at finding Dr Rigg ranged alongside Cardinal Manning and Canon Gregory.[1] Indeed there were now few Methodists who shared Rigg's devotion for Connexional schools; rather the views of the majority were expressed by one of the Wesleyan witnesses before the Commission who said that they were 'a deadweight in the circuits and injured all the Connexional funds'. Nevertheless, so powerful was Rigg's influence that it was not until 1891 that the Methodist Education Committee was able to declare unequivocally that 'the primary objective of Methodist policy is the establishment of school boards everywhere . . . and the placing of a Christian unsectarian school within a reasonable distance of every family especially in rural districts'.[2] The resolution was, in the words of the *Daily News*, 'a momentous decision, the most significant event which has occurred in the whole course of the educational controversy.'[3] For almost twenty years Methodists had divided their energies between maintaining their own schools and encouraging the expansion of the school board system. Now, at last, they had declared for a universal, unsectarian system.

The Free Churches had met the challenge of the Majority report with vigour and determination. They had succeeded in resolving long differences in educational policy and for the first time stood together in defence of the public system. Furthermore, they had, under the influence of Lyulph Stanley and in association with the Liberals, revived the old Education League under a new name, the National Education Association.[4] On the other side the story was very different. While Roman Catholics took up the cry for rate aid without hesitation or qualification, many Anglicans became apprehensive lest, particularly under a Liberal Government, the conditions governing such grants might endanger the independent existence of their schools. They, therefore, proceeded to repudiate even the tentative suggestions of the report, and diocesan resolutions in various parts of the country culminated, in November 1888, in the National Society's decisive rejection of rate aid.[5] The bolder policy was disavowed and Anglicans harked

[1] 10.5.88.　　[2] *Report of Wesleyan Education Committee*, 1891, 81.　　[3] 30.1.91.
[4] These developments are discussed in *British Journal of Educational Studies* (Allen Rogers 'Churches and Children'), vol. viii, No. 1, 40.
[5] *Report of the Conference of the Friends of Church Schools*, 6.11.88. N.S.

back to their old idea of piecemeal reform rather than place their schools on the 'slippery slope of the rates'.[1] There was the same dissension on the issue of free education, which was nevertheless effectively established in 1891 by the introduction of a uniform State grant of 10s. a year (the equivalent of 3d. a week) to all schools in lieu of fees. Naturally the two communities had reacted differently to the proposal for, while Roman Catholic schools with their low fees would benefit the most, Anglican schools charging higher fees would have to meet the deficits from other sources.[2]

Anxious as it was to befriend the voluntary schools, the Unionist Government (in the party realignment in 1886 the Liberal dissidents including Chamberlain had joined the Conservatives) was greatly embarrassed by denominationalist disunity. The minority group, the Roman Catholics, stood solidly for rate aid, but the Anglicans had a multitude of separate policies, some private and some diocesan, some for extra State aid, some for rate aid and still others for both kinds of aid. Ready and willing though it was to provide additional help, the Government could do little until the denominationalists had resolved their differences. Anglicans were especially hard hit by the free schooling measure of 1891 and soon exhausted every known form of raising money. Bazaars, sermons, appeals signed by Bishops, Deans and distinguished laymen, all were tried. Even by 1890 the Church of England had surrendered almost a thousand of her schools[3] and her losses were continually increasing. Moreover, the constant flow into the service of the school boards of teachers trained in Church training colleges was causing alarm, for the most highly qualified teachers were moving into board schools leaving the least qualified to staff the voluntary schools.[4] Roman Catholics, too, complained bitterly of their disabilities. As one Roman Catholic priest put it, 'I see our children left behind in the struggle for life. Our schools have given them only half a chance. I have wearied my congregations with appeals, the parents are not satisfied, the mistress is in poverty, the grant is low and even for

---

[1] The phrase was Dr Temple's.

[2] Almost a third of Anglican schools charged fees of 4d. and over. *Report*, 1891, P.P. [C.-6438-1] 300.

[3] *Ibid.*, xii.

[4] There was one two-year trained teacher to every 110 children in board schools, one to every 230 children in voluntary schools. Calculated from the statistical tables. *Report*, P.P. 1896 [C.-8249].

that low grant I feel I am indebted to some extent to the indulgence of the Inspector of the Education Department.'[1]

Year after year the Education Department, spurred on by the accomplishments of the larger school boards, was insisting on higher standards of education, more teachers, better school buildings and improved equipment.[2] Year after year the poverty of the churches compelled them to resist the new demands. By the early 'nineties it was clear that only large-scale remedy could meet denominational difficulties. For a decade the Roman Catholic hierarchy had looked to rate aid to save the situation and was prepared, in return, to allow ratepayers the rights of inspection and oversight over the expenditure of their money. Cardinal Vaughan was as keen as had been his predecessor, Cardinal Manning, to secure rate aid. He pointed out that public control of Catholic industrial schools had worked well for a period of twenty years. The ratepayers, he said, 'pay us annually considerable sums of money from the rates and we have found them to be neither filibusters nor invaders bent on annexation.'[3] Many Anglicans, too, longed for a more definite policy and in 1893 the *Guardian*, referring wistfully to Roman Catholic solidarity, appealed to the Bishops to give a clear lead instead of leaving the individual priest to take his own line and fight his own battles.[4] The Bishops, however, were extremely reluctant to consider the principle of rate aid which the Primate, Dr Benson, declared would in the long run be 'disastrous', 'dangerous', and 'lowering'.[5] What the Archbishop really feared as a consequence of rate aid was the introduction of a form of control which would 'unchurch the Church schools', the establishment of parents' committees which would be far more favourable to the homogeneous communities of Roman Catholics than to the Anglicans. During his lifetime, therefore, official approval of rate aid was out of the question. Nevertheless, the principle of rate aid became increasingly popular especially in Lancashire, where endowments were negligible[6] and where the blow of free schooling had struck with especial severity. As the movement gained ground throughout the

[1] The *Weekly Register*, 4.3.93.

[2] One topic of controversy was the regulation of the Code of 1889 requiring 10 (instead of 8) square feet of space for each child. Another was Acland's Circular 321, (1893) which forced into prominence the bad accommodation in voluntary schools.

[3] *The Times*, 10.6.96.   [4] 31.5.93.   [5] The *School Guardian*, 24.6.93.

[6] They amounted to 5¼d. a head, *The Times*, 3.8.96.

country, Anglicans became more and more impatient of official leadership in the Church and feelings of resentment and exasperation crystallised at the Church Congress held in Exeter in 1894 when, as one speaker put it, 'If our leaders will not lead, the cause is lost.'[1] The official reply in the New Year was cautious and restrained, a request merely for additional State aid in the form of an Exchequer grant to cover teachers' salaries.[2] In response to the cry of 'Our leaders must lead' the Bishops had made a gesture but they still sought to avoid the perils of rate aid.

In the meantime revival of religious controversy on the London School Board had attracted considerable interest. In February 1893 the denominationalists on the Board led by the High Anglican, Athelstan Riley, had taken the offensive and reopened the entire religious question. Riley was highly critical of the vague character of the religious instruction given in the London board schools and pointed out that the word 'Christian' had even been omitted from the original resolution of 1871. His new resolution, 'children are to be distinctly taught that Christ is God, and such explanations of the doctrine of the Holy Trinity are to be given as may be suited to their capacities,'[3] revived the old controversy. With the support of the Moderates under their leader, the Rev. J. W. Diggle, chairman of the Board, Riley succeeded in strengthening the original resolution and in securing the publication of a Circular to explain the change in School Board policy.[4] The repercussions were immediate for the teachers were deeply resentful and more than 3,000 of them applied to be relieved from giving religious instruction altogether.[5] The School Board election which followed in 1894 roused a fever of excitement with Dr Temple and Cardinal Vaughan coming out strongly in support of the Moderates, and Nonconformist leaders, like the famous Baptist preacher, Dr Clifford, rallying to the Progressives. The national 'Dailies' joined in the fray, *The Times*, the *Standard*, the *Evening News*, and the *Morning Post* on the side of the Moderates; the *Daily News*, the *Daily Chronicle*, the *Star* and the *Sun* on the side

---

[1] The *School Board Chronicle*, 13.9.94.   [2] *The Times*, 7.1.95.

[3] *Minutes of the Proceedings of the London School Board*, 38, 493.

[4] *Ibid.*, 39, 453, 15th February, 1894. The Circular directed the teachers 'to impress upon the children the relation in which they stand to God the Father as their Creator, to God the Son as their Redeemer, and to God the Holy Spirit as their Sanctifier'.

[5] *Report of the London School Board*, 1894, 17.

of the Progressives. Finally, after a crescendo of excitement and furore, the Moderates were returned to power but with a depleted majority. They took the lesson to heart and under the new chairman, Lord George Hamilton, modified their policy; in fact, the Circular was allowed to become a dead letter and before the next election Athelstan Riley announced his retirement from the Board. The episode, however, left a deep impression for it touched the delicate problem of the Cowper-Temple Clause, and long after the uproar and upheaval of the Circular controversy had died away the incident was recalled at the Board of Education as a warning against any interference with the clause.[1]

*   *   *   *   *

The summer of 1895 saw the Unionists in power again. In the preceding months party chiefs had been at pains to woo the denominationalists. A. J. Balfour, speaking at East Manchester in January, had given prominent place to 'the preservation of voluntary schools' and had declared that they should be treated 'tenderly, lovingly, as a most important part of the great division of education.'[2] At the Annual Meeting of the National Society in June, Lord Salisbury had declared his acceptance of the right of the parent to distinctive doctrinal religious teaching at the public cost. For the present, he urged the clergy to make the best of existing conditions 'by capturing the school boards' while, for the future, he promised them 'a better law which shall place you under no religious disability'.[3] The Government was naturally sympathetic towards the voluntary schools. Salisbury, referring to school board extravagance, said that he would 'like to see Mr. Forster's statement that the rate would never exceed 3d. in the pound written in letters three feet long and placed over every school board school in the country'.[4] However, keen as he was to relieve the voluntary schools, dissension among the denominationalists made progress very difficult. In vain The Times urged Churchmen to do everything in their power to strengthen the hands of the administration;[5] memorials presented in November

---

[1] 'Letter from Mr. R. L. Morant to Mr. A. J. Balfour', 3.1.02. Ed. 24, P.R.O.
[2] The School Guardian, 26.1.95.   [3] The Times, 13.6.95.
[4] Address to the Brighton Conservative Association, December 1895. Primrose League publication.
[5] The Times, 5.9.95.

1895[1] to the Prime Minister revealed that the two groups were as far as ever from agreement. Without a unanimous mandate from the denominationalists, the Government were in an embarrassing position. Politically, also, the delay was particularly unfortunate for as Home Rule receded the Unionist alliance showed signs of disintegrating and conflicts between the extremes became more noticeable. No single issue emphasised the differences so much as the education dispute. In March 1896 the Government introduced their Education Bill. The most significant of the proposals was the creation of new authorities for education, the counties and county boroughs, which for the present were given power to assist voluntary schools and control secondary education but which were clearly intended to absorb the school boards at some future date. The Bill also included proposals especially designed to assist the voluntary schools, namely the abolition of the 17s. 6d. limit, the exemption of schools from the rates, and a special grant to facilitate staffing arrangements in poor schools. One of the most controversial parts of the Bill was Clause 27 which, contrary to the Cowper-Temple Clause, permitted, under certain circumstances, denominational teaching in board schools.

In the light of Conservative pledges the Bill was a piddling, makeshift measure. The Cabinet had in fact considered a bolder, more comprehensive plan for the abolition of the school boards and the transfer of all schools, board and voluntary, to the county authorities,[2] but, at the Unionist request, the original proposals had been so drastically curtailed that they had become virtually worthless; the creation of new authorities would have added to the administrative confusion, the offer of 4s. per head (a 1d. a week) to poor schools, would merely have prolonged the agony of those schools. Nevertheless, even the modified Bill roused tremendous opposition from the Liberals and Nonconformists who claimed that Clause 27 would extinguish undenominational instruction in the nation's schools and hand them over to the clergy. As for the new aid grant, it would, according to Dr Clifford, put nearly half a million more money into the pockets of the priests. 'If the sons of Hampden and Cromwell are going to submit to this,' he wrote, 'then we may say farewell to Britain's

[1] Catholic Memorial presented 13th November, 1895. C.E.C. *Report of meeting of deputation of the National Society with the Prime Minister,* 20th November, 1895. N.S.
[2] *Parl. Deb.,* 4th Ser., vol. xi, col. 666.

supremacy in commerce, in love of justice and in religion.'[1] Though the Bill passed the second reading it had to be abandoned, so intense was opposition in the country and so prolonged the conflict at the Committee stage.

The Government had withdrawn their larger measure. But in the following year they introduced a Bill specifically for the relief of voluntary schools. In addition to the proposals of the previous year: the abolition of the 17s. 6d. limit, the exemption of schools from the rates and a special grant to poor schools, there was one new feature, the obligation to establish associations of voluntary schools, which were intended to distribute the new grant and to strengthen the weaker voluntary schools by providing a wider basis of organisation. Liberals and Nonconformists were once more in arms and in the north, where feeling was particularly strong, the newly founded branch of the National Education Association, the Northern Counties Education League, was especially active. The measure went through, but it was no more than a temporary expedient and as such was a grave disappointment to the Roman Catholics who regarded it merely as 'a further dole on account' rather than an acceptance of the principle that equal work was deserving of equal payment. 'We must', said Cardinal Vaughan, 'get rid of the reproach that our schools are charity schools, dependent upon casual alms; we want to have done with the whole sorry and degrading business which makes the salaries of the teachers in denominational schools hang upon the success of this or that grinning comedian or upon the pious audacity of some fraudulent bazaar.'[2]

For many years lack of a common policy had weakened the denominationalist cause so that even friendly Governments, without a unanimous mandate, had been unable to give anything more than temporary doles, sufficient to irritate the opponents of the voluntary schools, without giving commensurate relief to the schools themselves. However, the death of the Archbishop of Canterbury, Dr Benson, who had for so long led opposition to the principle of rate aid, brought a vital change. Dr Benson had refused to compromise; his successor, Dr Temple, taking a more realistic view, placed the need of a common policy before his personal scruples. While still Archbishop-designate he had, in

---

[1] Marchant, *Dr John Clifford*, 120.
[2] Snead Cox, *Life of Cardinal Vaughan*, II, 122.

November 1896, summoned a joint conference of the convocations of Canterbury and York to discuss the problem of financial aid to Church schools. The result, a resolution in favour of both forms of aid, rate aid to schools in school board districts as well as extra State aid for all schools,[1] was highly significant. At last, after years of wavering and indecision, rate aid had become the accepted policy of the Established Church; at last, therefore, denominationalists could speak with one voice.

Meanwhile, by the closing years of the century, many voluntary schools were in an extremely precarious position. The agricultural depression of the 'nineties had borne heavily on subscribers in the countryside, and everywhere rising education rates had widened the financial gulf between board and voluntary schools. In 1890 the difference in expenditure for each child in the two types of school had averaged 9s.; by the end of the decade it had risen to 11s. 6d.[2] In the city areas, of course, where rates were sometimes over 1s. in the £, the gap was much greater. Many schools had been crushed out of existence. Others had completely exhausted their credit and overdrawn their accounts; full maintenance alone would enable them to continue. The public system, on the other hand, was continually expanding. All through the 'nineties the number of children in board schools had been increasing at the rate of 100,000 a year and in the country as a whole there were by 1900 almost as many children in board schools as in voluntary schools. It was in the cities that school boards had made the most spectacular progress and particularly in London where the Board was educating over half a million children, more than twice as many children as all the voluntary schools put together. The great progressive school boards had built up immense and variegated school systems. They had widened and liberalised the curriculum, established school museums and libraries, and provided modern buildings and equipment. They had invaded the spheres of secondary and adult education by means of higher grade schools, pupil-teacher centres and evening classes. They had opened special schools, schools for the blind, the deaf and the dumb and for the mentally defective, as well as industrial schools for truant children. Their achievements were truly impressive but the school board system had one fundamental weakness, the lack of administrative cohesion between the individual units. Nor was

[1] Gregory, *Elementary Education,* Appendix, 201–2.   [2] See Appendix C.

it only the isolation of the school boards which needed to be broken down; voluntary schools must also be more closely associated with the public system before any general educational reform could be achieved. By the end of the century matters were rapidly being brought to an issue. Combined pressure from denominationalists for rate aid and from administrators for integration of the school systems were shortly to compel the Unionists to return to the problem. Clearly a new phase of religious conflict was about to begin with, on the one side, Churchmen looking to the Government for support and, on the other, Liberals and Nonconformists in close alliance. For a generation denominational schools had been on the defensive; the pending struggle would decide their fate.

Chapter 4

———————— ❊ ————————

The Act of 1902

The opening of the twentieth century coincided with a new urgency in the movement for educational reform. It was now clear that Britain was rapidly losing her industrial leadership and was in grave danger of being driven from the world's markets. Already by 1900 she had fallen to third place as a steel producing country, her exports had declined and her recent technological inventions had been negligible. It was significant that Germany and the United States, the most powerful of British rivals, had acted in the belief that commercial and industrial success was founded on educational efficiency whereas in Britain itself, though the lack of secondary and technical education had long been deplored, little had been done. It was only at the beginning of the twentieth century, when the irresistible pressure of events had driven the lesson home, that responsible opinion had at last awakened to the realisation that Britain's destiny depended as much on 'school power' as on 'sea power'.

The defects of the educational system were now very evident. In the field of secondary education the provision of schools was hopelessly inadequate; in the elementary system, which was necessarily the basis of secondary and technical education, there were glaring inequalities between board schools and voluntary schools; in administration there was duplication, inefficiency and extravagance. The need was for a recasting of the entire educational system. The basic problem, and at the same time the most controversial, concerned the elementary system of education and, in particular, the voluntary schools within the system. For these schools, which were educating rather more than half the nation's children, were in urgent need of improvement. Not only were many of them inferior themselves, but their effect was to drag down the general level of education. Exhausted financially, the denominations were incapable of making the necessary improvements.

What was to be done about the voluntary schools? In 1900 they numbered over 14,000 with a school population of nearly two and a half million.[1] Some of them, it was true, were maintained merely to avoid the costly machinery of a school board, but many were the products of strong religious feeling. Opponents of the voluntary schools would have preferred to leave them to die a natural death but, other considerations apart, such a policy was thoroughly unpractical. For, although voluntary schools were closing at the rate of sixty each year, a decline which might well accelerate in urban areas, the bulk of the schools would be likely to remain open for a very long period. Even if they were left to struggle on under existing conditions the majority would not disappear; they would simply linger on and remain a perpetual source of weakness to the entire educational system. Nor was it of any use tinkering with the problem by granting additional Government doles to voluntary schools, for experience had proved that such doles were absorbed in day-to-day expenditure almost as soon as they were given. Already, within three years of the Aid Grant of 1897, the benefits had been almost entirely swallowed up. The need was for a settlement which would offer permanent prospects of help.

In the towns the condition of voluntary schools was grave indeed, and many were in imminent danger of extinction. The Bishop of Rochester wrote frankly to the Prime Minister, Lord Salisbury, in December 1901,[2] 'If the schools are not in some way relieved many will go within the year — enough to greatly weaken the cause, and, by creating the impression that "the game is up", to bring down others in increasing numbers and at an accelerating rate. I am speaking of what I know.' Reports from northern cities similarly stressed the imminence of large-scale surrender. The position of the rural voluntary schools was different. Village schools were usually Church schools, but whether they were Church schools or board schools there was the same apathy, the same reluctance to spend money and the same indifference to standards. Throughout rural society education was regarded with contempt and even hostility since it deprived employers of a large supply of cheap labour, and the individual

[1] See Appendix C.   [2] 4.12.01. Ed. 24. P.R.O.

schools in their poverty and isolation afforded village children little chance of escaping the depressed existence of their fathers.[1]

Denominationalists in recent years had been prolific with suggestions for the reform of the dual system. Anglicans, who had at last reluctantly accepted the necessity of rate aid, produced a number of schemes, all asking for rate aid and for some relaxation of the rigours of the Cowper-Temple Clause.[2] Roman Catholics held firmly to their claim of rate aid for the maintenance both of existing schools and of new schools which they might build in the future.[3] In support of their claim they pointed to other aspects of the social system, to Reformatory schools and to the Army, Navy and Poor Law institutions, where those who desired denominational influences did not have to bear unfair burdens. The denominational cause was weakened by division of opinion. There were two distinct theories of the function of religion in the schools: 'the religious atmosphere theory' and 'the regulated hours theory'.[4] The first was held by members of the Roman Catholic minority. It was held also by the many Anglicans who wanted the Church 'atmosphere' to permeate the entire life of the school, who desired, in the words of Lord Hugh Cecil, 'schools with two doors',[5] one leading to the world and the other leading to membership of the worshipping community. On the other hand, some Anglicans held that dogmatic instruction and secular teaching were completely separate.[6] Indeed, in the past Churchmen of this school of thought had pointed to the Conscience Clause as a complete protection for Nonconformist children attending their schools, and had even solicited Nonconformist support for them on the purely secular ground of economy.

As for the Nonconformists themselves, they had during the years modified their views very considerably. In 1870 they had been extremely suspicious of the very clause, the Cowper-Temple Clause, which by experience they had now come to regard as their most effective safeguard. In 1870 they had wavered between secular and undenominational teaching in public schools and had weakened

---

[1] The *Manchester Guardian*, 1.2.99. Article on 'Education in Country Districts'.

[2] Gregory, *op. cit.*, Appendix, 203–6.

[3] 'Statement of the Catholic claim in the matter of a National System of Education', 29.11.01. C.E.C.

[4] J. A. Spender, The *Contemporary*, vol. 82, 811.

[5] *Parl. Deb.*, 4th Ser., vol. cvii, col. 845.

[6] Speech of the Bishop of Leicester at Church Congress. *The Times*, 8.12.02.

their cause accordingly; now they were united and firm in defence of the undenominational principle. In 1870 they had themselves owned large numbers of schools; now they were stalwart champions of the school board system and had transferred to the local boards large numbers of their schools. In urban areas, where there was a choice of school, they had no feelings of grievance, but in the country parishes they bitterly resented the Anglican monopoly. For it happened so often that the only school their children could attend was, in Halévy's words, 'built with the squire's money and taught with the parson's catechism. And woe to the Wesleyan or Baptist child who refused to attend the religious lesson.'[1] There were many complaints of the ineffectiveness of the Conscience Clause, for it was not an easy thing for a labourer to set himself in opposition to the squire and parson. Nonconformist suspicion and hostility were intensified by the enthusiasm of overzealous clerics. One rural diocesan inspector, for example, reported that it was his custom to single out Nonconformist children and question them on denominational instruction. 'Thus', he wrote, 'we are training the children of Nonconformists to be children of the Church.'[2] With the growth of the High Church movement conditions had deteriorated in late years. It was one thing for Nonconformists to accept Catholicism as a thing apart, but it was quite another matter for them to view calmly the 'Romeward tendency' in institutions which affected their own children. To be a Roman Catholic was 'to deserve the pity due to the sufferers from an hereditary disease'; to be a Ritualist was 'to be guilty of the deliberate importation of that disease'.[3] While the former could be regarded with a measure of tolerance, the latter excited suspicion and hostility.

Nonconformists also resented the restrictions placed on their members within the teaching profession who were excluded from the 14,000 headships controlled by the Church of England, and virtually altogether from schools in single-school areas. So far as the denominational schools were concerned, teaching was a close profession restricted to members of the controlling sects and it was all the more galling that many teachers in Church schools, paid very largely from public funds, were appointed as much for parochial duties as for educational work. Above all it was the

---

[1] Halévy, *History of the English People in the Nineteenth Century*, V, 166.
[2] The *Guardian*, 4.8.97.   [3] *The Nineteenth Century and After*, vol. lix, 757.

injustice and illogicality of the Anglican ascendancy in the schools which was resented for it was not unusual to find that the majority of pupils attending the village National school were the children of Nonconformists.[1] Free Churchmen, therefore, were united in urging the provision of undenominational schools in all districts. Denominational teaching they regarded as an extra which should be paid for by those who wanted it, for they felt that minorities should suffer rather than that the conscience of the majority should be offended by the propagation of sectarianism in publicly maintained schools. They were very suspicious, too, that the inspiration behind denominational claims was not the parent but the priest, a thought which led them to reflect darkly on the threat to liberty and cherished rights. They were, therefore, implacably opposed to additional subsidies for denominational schools and were hopeful that these schools would gradually be starved out of existence. The paradoxical situation at this period has perhaps been best summed up by the foreign observer, Halévy, who wrote, 'there were State schools favoured by the Free Churches; free schools favoured by the State Church.'[2] Thus in the re-organisation of the national system of education, the religious question was the most intricate and thorny problem to be faced. Essentially it touched men's consciences and the greatest difficulty was the inability of either side to appreciate the conscience of the other.

Significant political changes had occurred since 1870. The parties themselves had undergone transformation and the issues of conflict were different. Politically, the Nonconformists counted for less than they had a generation ago. In 1870 they had been solidly Liberal; now, following the Home Rule controversy, they were divided in party allegiance. Moreover, with the removal of the last of their civil disabilities their passionate interest in politics had declined. To the Liberals the reopening of the religious conflict came as an unmixed blessing. For many years they had been in the wilderness; divided in leadership, disrupted and disorganised by the issue of the Boer war, their fortunes had sunk to a low ebb. Here was an issue on which all could unite, a challenge to be taken up without hesitation or qualification. The

---

[1] This was true, for example, of some of the Lincolnshire villages. The *Eastern Morning News*, 16.7.97.

[2] Halévy, *op. cit.*, 165.

position was very different for the Unionists. For years the powerful coalition had worked well under the dual leadership of Salisbury and Chamberlain. Only recently in the tense war-time atmosphere of 1900, the country had renewed its mandate. But to an alliance of Tory Churchmen and ex-Liberal Dissenters the education issue was fraught with danger. Here the party was most vulnerable.

Already, officials at the Education Department (soon to become the Board of Education) had been making preliminary preparations for large-scale reforms. The moving spirit was Robert Morant, Secretary to the Vice-President, Sir John Gorst. Morant was determined to substitute for the existing complexities of educational administration a more centralised and logical system and his ideas were reinforced by the publication, in January 1901, of the Fabian Tract, 'The Educational Muddle and the Way Out'.[1] This was a bold plan to make the county councils the authorities for education with jurisdiction over board and voluntary schools alike. Both types of school were to be rate aided. The Fabian policy for the voluntary schools was 'to put them under the control of the local education authority; to improve and strengthen their committees of management; to raise their efficiency; and especially to provide better salaries for their teachers; to make impossible the tyrannical vagaries of foolish clergymen in the village schools; and to bring these into co-ordination with the rest of the educational system'. Morant never seriously contemplated the abolition of the voluntary schools for, other reasons apart, the cost of replacement would have been prohibitive.[2] Indeed some school boards were already becoming alarmed at the rate of closures and were anxious to provide assistance to keep the church schools going. Clearly the most practical reform would be the establishment of larger units of local administration with control over all schools. Sir John Gorst foresaw the outcry which would come from the stalwarts of the school board system, but he was determined to take a firm line. He had never regarded school boards as permanent institutions for they were a modern anomaly in local government and would never have been created if the county councils had existed in 1870. In his opinion there

[1] Tract, 106, 14.
[2] 'Note (by R. L. Morant) on the cost of replacing all voluntary schools by board schools', undated. Ed. 24. P.R.O.

should be one administration for all local purposes, the one body having entire control of local finance.[1]

In 1900 the whole question was precipitated by the Cockerton Judgment, which pronounced illegal the activities of the London School Board (and therefore every other school board) outside the field of elementary education. In order to regularise the position a Bill was introduced on 2nd July empowering the county and county borough councils to take control of the 'Cockerton' schools. The Liberals thereupon rallied to the defence of the school boards. To them this was 'a trumpery Bill', designed to humiliate the school boards, to 'truncate' them and 'tie them down to the rudiments'.[2] If, they said, these bodies had trespassed on the field of secondary education, it was only because there had been a void which no one else had been anxious to fill. The *Daily News* warned its readers, 'There is no time to lose. The Church party have been working steadily and remorselessly by every underground method known to them and now they have sprung a mine which threatens the very citadel of popular education.'[3] The Unionists, however, were in a strong political position; realising they had acted prematurely they withdrew their interim Bill on 30th July. Inevitably it was then only a question of time before they tackled the entire problem of educational reform.

Outwardly 1901 was a skirmishing year, while behind the scenes planning and preparations continued intensively. By the end of the year the atmosphere was one of expectancy. The denominationalists were now agreed on the need for rate aid. They insisted that the school managers should retain control of religious instruction and the appointment of teachers, though they were prepared to concede minority representation to the local authority.[4] Anglicans, in addition, still hankered after some modification of the Cowper-Temple Clause which would allow them access to their children in the board schools. The Nonconformists, meanwhile, rallied to the Liberal opposition in defence of the school boards.

Morant was deeply engaged during these months with the crucial problems of administration and finance. He was concerned

[1] 'Letter from Sir John Gorst to the Duke of Devonshire,' 13.12.00. Ed. 24. P.R.O.

[2] *Parl. Deb.,* 4th Ser., vol. xcvii, cols. 475 and 499.   [3] 26.3.01.

[4] (1) Resolutions approved by the National Society, 29.11.01. *Minutes of the Standing Committee.* N.S. (2) See note 3, p. 71.

to devise efficient units of administration and was therefore engaged not only in the collection of statistical information but also in sounding the councils of the big county boroughs to discover how far they would be prepared to accept large new duties.[1] At the same time he consulted representatives of the denominations in order to obtain their views. Within the Government he found vacillation and confusion. In the first place, Balfour, the leader of the Commons and successor designate to Salisbury, had to be weaned from a preference for dealing with secondary education in isolation.[2] In the second place, there was powerful opposition to the principle of compulsory rate aid. It was a vital question whether the new authorities should be compelled or merely empowered to aid the voluntary schools in their areas. Salisbury, as a staunch Churchman, was opposed to compulsion on the grounds that it would destroy the voluntary principle.[3] Chamberlain and Balfour, on the other hand, had in mind the political consequences of the imposition. Indeed, Chamberlain was unwilling to contemplate rate aid in any form, and was convinced that compulsory rate aid would be wholly disastrous for the Unionist coalition and would bring 'rate war in every town'. In an effort to break the deadlock, Morant travelled to Birmingham in early December to see Chamberlain. The interview which followed was one which Morant was to regard as the most important single achievement of his entire life.[4] Still a young man in his thirties, he was face to face with a formidable veteran of immense political experience and authority. With devastating logic he answered one by one the objections to rate aid, reminding the Colonial Secretary that it was his South African war which had made further Exchequer aid impossible. 'We have tried to build you a bridge,' he said, referring to permissive rate aid, 'I admit that it is shaky. But . . . it is the least unsafe bridge that can be built.' Within a matter of days Chamberlain yielded so far as to accept this less obnoxious form of rate aid but he did so with extreme reluctance and with a deep sense of foreboding for future political prospects.

---

[1] 'Notes on aspects of educational administration', 1.8.01. Ed. 24. P.R.O.

[2] 'Letter to the Duke of Devonshire', 28.8.01. Ed. 24. P.R.O.

[3] Amery, *Life of Joseph Chamberlain*, IV, 485.

[4] 'Notes of conversation between Mr Chamberlain and Mr Morant on Education Bill', 12.12.01. E. 24. P.R.O. The interview is described in *Amery, op. cit.*, 483–7 and in Allen, *Sir Robert Morant*, 167.

Balfour himself was fully aware of the disadvantages of the 'adoptive principle' but, in his anxiety to keep the Unionist alliance, he still sought to avoid compulsion. Instead he made various ingenious suggestions. He proposed, for example, that in return for rate aid the voluntary schools should make some financial contribution to the local authorities.[1] On another occasion, he suggested that authorities should be left to make their own arrangements with the individual schools in their areas.[2] The rate aid controversy confronted the Conservatives with a dilemma. On the one hand, they feared that compulsion would disrupt the Unionist alliance; on the other hand, they were conscious that local option offered no security to their own supporters. Politically it was very tempting to keep the adoptive principle, but as a matter of justice it was hardly fair to leave the denominations dependent on local favour. Meanwhile, Morant, who had conducted his own investigations into the finances of the voluntary schools, was emphatic on the need for action. 'Some drastic treatment must be found', he wrote, 'unless a large number of voluntary schools are to be extinguished and board schools to take their place.'[3] It was no wonder that Balfour complained that he was 'in the lowest possible spirits about the whole question' and had come to regard it as 'far more insoluble than the South African problem'.[4]

By the New Year of 1902 Morant felt that the time had come for firm decision. He urged the Government to deal boldly with the problem before them. 'If we cannot let the whole subject alone', he wrote, 'we cannot possibly get over the various difficulties that inevitably crop up one after the other directly one bit of the problem is touched except by grasping the *whole* problem, setting up a new system and abolishing at one stroke all the causes of all the difficulties, and substituting one symmetrical and consistent organisation instead.'[5] Administration, finance and religion were the three main issues. On the first two, Morant advocated a complete departure from the Act of 1870 by the establishment

[1] 'Mr. Balfour's Instructions (to R. L. Morant) as to lines of Education Bill', 20.12.01. Ed. 24. P.R.O.

[2] 'Mr. Balfour's Draft Scheme', 3.2.02. Ed. 24. P.R.O.

[3] 'Memorandum by Mr. Robert Laurie Morant on financial condition of voluntary schools', February 1902. Ed. 24. P.R.O.

[4] 'Memorandum to R.L.M. by A.J.B.', undated. Ed. 24. P.R.O.

[5] 'Letter from Mr. R. L. Morant to Mr. A. J. Balfour', 3.1.02. Ed. 24. P.R.O.

throughout the country of education authorities levying education rates. The third issue was by far the most complicated. Here there was a close parallel between the position of the Governments in 1870 and 1902. The Unionists of 1902, like their Liberal predecessors, would have preferred the adoptive principle for rate aid to denominational schools. In the event the statesmen of 1870 had fallen back on extra State aid for the voluntary schools and the Cowper-Temple Clause for the rate aided schools. In 1902, however, the heavy war debt excluded all possibility of extra State aid and Morant had by now become firmly convinced that the new basis of rate aid must be complete and permanent.[1] As for the Cowper-Temple Clause he was not prepared to risk a direct assault, although he would have liked, in the Anglican interest, to secure some slight modification in special cases. Morant had got to the very heart of the problem. He wanted the Bill to be framed on bold lines so that the new settlement should be 'complete, consistent and workable'. In particular, he advocated 'complete rate maintenance', as the only way of ensuring responsibility by the local authorities for the efficiency of all recognised public elementary schools in their areas.

Balfour and Chamberlain were still anxious to avoid compulsion and Chamberlain revived the famous Canadian plan whereby ratepayers allocated their rates to the schools of their choice.[2] Denominationalists had often suggested it in the past; and in 1896 it had been considered worthy of examination at the Education Department but Michael Sadler, after detailed investigation, had reported against its adoption in this country. Now in the New Year of 1902 it was scrutinised once again and once again it was pronounced unworkable.[3] The greatest practical difficulty was the existence of large numbers of compound householders who would have no chance of exercising the option. For example, few Irish Catholics in London or Liverpool paid rates direct, nor did the majority of agricultural labourers in country districts. Altogether, the difficulties were insuperable.

The Education Bill was introduced in the Commons on 24th March by Balfour, who assumed personal responsibility. It was

---

[1] 'Memorandum by Mr. R. L. Morant on Free Optional Aid versus Complete Rate Maintenance', 28.1.02. Ed. 24. P.R.O.

[2] 'Rough Draft by Mr. Chamberlain', January 1902. Ed. 24. P.R.O.

[3] 'Comments by Mr. T. Llewelyn Davies of the Local Taxation Commission', 10.2.02. Ed. 24. P.R.O.

almost wholly the work of Morant and included, on his advice, the retention of the Cowper-Temple Clause. Contrary to his advice, however, it included the 'adoptive principle' on rate aid which party chiefs had felt unable to discard and which was an obvious source of weakness. The emphasis in the Bill was on the welding of secular education into an organic whole under new local authorities, the county and county borough councils. For the first time, control and responsibility for education was to be vested in popularly elected bodies and, in return for rate aid, an element of popular control was to be infused into the management of voluntary schools which were to have up to one-third of their managers appointed by the new authorities. Balfour was at pains to defend the new provisions for church schools; he stressed the rights of parents to have schools of their choice, and the necessity, therefore, for recognising the right to denominational teaching as well as the right to undenominational teaching. He declared that 'the idea of the voluntary schools being swept away by an Act of Parliament or by any other method, is absurd. The mere magnitude of the forces with which you have got to deal renders it impossible, the mere magnitude of the gap which would be created in the system of national education renders it impossible. Voluntary schools must remain and, that being the case, they must be reinvigorated'.[1]

The Opposition attacked the Bill with great fire and fury. The abolition of the school boards would, they declared, kill local interest, while the granting of rate aid to denominational schools would outrage Nonconformist feelings and bring strife in every parish throughout the land.[2] The Liberals were in good heart. Here at last was a rallying point to unite them. The clarion resounded in their press; school boards were to be destroyed, said the *Daily News*, simply because they stood for 'enlightenment and progress'; education instead was to be 'crowded in on the tail of drainage and police, to be controlled by a subordinate committee of a body elected on another issue, chosen by the political caucus and holding its meetings in secret. Education is to be withdrawn from the light of day'.[3] After heated debate, the option clause was

[1] *Parl. Deb.*, 4th Ser., vol. cv, cols. 854–5.
[2] Speech by Lord Rosebery at National Liberal Club, 23.5.02. Liberal League Publication, No. 38.
[3] 25.3.02.

struck out by a free vote of the House on 9th July.[1] Balfour explained his own conversion to the compulsory principle on the grounds that it would provide the only safeguard against religious conflicts recurring at every local election. Chamberlain, the principal opponent of compulsion on the Government benches, was out of action and in hospital at the time, but his son registered his protest by voting with the Opposition.

In the country the repercussion was immediate. So long as Nonconformists had power to prevent the local application of rate aid they were scarcely justified in raising a great commotion. Now that it was to become a national levy they could denounce it as a compulsory Church rate. For years Nonconformists had demanded a universal system of board schools and had looked forward to the gradual disappearance of church schools. Now it seemed that these schools were to be given a new lease of life and the way made clear for their unlimited extension. The Balfour Bill worked miracles with the Nonconformists. Dr Parker of the City Temple declared that it 'had aroused the very dead', and he went on to say that seldom in his fifty years' ministry had he known Nonconformity 'so thoroughly awakened or so justly angry'.[2] The agitation in the country reached its height during the Parliamentary summer recess. Once again Dr Clifford came forward as the great champion of Nonconformity and in the *Daily News* launched a passionate attack on the Bill in the form of a series of letters which were read throughout the length and breadth of the land. He appealed to the old Puritan Spirit of 'No surrender' to Clericalism and Romanism for he was convinced that the forces at work were 'the same as those which gave our Fathers the Act of Uniformity, the Test and Corporation Act . . . the genealogy is indisputable'.[3] Published subsequently in pamphlet form, the Clifford letters had a tremendous sale and were thought worthy of reply by Balfour himself.[4]

In his campaign Dr Clifford was joined by other leaders of Nonconformity, by Dr Hugh Price Hughes and Dr Scott Lidgett of the Methodist Church and by the Congregationalists, Dr Parker and the Rev. J. Hirst Hollowell. The latter, as secretary of

---

[1] *Parl. Deb.*, 4th Ser., vol. cx, cols. 1240–3.   [2] The *Daily News*, 9.9.02.
[3] *Ibid.*, 10.9.02.
[4] Pamphlet 'Letter from the Rt. Hon. A. J. Balfour, M.P. on the Criticisms of an opponent of the Education Bill'.

the Northern Counties Education League, was responsible for the agitation in the north which reached its peak on 20th September at a great meeting in Leeds. Demonstrators from all parts of the West Riding arrived in sixteen special trains and formed a procession a mile long through the city streets *en route* for their great gathering on Woodhouse Moor, where they unanimously resolved 'to kill the Bill'.[1]

Clifford's picturesque expression 'Rome on the rates' was a fine rolling phrase for the agitators. It sounded bloodcurdling to ardent Nonconformists, but it was largely delusive for it was not the Roman Catholics but the Anglicans with ten times their number of schools who stood to gain most from the Bill. Nevertheless, it was the Roman Catholic community which gave it the most enthusiastic reception; no class of school was more in need of equipment and better salary scales than their own, which would reap enormous benefits. Cardinal Vaughan welcomed the proposals as 'a distinct step in the right direction',[2] though he was not entirely happy about the powers to be given to the new local authorities and had misgivings about the standard of school buildings they might demand. If, for example, city authorities insisted on buildings equal to those of their own board schools, the Roman Catholics would find themselves in great difficulties. The Cardinal was himself perturbed by the proposal for public representation in the internal management of the schools, though he consoled himself with the thought that a two-thirds majority of Church managers would leave the denominational control secure. Despite minor objections, he was prepared to accept the Bill as a good bargain, and he took a firm line with those members of the Catholic Poor School Committee who expressed their preference for Exchequer grants rather than rate aid. 'We must remember', he said, 'that we are an unpopular and insignificant minority in this country and must take care lest by seeking to obtain the ideal we do not lose what we have hitherto gained.'[3]

Balfour found the Anglican reception of the Bill rather disappointing. It was true that the Archbishop of Canterbury described it as 'an honest and statesmanlike measure',[4] but High

---

[1] *The Times,* 22.9.02.   [2] 'Letter to A. J. Balfour', 16.11.01. Ed. 24. P.R.O.
[3] 'The Cardinal's Note. Proposed Catholic attitude to the Education Bill' (undated). Ed. 24. P.R.O.
[4] *Parl. Deb.,* 4th Ser., vol. cxv, col. 1225.

Anglicans were more grudging in their praise. 'We will not pretend for a moment that it is a final settlement of our claim', said the *Church Times*, 'nor adulate the Government because it offers us after so many years a moiety of that which is our right.'[1] In Parliament the High Anglican spokesman, Lord Hugh Cecil, made it clear that the Bill did not go far enough, and demanded 'facilities' for giving denominational instruction to Church children in local authority schools.[2] In the Church of England the High Anglicans were a small but aggressive minority and even to their own Bishops they were not infrequently a source of embarrassment. Yet on the schools' question they were often more realistic than many of their leaders; they foresaw the inevitable decline in the number of Church schools and the attendance of an increasing proportion of Anglican children at council schools, so they preferred to concentrate their energies on securing 'facilities' in council schools rather than struggling to preserve the dwindling number of denominational schools. The Nonconformists, however, reacted violently to the Anglican proposal. They had themselves no interest in 'facilities', and deplored the separation of school children into denominational pens. David Lloyd George, a rising back bencher, declared that 'facilities' would lead to all sorts of canvassing and that in the long run it would be a question not of 'superior dogmas', but of 'superior buns'.[3]

Within the Church of England there was wide diversity of view. Whereas Anglo-Catholics thought that the Church was not gaining enough, Liberal Churchmen thought that she was getting too much. The Bishop of Hereford, for example, condemned the Church's policy of 'aggressive grasping' which, he said, was threatening to destroy her spiritual influence. He considered that her educational policy was bringing a 'miserable bone of contention' into English life and he urged that she should meet the Nonconformists by yielding very much more to public control.[4]

Meanwhile Balfour, who had become Prime Minister on Salisbury's resignation in July, was concerned at developments during the recess. Appeals of wild oratory and hysterical agitation

---

[1] 23.5.02.   [2] *Parl. Deb.,* 4th Ser., vol. cvii, col. 845.
[3] *Parl. Deb.,* 4th Ser., vol. cxv, cols. 439–40.
[4] *Ibid.,* 4th Ser., vol. cxvi, cols. 341–6. (The Bishop had produced his own scheme designed to end exclusive control by the Church of single-school areas. Letter to *The Times,* 30.7.02.)

he could afford to dismiss, but the resounding defeat of the Government candidate at the North Leeds by-election was a serious indication of public feeling. Before Parliament reassembled in the autumn, he addressed a gathering in Manchester. Though it was his first important public speech as Prime Minister and his first since the end of hostilities, he devoted the whole of a long address to a resolute and powerful defence of the Education Bill. What, he asked, was the alternative? The slow and gradual extinction of the voluntary schools and, so long as that process lasted, the degradation of the whole system of education. 'There is at stake', he told the crowded Manchester gathering, 'the education of your children for a generation.'[1]

Back in Parliament the Bill was disputed line by line. The Liberal Unionists were in poor spirits. Chamberlain left for South Africa in the autumn but before his departure he wrote gloomily to the Duke of Devonshire, 'Our best friends are leaving us by scores and hundreds and they will not come back. I do not think the Tories like the situation but I suppose they will follow the Flag. The Liberal Unionists will not.'[2] In a private memorandum Balfour expressed doubts whether the Bill would survive 'the hatred of its enemies and the indifference of its friends'.[3] Nevertheless he was resolved to deal firmly with all extremists, and resisted demands, from the one side for 'facilities', and from the other for compulsory purchase of voluntary schools. He would not hear of an amendment permitting voluntary schools to contract out of the new settlement,[4] nor would he tilt the balance against them by depriving managers of the right of appointing and dismissing teachers.[5] However, he endeavoured to ease Nonconformist grievances by accepting an amendment which would mitigate the hardships of their young teachers, and he was at pains to stress to Nonconformists their total gains under the Bill. 'For the first time', he said, 'it enables the local education authority to provide secondary education for Nonconformists; for the first time it thrusts aside the trust deeds of voluntary schools so that Nonconformists can be elected to all posts except to headmasterships.'[6] Similarly, it was to pacify the Nonconformists that Balfour

---

[1] *The Times*, 15.10.02.　　　　[2] Holland, *Life of the Duke of Devonshire*, II, 284.
[3] 'Memorandum (initialled A.J.B.) about Kenyon-Slaney Clause', 6.12.02. Ed. 24. P.R.O.
[4] *Parl. Deb.*, 4th Ser., vol. cxiii, cols. 258–60.　　[5] *Ibid.*, 4th Ser., vol. cxv, col. 836.
[6] *Ibid.*, 4th Ser., vol. cxiii, col. 1277.

risked the wrath of the Church party and accepted the Kenyon-Slaney amendment.[1] Henceforth, whatever the stipulation of the trust deed, responsibility for religious instruction in voluntary schools was no longer to rest with the parish priest alone but with the whole body of managers. The clause was deliberately directed against individual Ritualists in single-school areas. It was, in the words of The Times, 'highly desirable that the pranks of wrong headed, if well intentioned, clerics should be subjected to some real and wholesome check.'[2] In fact, all the amendment did was to make explicit something which had already been implicit in the Bill itself, yet it raised an 'ecclesiastical tornado'.[3] The Church Times was furious at what it called 'the wanton insult' of the amendment, and still more wrathful against the Bench of Bishops who had accepted it.[4] Even Morant was perturbed at the Anglican fury and warned Balfour in some alarm that it was 'horribly dangerous' to alter the trust deeds.[5]

What both Anglicans and Roman Catholics were anxious about was the extent of their financial obligations under the Bill. Since the passing of the 1897 Act the Government had assumed responsibility for 'minor improvements' and it was now felt that the local authorities should undertake similar obligations. Cardinal Vaughan urged the Prime Minister not to 'spoil the ship for a ha'porth of tar'.[6] Anglicans were similarly concerned, and in the Upper House they inserted a new clause placing on local authorities the responsibility for 'fair wear and tear'[7] which, despite further outcry from the Opposition, was accepted by the Commons and incorporated into the Bill.

During the final stages of debate Balfour dealt sternly with all malcontents. He reminded those denominationalists who pleaded inviolability of trust deeds that they were now accepting aid to a degree never foreseen when the trusts were made. He was equally forthright with the Liberal Opposition, which, as he pointed out, had produced no alternative workable scheme but was apparently content to await the gradual extinction of the voluntary schools.[8] At last, after debates lasting fifty-nine days, the Bill was passed

[1] Ibid., 4th Ser., vol. cxiii, cols. 1311 et seq.   [2] 8.12.02.
[3] Asquith's description. Parl. Deb., 4th Ser., vol. cxvi, col. 335.   [4] 7.11.02.
[5] Allen, op. cit., 327.
[6] 'Letter from Cardinal Vaughan to A. J. Balfour', 16.11.02. Ed. 24. P.R.O.
[7] Parl. Deb., 4th Ser., vol. cxvi, col. 362.
[8] Ibid., 4th Ser., vol. cxv, cols. 1178 et seq.

and received the Royal Assent on 18th December. Its successful passage had been due in no small measure to the powerful combination of personalities, to the careful and detailed planning of Morant on the one hand and to the skilful political strategy of Balfour on the other. But the conflict had been unbelievably bitter. Time and time again arguments had been stated and restated, solutions proposed and rejected, and amid all the turmoil and excitement the educational aspects of reform had been very largely overlooked. Yet the changes were significant; education was for the first time brought into the main stream of local government, county councils and county borough councils were to be the new local education authorities responsible for all kinds of education in their respective areas, while the councils of the larger boroughs were given responsibility in the elementary field. Thus the school boards were to disappear and with them the wilder enthusiasms and extravagances which had often been associated with direct control. A new fusion of public and private enterprise was to place voluntary schools, now to be called 'non-provided' schools in contrast to the local authority or 'provided' schools, on a firmer footing and secure their effective control. In fact, the 1902 Act created a new national framework within which education could be adapted to meet the needs of the day.

The school board era had ended. More than a generation had passed since the foundation of the early boards; in the meantime they had spread over the country until they covered an area representing two-thirds of the population. They were now providing elementary education for over 2,000,000 children and had even invaded the sphere of secondary and higher education. Behind the unedifying spectacle of religious conflict at election times and at school board meetings, there had been a very real conflict of principle. Undoubtedly the more extreme supporters of the school boards had endeavoured to drive the voluntary schools out of existence, for in their enthusiasm for direct control they had tended to assume that a local authority, elected by popular vote, held the monopoly of educational wisdom. Nevertheless, in their devotion to public representation they stood for a principle which was firmly rooted in English life. On the other hand there was the principle, steadfastly maintained by denominationalists, that education was too closely linked with private conviction to be brought wholly under the direct control of public authority. The two types of school, voluntary and board school, represented two ideals, two ways of thought deeply grounded in national tradition.

Both points of view were respected in the Act of 1902. Essentially the measure was designed to end the existing conflict and competition and to secure all-round efficiency. By a new compromise the balance between undenominational and denominational schools was maintained; the provision and repair of school buildings remained the responsibility of the denomination while the cost of their maintenance, including teachers' salaries now came from the public purse. The national gain was indisputable; for the first time the entire country came under local authorities responsible for standards of secular education in both types of elementary school, for the first time public money was available for the proper payment of all teachers, for the raising of standards in all elementary schools and for supporting secondary education. National education was at last to be in the hands of experts instead of amateurs.

Anglicans and Roman Catholics were on the whole well satisfied. They were now assured of a form of aid which would be automatically adjusted to changing costs and which would be available for any new schools which they might build in the future. Their schools were recognised as a permanent and essential part of the national provision for education. Nonconformists, however, girded themselves for resistance. It had been supposed in 1870 that Forster's Act was the worst that could have happened to Nonconformity. Now, a generation later, his Act was regarded very differently and his institution of the board school system was hailed as the best thing that had happened in this country since the Reformation. The new measure was denounced for establishing a form of public control which was both remote and diluted, and for the endowment of ecclesiastical institutions and the perpetuation of theological tests for teachers.[1] Indeed, it seemed to Nonconformists that the Cowper-Temple Clause was all that remained of the 1870 compromise and that the Church 'had gobbled up everything else'.[2] And yet Nonconformists had much to be thankful for. For years they had clamoured for public control of education in the form of a universal system of school boards. Now public authorities for education were to be set up

---

[1] *Parl. Deb.*, 4th Ser., vol. cxv, cols. 937 *et seq.*
[2] Birrell, The *Independent Review*, October 1903.

everywhere and popular control of secular education was complete. The significance of the Act, however, was insufficiently appreciated and Nonconformist extremists proceeded to launch a movement of 'passive resistance' against the payment of rate aid to denominational schools. The Passive Resistance League came into existence with the *Crusader* as its press organ and with Dr Clifford as its leader. But among Free Churchmen there were many who shrank from militant measures. Methodists, for example, were divided on policy and it was one of the Methodist leaders, Dr Scott Lidgett, whose moderating influence prevailed at the decisive meeting of the National Free Church Council when passive resistance as a method of protest was renounced.[1] Despite their misgivings the main body of English Free Churchmen were not prepared to go to extreme lengths.

Rate aid had been singled out as objectionable by the passive resisters, but it is difficult to see why a particular class of school should have been regarded as eligible for Imperial grants coming out of the tax-payer's pocket and ineligible for local aid coming out of the ratepayer's pocket. Dissenters had never demurred against the payment of taxes out of which money had long been given to denominational schools. Why did their consciences now rebel against the payment of rate aid? They themselves made a distinction which was practical though hardly logical, that it was possible to discover the amount allocated out of the rates to a particular object, but impossible to calculate the proportion allocated out of the taxes. The truth was that rates came home to the individual much more forcibly than taxes, which were largely indirect and therefore impersonal. In both England and Wales passive resisters launched a rate war as an organised campaign against the 1902 Act. In England, where resisters were confined to a minority of noisy extremists, the movement never jeopardised the settlement, but in Wales the situation was more serious. Here it was the new local education authorities who defied the Government by collecting the new education rate but leaving the denominational schools exactly as they had been before the Act. The leader of the revolt was the vitriolic David Lloyd George, the slogan, 'No control — no cash.'[2] Wales was in the grip of a religious revival and Lloyd George's meetings of political protest

[1] Pritchard, *Symposium. Rev. John Scott Lidgett*, 27.
[2] Edwards, *David Lloyd George*, I, 258.

were impassioned by the evangelistic fervour of the time. Faced with the Welsh crisis Morant saw the need for firm action lest the more truculent English authorities should be encouraged to follow suit and so, on his advice, the Default Act[1] was passed to save the situation for the voluntary schools. Lloyd George's reply was an act of defiance, the setting up of a Campaign Fund in order to establish 'revolt schools'. Gradually, however, the movement subsided as one by one the Welsh authorities surrendered, though it was not until Montgomeryshire yielded in 1906 that the revolt was finally extinguished.[2]

Slowly the welter of controversy died down. It is hard to forgive the fanatical extremists on both sides who had degraded national education to a miserable quarrel between Church and Chapel. For, once it was given a fair trial, the 1902 Act was to prove thoroughly sound and constructive. The recognition of voluntary schools as full members of the national system of education was a considerable achievement, but it was only a small part of the general intention underlying the Act, namely, to secure greater unity in educational administration. Politically, the repercussions were significant for, as in 1870, the education issue helped to change party fortunes. Then Nonconformist desertions had driven the Gladstone Government on the rocks; now, once again, the rekindling of religious fires had weakened the party in power. Indeed, the Unionist coalition never recovered from the blow for some of the Liberal Unionists faded into private life, leaving a remnant which was henceforth indistinguishable from the main body of Conservatives. Liberal Unionism now belonged to the past and the long monopoly of one political party was over. On the other hand, members of the Liberal Party were buoyant with new hope and vitality and lost no time in launching an active political campaign in the constituencies. Identifying themselves completely with the Nonconformist cause, they made the most of religious fears and antagonisms. 'To read the Liberal newspapers of the day,' says Halévy, 'you would imagine that the Cecils were preparing to revive the policy of Laud if not of Strafford, and that in every village a Nonconformist Hampden was about to rise against their persecution.'[3]

[1] See Appendix B.

[2] *British Journal of Educational Studies*, vol. x, No. 2, 174. (E. Eaglesham, 'Implementing the Education Act of 1902.')

[3] Halévy, *op. cit.*, 210.

The 1902 Act provoked the last great outburst of public controversy between Anglicans and Free Churchmen. For a brief moment it seemed that the Act had revived the power of political Nonconformity, but it was an illusion which was soon dispelled. Despite the noisy resistance and prolonged agitation, passive resistance never seriously imperilled the settlement and as a topic of political controversy it was soon superseded by Imperial Preference. Perhaps its greatest effect was to restore the morale of the divided Liberal Party and to put it in good heart for the greater struggle which lay ahead. Certainly Nonconformity never recovered its old political influence and the growing secularisation of English life continued to sap its strength until public opinion became deaf to the old war cries. A new age had begun, an age of growing indifference and of changing values. During the next generation the Nonconformist phalanx of the Liberal Party gradually disintegrated until with the advent to power of the new Labour Party it disappeared completely.

Chapter 5

———————— ❋ ————————

The Liberal Bills, 1906–8

In December 1905, Parliament was dissolved and the Unionists went to the country. Although education was by this time only one among many issues of conflict, for electioneering purposes it was a godsend to the Liberals. Most eloquent of his party, Lloyd George spoke ominously of the fearful reckoning which was coming to his opponents for their oppression of the Nonconformists, but despite all the sound and fury the real conflict between the parties was on quite a different issue, that of Free Trade versus Protection. Nothing since Gladstone's conversion to Home Rule had caused such a sharp cleavage of policy.

The result, in January 1906, was an overwhelming electoral victory for the Liberals. For the first time since the passing of the Third Reform Bill the Liberal Party had a clear mandate and Campbell-Bannerman as Prime Minister headed a Cabinet of unusual strength and character. The Conservatives had been routed, and it was with dismay and apprehension that their leaders viewed the prospect of government by men like Lloyd George who did not belong to the old ruling order and whose programme threatened political and social upheaval. Despite their crushing defeat, therefore, they determined to defy the party in power and use their majority in the Upper House to defend the *status quo*. The first real clash was to come on education. The Liberals, with exuberant energy, were anxious to lose no time in fulfilling election pledges, and the new President of the Board of Education, Augustine Birrell, was soon absorbed in the complexities of the education issue. Birrell was a man of unusual talent and ability, who on the education issue had wide sympathies and a depth of understanding. The son of a Baptist minister, he was himself acutely aware of the feeling of Free Churchmen and particularly of their resentment of the Anglican monopoly of the village schools. 'The ivy-mantled tower of the church, the pleasant rectory, and the eaves and gables of the schoolhouse,' he said, 'instead of being to the Nonconformists symbols of a common Christianity, have been symbols of strife and contention.'[1] Nor did he consider that the Conscience Clause had helped very much, for the exercise of the right of withdrawal made the child unpleasantly conspicuous. With his own youthful experiences in mind he observed that 'Uniformity is the uniform creed of childhood and any reasonable child would rather be wicked than singular'.[2] However, Birrell had also an appreciation of other points of view. In his autobiography he confessed to having 'a soft place' in his heart for religious minorities, Roman Catholics, Jews and High Anglicans in the large towns. 'I had seen the schools belonging to these creeds in Liverpool, London and elsewhere', he wrote, 'and had a great admiration for them.'[3]

Like all reformers since 1870 Birrell and his party had to decide whether to build on existing foundations or to restart from fundamental principles. If they decided to begin afresh there were two possible solutions, both logical and both drastic. The one was the purely secular solution, the teaching of no one's religion in public elementary schools; the other, the frankly denominational solution, the teaching of everyone's religion on equal terms. The first alternative, total secularisation, seemed the easy way out of a perplexing situation, but such an idea was violently opposed to the religious tradition of the country. Though widely supported in 1870, it had been discarded then and had never been seriously considered since. The second alternative, the teaching of everyone's religion, had always daunted the educational administrator; it involved so many undesirable features, the taking of a religious census, the segregation of children into denominational pens and the difficulties of the 'right of entry'. It was true that the problem had narrowed down to the teaching of three forms of religion, undenominational Christianity, distinctive Anglican or distinctive Roman Catholic teaching. In Roman Catholic schools and the more homogeneous of the Anglican schools there would be no difficulty, but elsewhere the administrative problem would be insuperable; to bring in well-meaning amateur teachers would disrupt school organisation and the only alternative, religious tests for teachers,

---

[1] *Parl. Deb.*, 4th Ser., vol. clvi, col. 163.   [2] *Ibid.*, 4th Ser., vol. clv, col. 1029.
[3] Augustine Birrell, *Things Past Redress*, 189.

was undesirable. Both logical solutions, therefore, were out of the question.

It was customary and, indeed, politically expedient to treat all denominational schools alike but there were really two types of denominational schools: the Anglican schools, which drew, for the most part, on heterogeneous school populations and which varied enormously in the denominational instruction they gave and the Roman Catholic schools, where distinctive doctrinal teaching was given only to children of Roman Catholic parents. In the debates of 1902 several Liberal speakers had distinguished between the two types and had referred to the need of a separate settlement for the Roman Catholics. Neither of the political parties could afford to ignore the Roman Catholic minority for both were pledged to retain at least fifty Irish members in the Imperial Parliament, a solid phalanx which would always rally loyally to the support of co-religionists in England. It was clear that great skill and ingenuity would be required in devising a settlement. In anticipation of a new measure Nonconformists in March stressed three main principles: a uniform system of public elementary schools, provided and controlled entirely by public authority, the abolition in these schools of all distinctive religious teaching within school hours, and the abolition of religious tests for teachers.[1] Simultaneously, denominationalists reaffirmed their position and emphasised the right of parents to obtain for their children instruction in their faith.[2] Both Anglicans and Roman Catholics, however, were reasonably satisfied with the existing settlement. Some were still a little nervous about the enormous powers of the local authorities, but in general relations had been friendly and cordial.

The Liberals for their part considered themselves bound by their election pledges, the establishment of popular control over all schools maintained out of public money and the abolition of religious tests for teachers. They must, therefore, transfer all nonprovided schools to the local authorities, and release the teachers from the necessity of giving religious instruction. In this way they would meet Nonconformist grievances, but the problem was

---

[1] Resolutions of the National Council of Evangelical Free Churches, 6.3.06.
[2] (a) Resolution of the Upper House of Canterbury Convocation, 22.2.06.
  (b) 'Statement of the Catholic position with regard to Education', March 1906 (issued by the Catholic Education Council). C.E.C.

to reconcile the denominationalists. 'Facilities' seemed to offer the only solution to the dilemma. Indeed, the Prime Minister, a Scotsman, favoured the logical Scottish solution of teaching everyone's religion. He would have preferred to confine State education to secular instruction and to give equal 'facilities' to all denominations to teach their tenets in all public elementary schools[1] but the difficulty was that 'facilities' on such a scale would completely violate the Cowper-Temple Clause. To take the sting out of the proposal Birrell explored the possibility of restricting 'facilities' to out-of-school hours and certainly the preliminary plans which were shown to the Archbishop of Canterbury included provision for such 'facilities',[2] but in the end the idea was dropped and nothing further was heard of it.

On 9th April Birrell introduced the Liberal Bill. The main feature was the abolition of the dual system and the establishment of a single system of schools under complete public control. Local authorities were empowered to take over all existing denominational schools, which were to be divided into two types, the moderate denominational schools and the extreme denominational or 'atmosphere' schools. Corresponding to the two types of school there were to be two types of 'facilities', 'ordinary' and 'extended', for giving denominational instruction. Ordinary 'facilities' were to be restricted to two days a week with Cowper-Temple instruction on the remaining days; extended 'facilities' were permitted on every day of the week. In the first type of school the regular teachers were expressly excluded from giving denominational instruction, in the second type the local authorities might, if they thought fit, permit the teachers to give such instruction. In both types of school the option of granting 'facilities' as a result of transfer was to rest with the local authorities, who were to pay rent for the schools transferred.

The first category of schools, described in Clause 3 of the Bill, was intended to include the majority of Anglican schools; the second category, described in Clause 4, was designed for the smaller number of Roman Catholic and Jewish schools,[3] as well as a minority of Anglican schools. The intention was to make the undenominational or 'moderate' denominational school the normal type, and to allow the purely denominational school only

[1] Spender, Life of the Rt. Hon. Sir Henry Campbell-Bannerman, II, 76–7.
[2] Bell, Randall Davidson, I, 517.   [3] There were only 12 Jewish schools.

where it existed over and above the ordinary school supply of the district. Two rigorous conditions were laid down before a school could qualify for extended 'facilities'; firstly, four-fifths of the parents of the children attending the school must ask for these 'facilities' and, secondly, the school must be situated in an urban area with over 5,000 inhabitants. In general, any existing church school, wherever it was situated and however small the demand, might apply for ordinary 'facilities', but before a school could claim extended 'facilities' it must be both urban in situation and homogeneous in character. With his Nonconformist background Birrell had a special interest in strengthening the Conscience Clause, and accordingly Clause 6 stated that a parent should not be under any obligation to send his child to school, 'except during the times allowed in the time-table exclusively to secular instruction.' In this way Birrell hoped to make the Conscience Clause, which he considered had hitherto had 'a useless career', much more of a 'genuine reality'.[1]

Described by the Prime Minister as 'an undenominational Bill, setting up an undenominational system',[2] the measure had been deliberately designed to eliminate the Anglican monopoly in the single-school areas. But it was precisely the undenominational principle behind the Bill which roused the fury of the Opposition members. To them it seemed like the endowment of a new religion, 'Birreligion'. Indeed, in its original form the Bill dealt harshly with the denominations, for it gave them no security that their schools would be accepted either as Clause 3 or as Clause 4 schools. Nor did Birrell give them much encouragement when, referring to those who wanted denominational instruction as minorities, he said, 'All minorities must suffer, it is the badge of their tribe.'[3] Anglicans found little comfort in the terms of Clause 3, especially in 'the compulsory silencing' of the teacher and the confiscation of property bequeathed on trust.[4] Roman Catholics, on the other hand, concentrated on Clause 4 complaining that the 'facilities' offered would be wholly illusory, half their schools would be cut out by the statistical qualifications and the character of the other half would depend on the favour of the local authorities.

---

[1] *Parl. Deb.*, 4th Ser., vol. clxvi, col. 1587.   [2] *Ibid.*, 4th Ser., vol. clix, col. 838.
[3] *Ibid.*, 4th Ser., vol. clv, col. 1033.
[4] Archbishop of Canterbury in a letter to the Secretary of the National Society, published in *The Times*, 11.3.06.

Tim Healy scathingly suggested as a suitable preamble for the Bill the words, 'Go and teach all nations, with the consent of the County Councils.' 'The Catholic convict, the Catholic pauper, the Catholic soldier and even the Catholic corpse', he said, 'is looked after with extraordinary punctilio by the great Parliament of England. So I must be either a pauper or a foundling in order that the rites of my religion may be conserved.'[1]

In the country as a whole there was a deluge of criticism. To the Nonconformists it was Clause 4 which was particularly objectionable. The old leaders of passive resistance denounced the principle of rate aid to denominational schools and at a meeting with the President in June threatened the Government with their defection. In vain Birrell argued with them, explaining that Clause 4 was a consequence of their own rejection of the secular solution. 'You cannot deal with education in this country, unless you adopt boldly the secular course', he said, 'you can only deal with it in a spirit of compromise.'[2]

Denominationalists, too, were up in arms. The Primate, Dr Davidson, himself gave a strong lead but the most forthright of the Anglican Bishops was Dr Knox of Manchester, who talked of 'racks and thumbscrews'. Clause 4, he said, had been 'purposely drawn to favour as many Roman Catholic schools and as few Church schools as possible', while the terms of Clause 3 would be satisfied if the authorities allowed the children 'to receive their Church instruction in the playground or on the street'. To one of his audiences he declared, 'Your tea, your sugar, your beer and your incomes are to be taxed that the children of the Church may be robbed of their Church education and that your schools, built by your own free contributions, may be made useless for your own requirements.'[3] Under his leadership the Church Schools Emergency League, founded to oppose passive resistance, was revived in Manchester and so intense was the feeling in the diocese that thirty-two trains full of Lancashire Churchmen travelled up to London in Whit week to demonstrate their indignation. Roman Catholics were no less alarmed and the *Tablet* denounced the Bill as 'a new penal law' which would impose

---

[1] *Parl. Deb.*, 4th Ser., vol. clvi, cols. 1528–31.
[2] Minutes of meeting of deputation of the National Passive Resistance Committee with the President, 18.6.06. Ed. 24. P.R.O.
[3] Bell, *op. cit.*, I, 519 *et seq.*

'surrender or starvation'.[1] The Catholic Education Council (the Poor School Committee had changed its name two years before) was divided on policy. Some members preferred to stand out of the new arrangements altogether and return to the pre-1902 conditions of State aid since they feared that facilities under local control would mean 'pawning the atmosphere in order to buy the words of the catechism.' Others, like Monsignor W. F. Brown, were hopeful of establishing good relations with the local authorities. The Monsignor spoke with considerable authority on education; as a Scotsman he was familiar with the Scottish system and his membership of the old London School Board had given him experience of English local administration. He was emphatic that to return to the days of large classes and small salaries would be suicidal; while he could see some prospects under an amended Bill, he could see no future whatsoever in contracting out.[2] His view prevailed and on 18th June the Catholic Education Council resolved on the appointment of a Watching Committee[3] to work closely with the Irish members in order to secure amendments to Clause 4.

The Liberals, anxious to retain the allegiance of the Irish Party, sought to make the clause more palatable, but they were in a quandary, for their Nonconformist supporters were already very restive. The real difficulty was how to reconcile the Liberal pledge of 'no tests for teachers' with denominational insistence on the fitness of teachers to teach religion, since if Clause 4 was to work effectively the regular teachers must be practising members of the denomination concerned. Birrell had assured the denomination-alists that 'the intention of the clause really is that the schools which come within its conditions should be carried on just as they are now'.[4] But he had given no safeguards. From the Roman Catholic point of view there were three gaps in the clause: firstly, local authorities were not obliged to take over their schools, secondly, where they did take them over they were not obliged to grant extended 'facilities', and thirdly, where they granted extended 'facilities' they were not obliged to permit the regular staff to give the 'facilities' instruction. The first gap Birrell refused to bridge.

[1] 12.4.06.
[2] Minutes of the Executive Committee of the Catholic Education Council, 25.4.06. C.E.C.
[3] Ibid., 18.6.06. C.E.C.
[4] Statement to a Jewish deputation. The Jewish World, 4.5.06.

He had always contemplated, he said, 'that schools would be willing to come over and that the authorities would be desirous to take them,' but it would, he thought, be wrong to compel the authorities, irrespective of the school provision of the area, to take over a school 'simply because it was there'.[1] The other gaps he was prepared to do something about and on 25th June he announced two Government amendments. The first put indirect compulsion on the local authorities to grant extended 'facilities'. The second referred specifically to the 'facilities' instruction and gave dissatisfied parents the right of appeal to the Board of Education; the Board could, if it thought fit, transform a school into a contracting out school.[2] Both were elaborate ways of surmounting the difficulties, but inevitably so if the election promises were to be kept. Roman Catholics, however, were far from satisfied for, as the Irish members pointed out, the local authorities could still evade their responsibilities. Nor had they any liking for the contracting out or, as they preferred to call it, 'the kicking out'[3] provision. Birrell was clearly unimpressed by the more extravagant propaganda of Roman Catholics in the country at large and refuted sharply their favourite argument that Catholic elementary schools should be placed on the same financial footing as Catholic industrial schools and provided wholly from public funds. 'It is monstrous to say that the State stands in *loco parentis* to children attending a day school where (they go) for five days a week from nine to four,' he said, pointing out that in industrial schools it was due to the default of the parents that 'the children are taken away . . . and are put into schools where they have no holidays and where they live all the days of the week and all the hours of the day'.[4]

Anglicans put forward numerous amendments designed to secure modifications in both Clause 3 and Clause 4. Lord Robert Cecil's proposal to give every denomination 'facilities' in Clause 3 schools had strong Conservative backing. It would, said Balfour, be the 'first, but long step in the direction of freeing local authorities from the Cowper-Temple Clause'.[5] The Liberals, however, refused to consider the amendment; nor would they hear of the regular staff giving ordinary 'facilities' instruction, which would,

[1] *Parl. Deb.,* 4th Ser., vol. clix, col. 200.   [2] *Ibid.,* 4th Ser., vol. clix, cols. 674 *et seq.*
[3] *Ibid.,* 4th Ser., vol. clix, cols. 815–16.   [4] *Ibid.,* 4th Ser., vol. clvii, col. 461.
[5] *Ibid.,* 4th Ser., vol. clix, col. 255.

H

in Birrell's words, 'knock the bottom out of the Bill.'[1] On Clause 4 it was the stringency of the conditions to which Anglicans objected. They sought to make it applicable in all areas, rural as well as urban, and they suggested that 'a reasonable number' of parents should replace the original four-fifths majority.[2] Birrell, in reply, emphasised that 'this was a highly exceptional clause dealing with highly exceptional circumstances. . . . A school must be beyond all question a denominational school'. There must be no question of 'nice enquiries or fine discriminations'.[3] He was, however, prepared to compel local authorities to take over both Clause 3 and Clause 4 schools if, in return, the owners of all voluntary schools would similarly accept compulsion to hand over their schools.[4] The obligation was to be bilateral. This offer, though acceptable to the Roman Catholics, was rejected by the Anglicans and, after much discussion, was abandoned.[5]

At the third reading, in December, the Government had a majority of more than two to one. Except for the two important amendments to Clause 4, amendments which in no way modified the stringency of its conditions, their Bill had retained its original form, and its opponents therefore remained completely irreconciled. In the Commons a Conservative minority had attacked and obstructed the Bill at every stage. In the Lords a Conservative majority set out to transform the measure in the Anglican interest. The Archbishop of Canterbury, Dr Davidson, felt that the Bill was based on a policy born of 'impatience and despair'. He led the attack and endeavoured to secure for his community conditions at least as advantageous as those which were to be tacitly accorded to the Roman Catholics. 'What does the Bill do?' he asked, 'It takes 14,000 existing schools, with their trusts, and demolishes, not the mere wording of the trusts, but the very essence and pith of them . . . the school is handed over to the local authority which may, if it likes, refuse to take it or, if it does take it, may practically secularise it save for some two hours a week and may appoint teachers who are unwilling to give, or untrained to give, religious teaching.'[6]

During the course of debates in the Lords it became clear that there were two groups in the Established Church each pressing

---

[1] *Ibid.*, 4th Ser., vol. clix, col. 1652.   [2] *Ibid.*, 4th Ser., vol. clix, cols. 851 and 990.
[3] *Ibid.*, 4th Ser., vol. clix, col. 993.   [4] *Ibid.*, 4th Ser., vol. clviii, col. 839.
[5] *Ibid.*, 4th Ser., vol. clviii, cols. 848 *et seq. Ibid.*, vol. clxi, col. 227.
[6] *Ibid.*, 4th Ser., vol. clxii, col. 934.

for amendments; there were the backwoodsmen, who were all the time seeking to preserve Anglican predominance in the village schools, and there were the more progressive, who, thinking of the urban areas, were anxious to secure 'facilities' in all schools.[1] In the event both groups secured amendments and in the process completely transformed Clause 4. It now became mandatory on the local authorities to accept the clause, all restrictions limiting extended 'facilities' to urban areas were swept away and, in place of the four-fifths proportion, a bare majority of parents was now sufficient to preserve the fully denominational character of the school. There was also an amendment to permit the teachers, if they wished, to give denominational instruction, and, further-more, the famous Cowper-Temple Clause was to be relaxed so that authorities could provide denominational teaching in council schools. In effect by seeking simultaneously to preserve her exist-ing schools and to extend her teaching to local authority schools the Church of England was claiming the whole of what ought to have been alternative groups of amendments.

The Bill as it emerged from the Lords was a strictly denomi-national measure. Clause 4 had been deprived entirely of its original significance; church schools were to be left practically undisturbed while for the first time local authorities were en-couraged to open council schools to denominational influences. In the words of Lord Crewe, the Liberal Leader of the Lords, the Opposition 'had turned rules into exceptions and exceptions into rules'.[2] Birrell was bitterly disappointed. He described the Bill on its return to the Commons as 'a miserable, mangled, tortured, twisted tertium quid'.[3] Indeed, the action of the Lords in de-liberately reversing the decision of the Lower House drew attention to the privilege of their position. Birrell publicly attacked the anachronism of the situation. 'What is the good of winning great electoral victories', he asked, 'when you find on going a few yards down the lobbies of the House all the foes you routed in the open field, installed, established and apparently immovable, mutilating all your work and substituting something quite different.'[4] In the country Nonconformist feelings ran high

[1] *Ibid.*, 4th Ser., vol. clxiv, cols. 242-3, 270.   [2] *Ibid.*, 4th Ser., vol. clxvi, col. 1102.
[3] *Ibid.*, 4th Ser., vol. clxvi, col. 1581.
[4] Speech by Rt. Hon. Augustine Birrell at Bristol, 13.11.06. Published by the Liberal Publication Department.

and Dr Clifford urged the Government to overrule the 'episcopal oligarchy' by the creation of new Radical peers.[1] The situation was tense and for a time it even looked as though relations between the two Houses had reached a crisis. On 25th November the King intervened and urged Campbell-Bannerman to negotiate directly with the Archbishop of Canterbury.[2] The next day the Prime Minister saw Dr Davidson in an attempt to narrow the differences between them and, despite illness, which at this critical juncture confined the Primate to his bed at Lambeth, the two men continued in constant communication with each other. Dr Davidson's chief anxiety was that in Clause 3 schools the ordinary teacher should not be excluded from giving denominational instruction and so should not, as he wrote, 'be compelled to stand by in silence while some substitute attempts lamely to do what the teacher has been accustomed to do (and is eager to do) so well.' Otherwise he considered that the offer of ordinary 'facilities' would be 'a mere mockery'.[3] The Liberal veteran, A. H. D. Acland, on whom the Prime Minister relied a good deal for advice, commented discouragingly on Dr Davidson's stand for it was clear to him that the Anglicans would give up nothing, and he thought that the Liberals were in danger of being ridiculed if in addition to meeting the full Anglican demand they 'solemnly proceeded to pay rent to the Archdeacon, the Vicar and the other clergy'.[4]

When it came to the Commons' debate on the Lords' amendments on 10th December there still seemed a last-minute chance of saving the Bill. Though Birrell pressed for the rejection of the amendments *en bloc*, he did not exclude the possibility of new concessions. 'If', he said, 'the Lords were to feel at liberty to withdraw their amendments as a whole, if they could limit the scope, the purview and the operation of their amendments in any manner capable of coming within our scheme . . . why then, hope, I say, is still possible for us.'[5] The concessions he offered were considerable and indicated that the Liberals were prepared to tax the loyalty of their own supporters very severely in order to achieve religious peace. Firstly, he offered to substitute three-quarters

---

[1] *The Times*, 27.11.06.   [2] Spender, *op. cit.*, 302–4; Bell, *op. cit.*, 526–7.
[3] Memorandum from Dr Davidson to the Prime Minister, 5.12.06. B.M. Add. MS. 41252 ,ff. 8.
[4] Letter from Mr Acland to the Prime Minister. B.M. Add. MS. 41239. ff. 182–3.
[5] *Parl. Deb.*, 4th Ser., vol. clxii, col. 1596.

instead of four-fifths as the proportion of parents required for extended 'facilities' in Clause 4 schools; secondly, he agreed that the local authority should consult with a parents' committee and appoint teachers acceptable to them; finally, he was prepared to consider some modification in the position of the teachers in Clause 3 schools.[1]

Birrell's concessions were part of a general Liberal peace movement. Over fifty days of Parliamentary time had now been consumed and in the general desire for a settlement Liberal opinion had softened remarkably. In the ensuing three-day debate member after member, Nonconformist and secularist alike, indicated a willingness to concede points which at an earlier stage they would have considered essential. Roman Catholic objections would have been completely met by the proposed concessions.[2] When it came to the final vote, therefore, the Irish members, with the full backing of the English hierarchy,[3] sided with the Government. Anglican demands on Clause 4 had been largely met, while the gaps in Clause 3 had been so narrowed that the only points in dispute were now the single-school areas, where Anglicans themselves had long admitted the Nonconformist hardship, and the discretionary powers of the local authorities to allow teachers to give religious instruction.

Balfour, however, expressed great indignation at the Liberal action. The Government had, he said, adopted 'an insulting procedure' and he accused them of deliberately preventing an arrangement.[4] His words were echoed in the Upper House, where Lord Crewe, the Liberal spokesman tried in vain to conciliate the Opposition. He referred to Birrell's concessions and even indicated that the Government were prepared to accept something less than a three-quarters majority as the proportion of parents required for extended 'facilities' in Clause 4 schools, and that under Clause 3 they would allow assistant teachers to volunteer for denominational instruction in all except single-school area schools.[5] Simultaneously the Liberals engaged in further negotiations and

---

[1] *Ibid.,* 4th Ser., vol. clxii, col. 1597.

[2] John Redmond said that only about thirty R.C. schools would be excluded from becoming Clause 4 schools. *Ibid.,* 4th Ser., vol. clxii, col. 1615.

[3] The Archbishop of Westminster had made it quite clear that the hierarchy would prefer the Bill to pass. Letter to Lord Ripon, 8.12.06. Ed. 24. P.R.O.

[4] *Parl. Deb.,* 4th Ser., vol. clxvii, cols. 165–7, 466 *et seq.*

[5] *Ibid.,* 4th Ser., vol. clxvii, cols. 1387–8.

held two meetings with Dr Davidson and the Conservative leaders during the concluding stages of the Lords' debate.[1] Despite the narrow margin of difference the discussions foundered on Clause 3. The truth was that the Conservative leaders did not want a peaceful settlement and it was they, rather than the Archbishop, who remained hard and uncompromising. To them the Education Bill was part of a general Liberal offensive against the established order and they determined to exploit their ascendancy in the Lords in order to repulse the attack. The end came on 19th December with the Lords' decision to insist on their amendments.[2]

It was Balfour who, with cool and ruthless calculation, was directing operations.[3] He was well aware that the great mass of the electorate were becoming increasingly apathetic and indifferent to the religious controversy. His rejection of last-minute overtures was an act of defiance, a deliberate challenge to the Government to appeal to the country. 'They will not dissolve', he said, 'they know better.'[4] He was right. Despite their fury the Government yielded. Lloyd George and Grey were all for immediate dissolution[5] but in the end calmer counsels prevailed. Education was not in itself sufficient of a national question to rouse popular support and the Prime Minister let the occasion pass with a warning. 'A way must be found, and a way will be found', he said, 'by which the will of the people expressed through their elected representatives will be made to prevail.'[6] The mutilation of successive Liberal Bills was to make collision inevitable.

Had it succeeded the Birrell Bill would have anticipated the religious settlement of the 1944 Act. Both schemes distinguished between the two types of denominational school by bringing the majority into closer relationship with the public elementary schools and encouraging the remainder to play their part in the national system. Birrell's plan, however, would have been the more drastic. It would have unified the whole educational system from the administrative point of view and would have discriminated

---

[1] Bell, *op. cit.*, I, 529–30; Newton, *Lord Lansdowne*, 356.

[2] *Parl. Deb.*, 4th Ser., vol. clxvii, cols. 1415–18.

[3] Campbell-Bannerman described him as 'director-in-chief of both Houses', *Parl. Deb.*, 4th Ser., vol. clxvii, col. 157.

[4] Speech at the Junior Constitutional Club, 28th November, 1906.

[5] *History Today*, vol. 9, No. 3, 167. (Lucy Masterman, 'Recollections of Lloyd George.')

[6] *Parl. Deb.*, 4th Ser., vol. clxvii, col. 1740.

more searchingly between the two sorts of denominational schools. Anglicans would have had to surrender the denominational character of most of their village schools. Of their urban schools, large numbers would have qualified for extended 'facilities' and been strengthened by the new financial relief. The action of the Bill, therefore, would have been swift and drastic. It would have pruned the national system of those Anglican schools, the products of past benevolence, which no longer corresponded to present needs. It would have integrated fully into the national system those schools, both Anglican and Roman Catholic, which stood for firm religious conviction, and would have financed them entirely from the public purse. The measure offered prospects of permanent peace. Instead the future was to see a long war of attrition which gradually robbed the Anglicans of large numbers of their schools. More important still, as the financial basis of the 1902 Act became completely outmoded, Anglicans and Roman Catholics alike were compelled by reason of their poverty to oppose all educational improvements. Their resistance was to retard and impede the whole process of reform and as a result children in voluntary schools and council schools alike were the victims. In the years which followed, poverty and shabbiness became indissolubly associated in the public mind with church schools, for the average parent could not but contrast their buildings, dark and forbidding relics of the past, with the amenities of neighbouring council schools. No less sinister was the antagonism felt by teachers and administrators alike at the inflexibility of many denominational leaders whom they came to identify with obstructionism and reaction.

It is impossible not to regret the failure of Birrell's Bill. In the long controversy between Church and State here was the opportunity for an enduring settlement. But the occasion passed and with it the chance of establishing a system of education which would have been both unified and efficient. In the history of English education the Birrell Bill is unquestionably the great missed opportunity of the twentieth century.

*   *   *   *   *

Birrell was transferred in January 1907 to the Chief Secretaryship of Ireland. His Liberal successors, however, made further efforts to overcome the deadlock. Birrell had aimed at securing a unified system at the cost of considerable flexibility within that system. His successors, on the other hand, attempted to establish a rigid system, allowing at the same time certain means of escape from its restrictions. Contracting out provisions for denominational schools were, therefore, an integral feature of their schemes which, compared with Birrell's Bill, were makeshift measures, uneducational and retrograde.

The efforts of McKenna, Birrell's immediate successor, were fruitless. His Bill, introduced in February 1908, dealt ruthlessly with the voluntary schools;[1] all single-school area schools, almost 8,000 in number, were to be compulsorily transferred to the local authorities, while other schools might, if they wished, contract out and receive a Parliamentary grant of 47s. a head, a sum which they might supplement by charging fees. In the transferred schools 'facilities' for denominational instruction were restricted to single-school areas, where such instruction might be given out of school hours and by volunteers. In brief, McKenna proposed to use both 'facilities' and contracting out as means of dealing with the existing denominational schools, but the denominations were to have no choice; 'facilities' were confined to single-school areas, and contracting out to all other areas. Naturally, Anglicans and Roman Catholics were violently opposed to a measure which would make the majority of their schools outcasts from the national system. The Archbishop of Canterbury described his objections to the Bill as 'insuperable', since in the villages it would alienate the school buildings from the Anglicans to whom they belonged and would create 'the single-school area grievance in reverse'.[2] The Roman Catholic verdict was similarly conclusive; for them, a return to the poverty of the pre-1902 period was unthinkable.[3] Even the Nonconformists could raise little enthusiasm for the McKenna Bill.[4]

It was, indeed, completely destructive in character. Educationally it would have been disastrous for it would have wrecked the work of the local authorities, which had done so much to improve the efficiency of the denominational schools since

---

[1] McKenna had already made an unsuccessful effort to tackle the problem. See Appendix B.

[2] Letter of Archbishop of Canterbury to the President, 10.3.08. Ed. 24. P.R.O.

[3] Minutes of meeting of the Catholic Education Council, 28.4.08. C.E.C.

[4] *Parl. Deb.*, 4th Ser., vol. clxxxiv, col. 1429.

1902.[1] The contracting out schools were to stand apart from the whole structure of national education and to be excluded from participation in scholarship schemes as well as from the municipal provisions for medical and social care. The common feature of the Birrell and McKenna Bills was the destruction of the denominational character of the single-school area schools. The fundamental difference lay in the treatment of the urban denominational schools. Birrell would have accepted them as an integral part of the educational system and would have relieved them of all financial burdens; McKenna, on the other hand, would have degraded them to inferior status and driven them to rely once more on children's pence and gifts of charity. Perhaps the most crushing of the educational criticisms of McKenna's Bill came from an impartial body of observers, the Fabians, who condemned it as 'unique among the many Education Bills of the past fifty years, in not containing a single clause which even professes to make the school better or local government more efficient'.[2] Unregretted, McKenna's Bill perished in May after the second reading. By then, in the Cabinet reorganisation which followed Campbell-Bannerman's death in April, Runciman had replaced McKenna in the new Asquith Government.

Runciman took up the entire problem afresh. His method was to proceed by means of patient and deliberate negotiations so that all difficulties should be resolved before any publication of plans. To the task he brought qualities of diplomacy and tact which made his approach much more conciliatory than that of his predecessor. There was, moreover, a general lull in the public controversy which seemed to augur well for his success. The President's aim was to get representative bodies of both Anglican and Nonconformist opinion to make mutual concessions, and then to present the terms of the agreement to Parliament and to the country.

The Nonconformist leaders were the first to be consulted in the summer of 1908. In the preliminary discussions Runciman had to wean them from their preference for leaving things alone and convince them of the necessity for a contructive policy. Thereafter, he was able to work out with them points which might be used as a basis for negotiations with the Anglicans. They finally

---

[1] John Redmond quoted figures to show that teachers' salaries in R.C. schools had doubled in the years 1902-8. *Ibid.,* 4th Ser., vol. clxxxviii, cols. 1706-7.

[2] Fabian Society Publication, 23.2.08, 5.

demanded the general transfer of church schools to public authorities, leaving a small number of exceptional schools as contracting out schools while, in return, they were prepared to consider some relaxation of the Cowper-Temple Clause by allowing denominational teaching to be given, subject to certain conditions, in all council schools. The conditions were that denominational teaching must be limited to three mornings a week; it must not be given by the head teacher, nor be paid for by public money, nor must it oust Cowper-Temple instruction as the normal teaching of the school.[1] When Runciman came to approach the Archbishop of Canterbury and his advisers, he found that, though they were prepared to transfer their schools in single-school areas, they hoped for large-scale contracting out elsewhere. Furthermore, they demanded that the 'facilities' teaching in council schools should be given at any time during the day and by anyone from outside or inside the school without restriction. In the weeks that followed Runciman endeavoured to bridge the gulf between Anglicans and Nonconformists. Eventually only two points of conflict remained, whether the grant of 'facilities' in council schools should be mandatory or merely optional for the local authorities and whether 'facilities' teaching might be given by head teachers. Both sides had made substantial concessions, the Anglicans by agreeing to the transfer of their single-school area schools and the Nonconformists by accepting an infringement of the Cowper-Temple Clause.

In the meantime Runciman had indicated to Dr Bourne, the Archbishop of Westminster, his plans for a resettlement. He made no attempt, however, to negotiate with the Roman Catholics and merely used the occasion of his meeting with the Archbishop to appraise him of the facts. Dr Bourne summed up the situation realistically, 'He knew and I knew perfectly well that until he had squared the Anglicans it was no use speaking to us, because the whole arrangement depended upon that.'[2] Nevertheless, the Archbishop was considerably alarmed at developments which threatened to break the old denominational alignment and leave his own community isolated and impotent.

---

[1] 'Mr. Runciman's Speech at his Meeting with the Nonconformist M.P.s', 9.11.08. Ed. 24. P.R.O.

[2] Minutes of a Special General Meeting of the Catholic Education Council, 24.11.08. C.E.C.

As a result of continued discussion Runciman persuaded the Nonconformists to accept statutory 'facilities' which he was confident would reduce the number of contracting out schools. This was the absolute limit of Nonconformist concession, and Runciman now appealed to the Anglicans to respond by not insisting on the head teachers giving 'facilities' instruction. On the 10th November he wrote to the Archbishop, 'I have done my utmost and risked so much that I cannot go or carry any one else any further. I earnestly trust that you and other prominent Churchmen will not allow this opportunity to be destroyed.'[1] The reply was not unfavourable; the Archbishop indicated that he would be content if existing head teachers of transferred schools might continue to give denominational teaching. The negotiations had, except on one point, been thorough and exhaustive. The omission, however, was a serious one, namely, the financial terms to be offered to contracting out schools. Runciman had given repeated assurances that the conditions would be generous, but it was not until a few hours before the introduction of the Bill that he published the details. The blunder was a grave one. Indeed, in view of the careful preliminaries, it seems altogether remarkable that Runciman should have drafted a Bill before securing agreement on one of the most significant points.

On 20th November the compromise, which had been agreed to in preliminary discussion, was presented as a Parliamentary Bill. In his introduction[2] Runciman stressed the mutual sacrifices which had been made; the Nonconformists were permitting 'facilities' in every provided elementary school and the Anglicans, in return, were giving up their monopoly of country schools. He was at pains to describe the position of the new contracting out schools. Compared with the McKenna proposals they were to be strictly limited in number, but they were to come much more within the framework of national education. They were to be known as non-provided public elementary schools and to be supported by annual State grants of between 46s. 6d. and 55s. per child according to the size of school. Though they were excluded from rate aid, their pupils were to be admitted by the local authorities to courses of practical instruction in handwork, cookery and gardening, and their teachers were to enjoy the same rights of pension as

---

[1] The correspondence was published in a White Paper, Cd., 4421.
[2] *Parl. Deb.*, 4th Ser., vol. cxcvii, cols. 422 *et seq.*

those in provided schools. Moreover, Runciman attempted to hedge the new type of school with various precautions and assurances for continued educational efficiency. Contracting out schools, however, were intended to cater mainly for Roman Catholic needs and only for exceptional Anglican parishes. For the great body of Anglicans, therefore, Runciman stressed the advantages of 'facilities' teaching, which, for the first time, would become part of the regular curriculum in every public elementary school.

It was soon apparent from the general reaction to the Bill that Runciman had overestimated the success of his preliminary negotiations. Anglicans were incensed at the financial terms which the President had inserted at the last minute and were highly critical of their Archbishop's bargaining powers. He had, they alleged, made definite sacrifices and, in return, had received nothing save a promise of fair arrangements. The Bishop of Manchester was moved to describe the concordat as 'the peace of death',[1] while the National Society as a body determined on a policy of steadfast opposition.[2] Roman Catholics were thoroughly alarmed. They were now faced with an entirely new situation, the possibility, even the probability, of a settlement which would satisfy the Anglicans but would leave their own schools outside the national system. It was for them a frightening thought that, throughout the long months of bargaining, there had been no attempt to negotiate with their community. It seemed as though there was a deliberate intention to segregate their schools, to deprive them of the benefits they had enjoyed since 1902 and to condemn them to a state of semi-starvation.[3]

Neither Nonconformists nor teachers found much consolation in the Bill. Many Nonconformists considered it a very one-sided bargain. They pointed out that Anglicans would immediately be able to give denominational instruction in all council schools; all that they would be surrendering in return, and this not immediately, would be the right to appoint head teachers and staff in a proportion of Church schools.[4] Indeed, there was a feeling that Nonconformists would positively lose ground to the denominationalists. The teachers were no less suspicious of denominational encroachment. They objected strenuously to the right of

[1] The *Church Times*, 27.11.08.
[2] Minutes of a Special Meeting of the Standing Committee of the National Society, 27.11.08. N.S.
[3] The *Tablet*, 14.11.08.   [4] *Parl. Deb.*, 4th Ser., vol. cxcvii, col. 439.

entry in council schools as well as to the recognition of a class of
non-provided schools, and they were extremely suspicious lest
candidates seeking appointment under local authorities should be
pressed to give some form of denominational teaching.[1]

Altogether, the prospects of the Bill were not very hopeful. The
attitude of the teachers filled many Anglicans with dismay. They
realised that the value of 'facilities' instruction depended entirely
on the good will and co-operation of the teaching profession, and
in the circumstances they preferred to concentrate on securing the
continued existence of an unspecified and apparently unlimited
number of contracting out schools rather than trust the teachers.
Other Anglicans, however, urged restraint. The Bishop of Southwark, for example, spoke bluntly to his fellow clerics, 'Your
principal lever, that is the denominational schools, is weakening
yearly to an alarming extent in proportionate strength, in actual
amount and in reserves of resource.' On the other hand, the
promised right of entry would offer new opportunities, would
enable Churchmen to be 'no longer merely defenders of a
crumbling position', but partners 'in the expanding future'.[2]
Meanwhile the Primate was pressing for a revision of the financial
terms, and was particularly concerned to secure elasticity of
Exchequer grants in order to cover the contingency of increasing
costs. But, as the President's advisers were well aware, the proposed scale must not be made too attractive lest it encourage
contracting out. It must be 'a penalisation and not a privilege'.[3]

The Bill had a brief life. On the second reading, which began on
24th November, Anglicans and Roman Catholics joined in attack-
ing the contracting out clause. This, they alleged, would widen
the existing disparities and make many schools 'excrescences upon
the national system'.[4] In particular, Roman Catholic speakers
considered that their community had come off very badly indeed;
while Anglicans had been lured with right of entry during the
preliminary discussions, they had been completely ignored. Dread
of becoming educational outcasts weighed heavily with them
and their spokesmen harked back longingly to the provisions of
the Birrell Bill.[5] Nevertheless, despite denominational opposition,

[1] The attitude of the teachers is described by Michael Sadler, *Journal of Indian Education*, VII, 245.
[2] Copy of 'Statement by the Bishop of Southwark', 28.11.08. Ed. 24. P.R.O.
[3] Memorandum, 'Points for the Bill', 1908. Ed. 24. P.R.O.
[4] *Parl. Deb.*, 4th Ser., vol. cxcvii, col. 1158.   [5] *Ibid.*, 4th Ser., vol. cxcvii, col. 1163.

the Bill passed its second reading by a large majority on 30th November.

Thereafter, events moved rapidly. The decisive blow was in fact struck by the body of Anglican dissidents at a special meeting of the Representative Church Council.[1] Up to the last minute the Archbishop and the President struggled to save the Bill. Runciman, who was faced with formidable Nonconformist opposition, wrote to the Primate on the eve of the crucial meeting, 'I still see a glimmer of hope if you will agree that no more than 900 Church of England schools shall contract out, and will show means by which they will be secured.' The next day the Archbishop urged members of the Church Council to take a realistic view of the situation and, in particular, to consider the increasing numbers of Church children who were now attending council schools. 'What about the Church's care for these children?' he asked, and went on to plead that they should not lose 'the opportunity which may never recur, of securing by law that in every elementary school in the country — present and future — the right to give denominational teaching shall have a permanent place'.[2] The appeal was fruitless. The more extreme Anglicans remained irreconcilable. Their opposition to the Bill sprang from an intense dislike of undenominational religious teaching and from a fear lest, if the Bill became law, undenominational teaching would be the normal type of instruction in all elementary schools. It was this section which sponsored and carried the resolution condemning the entire compromise. The resolution was fatal to the Bill which Runciman had introduced as an agreed settlement. It was at once withdrawn, and the Government made no secret of the fact that the action of the Church Council had been decisive.

During its brief life of seventeen days the Bill had raised a mass of varied opposition, but the attitude of the Anglicans had been the determinative factor. Throughout, their persistent criticism of the financial terms had made the Liberals highly suspicious, for large-scale contracting out, which was evidently their intention, would frustrate the whole purpose of the Bill. None of the interested parties had been greatly enamoured of the measure and, when the Anglicans administered the final blow, there were few regrets. Runciman's attempt to settle the denominational question

[1] Formed in 1903 to recommend legislation to the Church of England.
[2] Bell, *op. cit.*, I, 538–9.

by agreement thus ended in failure, and disunity within the Established Church in the end proved fatal. Yet, despite the care and deliberation which he had devoted to preliminary plans, his Bill did not offer a statesmanlike solution to the problem of dual control and was in fact hardly worth saving; the 'facilities' it offered would have caused confusion and resentment in large numbers of schools while contracting out would have brought perpetual poverty to those which stood apart.

Three successive Presidents of the Board of Education had now spent themselves in vain endeavours to abolish the dual system, and the Liberals, who had entered office with high hopes, were in despair. It was indeed a sad retrospect to look back over three years of Liberal government and to acknowledge complete failure. Asquith, who, as Runciman's chief, had taken an intimate part in the discussions, felt the blow keenly and went so far as to describe defeat as the bitterest disappointment of his entire political life.[1]

The years which followed saw intermittent efforts to achieve a settlement. Both inside and outside Parliament there was activity on the part of individuals. Perhaps the most constructive contribution came from the Education Settlement Committee, a widely representative body with Michael Sadler as one of its secretaries. After careful consideration of the religious problem, the Committee published in 1910 a Report entitled 'Towards Educational Peace'. It contained a frank recognition, on the part of experienced administrators and educationists, of the need for diversity in the provision of schools. According to the proposed plan, parents were to have, in all except single-school areas, the right of choosing between two types of publicly maintained schools, the council school, controlled by the local authorities and the voluntary school, controlled by the denomination. In brief, the scheme was that in all parts of the country, urban or rural, public elementary schools under public management should form the groundwork of the national system of education, but that variety of efficient effort should be encouraged wherever possible. Government opinion, however, was opposed to reopening the issue. The Liberals, thoroughly weary and disillusioned with the whole business, were only too anxious to avoid further strife, and to avoid, also, the danger of dissension among their supporters,

[1] *Parl. Deb.*, 4th Ser., vol. cxcviii, col. 102.

between ardent Nonconformists on the one hand and convinced agnostics on the other. Moreover, in the country as a whole there was a lull in the public controversy. It was true that a minority of Free Churchmen, still brooding on their wrongs, continued their campaign of passive resistance, but their efforts had now dwindled to isolated gestures of defiance.

For the younger generation the old bitterness belonged to the past. Many of them were indifferent to the old religious struggles; they were much more attracted by the social evangelism of the rising Labour Party, for the new creed of socialism had a wide emotional appeal, and its adherents some of the zeal and fervour of members of a religious sect. The popular clamour now was for physical betterment and social equality. Above all, the 1902 settlement was working well. Quietly, almost unobtrusively, national and local administrators were erecting an efficient organisation and making good the arrears of past neglect. Unperturbed by the heat of public controversy, they were engaged in improving and expanding the education service by bringing the church schools up to standard, by building new secondary and technical schools and by providing for physical welfare. Already, thanks to Morant's foresight and initiative, the national system was becoming responsive to the needs of the twentieth century.

The Balfour Act had thus survived all Liberal onslaughts and within a decade had done much to transform English education. But the religious issue continued like an uneasy spectre to haunt the political imagination, and for many years to come statesmen could not contemplate the problems of dual control without a lively recollection of the warning offered by the Liberal reverses. Looking back they could see the fate of their predecessors, see, in the words of 'Omar Khayyám',

> *How Sultan after Sultan, with his pomp*
> *Abode his hour and went his destined way.*[1]

and, viewing their skeletons and their bones on the long desert route, they would hesitate to tread the same path lest they might themselves meet a similar fate.

---

[1] Quoted by Mr Butler during the debates in 1944. *Parl. Deb.*, 5th Ser., vol. cccxcix, col. 2257.

Chapter 6

Between the Wars

The crisis of war is a crucial test of a nation's values and way of life. In a most striking manner educational planning and advance in this country have coincided with major wars; it was the military successes of Prussia which in the mid-Victorian era strengthened the movement for national education, while in the twentieth century both world wars precipitated great reform measures. The first world war was a shattering experience to national pride. As the early optimism faded before the onslaught of an enemy superior both in technical efficiency and in intellectual training, hardships and suffering were inflicted on all classes of society. But the challenge of war provided the urge and vitality to plan for the future, and amid the ferment and crises of the times tradition was disrupted in 1916 by the entry into the Cabinet as President of the Board of Education of a man unknown to politics, but expert in the field of education, H. A. L. Fisher, the distinguished scholar and educational administrator.

Fisher was acutely discerning in his grasp of future educational needs. He realised that the intellectual wastage of the war must be repaired by the opening of all possible outlets to talent and ability, that more efficient technical training must be available to meet the economic competition which lay ahead and that, most important of all, adolescents must have something more than elementary education to prepare them for future responsibilities and to equip them for the complexities of life in the post-war world. Fisher was helped enormously by the newly awakened popular interest in education. In the past the general public had been largely indifferent or hostile to education, which was regarded as something provided from above by the benevolence of the upper classes or by the inexorable action of Governments; from time to time feeling had been aroused by religious controversies but even these upheavals had scarcely touched the masses. Already in the early years of the twentieth century education had come to the fore in the programmes of the Labour Party and the Trades Union Congress; politically it was seen as a means of challenging existing party predominance and socially as providing an opportunity for material advancement, the chance to 'get on' in life. The war stimulated a new interest in education and a demand for grammar school places, for the high wages of the time encouraged many working class parents to think in terms of secondary education for their children. The general enthusiasm for education and the pressure for higher standards in all types of school inspired Fisher to take the tide at its flood and launch a large-scale measure of reform. His Act of 1918 was specially directed towards the organising of post-elementary education by raising the school-leaving age, by expanding secondary schools and by establishing new central schools and day continuation schools.

The Fisher Act initiated a great forward movement in English education, but the religious settlement was deliberately left un-disturbed. Fisher himself had determined to avoid controversy lest a revival of bitterness should jeopardise his reforms. It was not, as he explained in his memoranda,[1] that he felt the issue was 'unimportant or irrelevant to the development of a national system of public education', but because he felt that 'it would be highly impolitic to attempt to deal with it, and perhaps impossible to deal with it, except on the basis of a wide general agreement'. Indeed, the religious difficulty was scarcely mentioned during the debates on the Education Bill. There was, apparently, a tacit understanding all round that the existing settlement should not be disturbed. Yet Fisher had already suspected that dual con-trol might impede the progress of educational reform, and so it was to prove. To a large extent the provision of the new types of post-primary school depended on the freedom of the local authorities to use the buildings of all existing schools to the best advantage and to control the selection, promotion and distribution of teachers throughout their areas. Difficulty soon arose over the organisation of a system of central schools in areas where church school managers could not afford to co-operate in the large-scale developments. Often, they could not even manage to extend their

---

[1] Much of the subsequent material is taken from this source. And later in a speech. See note 1, p. 118.

premises in order to provide the advanced and practical instruction advocated for senior pupils. Their only source of income was from dwindling subscriptions and donations and, far from being able to finance new extensions, they were finding it increasingly difficult to meet their commitments under the 1902 Act. As his measure was evidently in danger of becoming a dead letter Fisher in 1919 decided to reopen the religious issue.

He was hopeful that time had removed the old friction and that the new spirit of co-operation between Anglicans and Free Churchmen would be strong enough to overcome former difficulties. Already there were signs that the Anglicans were prepared to adapt themselves to new conditions. The National Society, for example, had indicated that it was, in certain circumstances, prepared to consider the transference of children from Church to council schools on condition that they received religious instruction 'in accordance with the wishes of their parents and at the hands of suitable teachers'.[1] A Free Church Memorial, submitted to the President in April 1919, strengthened him in his resolve to reopen the religious issue, but he was under no illusion as to the risks he ran. 'If I had consulted my own reputation', he said, 'I should have let it alone; but I felt it my duty at all events to afford a fresh opportunity for its exploration.'[2] In the summer, therefore, Fisher called the first of several conferences he was to hold with Anglican and Free Church representatives.[3] At the first meeting he submitted his proposals, which were based on the simple broad principles that the control of all non-provided schools should be placed unreservedly in the hands of the local authorities, and that in return the authorities should be obliged to provide 'facilities' for denominational instruction in all their schools at parents' request. (The proposals, in fact, were not unlike the Liberal schemes of 1908, and like his predecessors Fisher in the end had to fall back on contracting out for minority groups.) The President was impressed by the response he obtained at the first conference. He noted that there was a good deal of common ground between the two parties and that both Anglicans and Free Churchmen seemed to have moved a long way from the opinions they had

---

[1] National Society's publication, *The Education Act,* 1918.
[2] See note 1, p. 118.
[3] The meeting, held on 31st July, 1919, is described in Bell, II, *op. cit.,* 1126 *et seq.*

held in 1902. There were only two members who found themselves out of sympathy with the general temper of the discussions,
Dr Knox, the Bishop of Manchester, representing the Anglican
'exclusive' section, and Dr Clifford, the veteran diehard of Nonconformity; both withdrew from the conference discussions
before the end of the year 1919. The attitude of the Anglican
leaders was particularly encouraging for it was evident that they
were as keen to be rid of the embarrassments of the dual system
as were the representatives of the Free Churches. The old spirit of
bargaining had gone and, in return for an offer of 'facilities'
instruction in all types of school, they were now prepared to hand
over their own schools to the local authorities. Apparently they
were of the opinion that their money could be spent more
effectively on the denominational training colleges, which, by
providing religious teachers, would directly influence the life of
the schools. With their own schools dwindling at the rate of over
a hundred a year, and with the danger of the new educational
developments squeezing them out of the national system altogether, they were anxious to make terms while they still had
buildings to bargain with. Even the *Church Times* denounced the
existing system. '. . . the old sectarian strife must be forgotten', it
declared, 'for the issue has changed. In bygone days it was whether
one or another form of Christianity would get the best of a
bargain. Now, the issue is whether Christianity or secularism shall
be the future creed of England.'[1] Indeed, so anxious were the
Anglicans to respond to overtures that, before the date of the
second conference, they themselves submitted proposals designed
to fill the gaps of Fisher's outline scheme.

The situation was, however, extremely delicate. The President
could not exclude the possibility of reaction within the Anglican
Church, nor could he disregard the reluctance of the Nonconformists to surrender the Cowper-Temple Clause. Moreover,
Roman Catholics would certainly oppose a measure which did not
ensure the religious atmosphere of their schools. Nevertheless,
Fisher was resolved to go ahead. His first object was to secure
substantial agreement between the two main parties so that he
could get the great body of Anglicans into the scheme. Thereafter,
he intended to devise special terms for minority groups.

During the negotiations the Secretary of the National Society

[1] 12.12.19.

had suggested the Scottish solution as a way out of the difficulty, and officials of the Board were at pains to investigate the possibility of applying in England the principles of the Scottish settlement of 1918. In Scotland the vital point was that by a system of tests for teachers the denominations were given absolute security that their children would receive efficient denominational teaching, as the Education (Scotland) Act of 1918 stipulated that teachers must be approved for 'their religious belief and character by representatives of the church or denominational body in whose interest the school has been conducted'.[1] However, the historical background of the problem in Scotland was completely different from that in England; firstly, there had never been any Cowper-Temple Clause, and denominational education from 1872 onwards had been an inherent part of the educational system; secondly, only two Scottish denominations, the Presbyterians and the Roman Catholics, were interested in giving denominational instruction, and the country fell neatly into compartments in which one or other of them was predominant; thirdly, the scale of the problem was entirely different, as voluntary schools in Scotland catered for less than 10 per cent of the children. In Scotland, therefore, it had been possible to apply in 1918 a simple solution, the transference of all voluntary schools to the local authorities by sale or lease. In England the cost of transference of half the nation's schools would be prohibitive. More significant still, the principle of tests for teachers, which was embodied in the Scottish settlement, would offend large and important sections of English opinion.

Fisher therefore discarded the Scottish solution and fell back instead on the old idea of contracting out for those who insisted on denominational atmosphere schools. Contracting out, however, was to be restricted to existing schools and there was no provision for new schools of this type. The scheme did not meet with encouraging response from the Anglican and Free Church leaders, and Fisher did not even get as far as suggesting it to the Roman Catholics themselves, though he later included contracting out in his public statement of proposals. Despite the fact that the negotiations were still incomplete, the President was anxious to test the general atmosphere in the country, and in March 1920, he prepared a public statement on the future of the denominational

[1] See Appendix C.

schools.[1] Taking as the title of his address, 'The Development of Elementary Education', he set out for consideration his suggested solution of the problems of the dual system. The immediate response was unpropitious. On the very morning of the speech the *New Statesman* sounded the alarm, and even before the day Dr Clifford had taken the offensive by intervening in a critical by-election in Camberwell. In the weeks that followed, it was clear that members of the old wing of Nonconformity had learnt and forgotten nothing. The *Christian World* talked suspiciously of 'the collection of coupons by parsons' and declared, 'the price (the sacrifice of the Cowper-Temple Clause) is too big to pay. The dual system is disappearing. Gradually, but surely, the voluntary schools are going under and that is why the Church wants to make the bargain.'[2] Dr Clifford's intervention at Camberwell had showed that the Nonconformists were prepared for action, and at a moment when the Government seemed to be losing its hold in the constituencies the prospects looked serious. Fisher therefore held full and frank discussions with the representatives of the Free Church Council. In vain he sought to disabuse them of the notion that the Church schools were about to fall into the laps of the local authorities like so many 'ripe plums'.[3] The representatives remained unmoved and the meeting ended with Dr Clifford gloomily warning the President that he must not imagine he had a 'free course before him'.[4]

Nonconformist opposition was disappointing; less surprising was the emphatic rejection of the plan by Roman Catholics.[5] They had been left out of the negotiations entirely, though Fisher had privately acquainted individual leaders with his proposals. For them the scheme meant the surrender of the solid ground of 1902 without any definite compensation, since they could hardly be expected to attach much value to the privilege of teaching the few Roman Catholic children in council schools. Though Free Church-

[1] Copies of the speech which the President was not able to give on 27th March, were sent to the Press.

[2] 1.4.20.

[3] He quoted the relevant figures. Between 1902 and 1920, voluntary schools had decreased by 2,000. Between 1912 and 1920, the Established Church had lost 1,140 schools, but had still over 10,500 and at an average rate of 100 closures a year it would take 105 years to complete the process of transfer.

[4] A week later the Education Committee of the National Council of Evangelical Free Churches condemned Fisher's proposals, 14.5.20.

[5] The *Tablet*, 3.4.20.

men and Roman Catholics had come out strongly against the proposals, and Anglicans, who might have been expected to respond enthusiastically, had been restrained in their approval, it was in fact the teachers who administered the decisive blow.[1] They were unanimously opposed to the right of entry, and they were apprehensive, despite all assurances to the contrary, lest they should find themselves under strong pressure to give denominational instruction. Their fear was that local authorities would prefer to appoint candidates who expressed a willingness to impart a certain type or types of religious instruction, so that there would in fact be tests for teachers.

Fisher had hoped that the general spirit of co-operation would be sufficient to carry him over and past the old obstacles. His approach to the problems of dual control had been empirical, based on the desire for a give and take arrangement, but his negotiations had revealed unexpected prejudice and suspicion, and instead of reaching a simple solution he had been driven back on contracting out. The result was a patched up and superficial compromise, incapable of achieving educational peace. The economic difficulties which beset the country at the end of 1920 put an end to official negotiations[2] and Fisher, in despair, wrote, 'It seems to me most doubtful whether it will ever be possible that the religious problem in our schools can be solved without inciting a violent controversy, and, though there are few sacrifices which I would not make to get rid of the dual system, I am not prepared to invite a raging, tearing controversy on the religious question.'

Perhaps the most significant feature of the entire period was the eagerness of the Anglican leaders to negotiate. In return for 'facilities' their spokesmen were now apparently prepared to sacrifice all the securities of the dual system. This desire was not confined to the Archbishop of Canterbury and other members of the Episcopate; the National Society had supported the plan, and the *Church Times* presumably represented the High Church view when it declared that 'the proposals put forward by Mr. Fisher are on sound lines and such as the Church will be able to accept'.[3] Even the Bishop of Manchester, despite his withdrawal from the

[1] Resolutions of the N.U.T. Easter Conference. The *Times Educational Supplement*, 8.4.20.

[2] A private member's Bill, the Davies Bill, introduced on 1st November, 1921, followed the lines of the Fisher proposals.

[3] 30.4.20.

discussions in April, moved a resolution of the northern convocation in favour of the scheme.[1] Indeed, many Anglicans were
reluctant to see the proposals drop and on several occasions tried
to revive them. Dr Davidson indicated his own views with complete frankness, 'I have come to the pretty sure conclusion that,
taking England and Wales as a whole, for every Church of England
child in our schools, we have two Church of England children in
provided schools.'[2] For the first time it seemed that the great body
of Anglicans were agreed on a solution, unity of administration
under local authorities with variety of type. Nevertheless, there
were some who refused to contemplate the surrender of their
schools and were prepared to put up fierce resistance; Lancashire
Churchmen, for example, again revived the Church Schools
Emergency League to the dismay of both the *Church Times* and
the *Guardian*. In the words of the *Guardian*, it was 'an organised
effort not to secure satisfactory terms in the event of any change,
not to suggest any alternative plans, but simply to oppose any
change and let things drift'.[3]

Fisher's resignation in 1922 marked the end of official sounding
on the religious issue, but efforts continued at a different level.
There was, for example, a serious attempt at a local settlement in
Wales, where the geographical distribution of elementary schools
was obsolete and many of the voluntary school buildings in the
villages were dilapidated and out of date. A plan of consolidation
was urgently needed in order to eliminate the unnecessary schools.
The initiative for discussion between the Welsh churches was
taken by the Nonconformists, whose views had changed with the
years. In the past they had maintained that religious instruction
was the business of the Sunday school and should therefore be
excluded from the public elementary schools. Now, however,
faced with the decline in Sunday school attendance, they realised
that the majority of children would be brought up in entire
ignorance of religion unless it were taught in the day schools.
Discussions begun as early as 1921 continued for the next two
years between churchmen, administrators and teachers.[4] Perhaps
the most astonishing thing was the almost entire lack of public

[1] The *Yorkshire Post*, 29.4.20.
[2] Address to the Canterbury Diocesan Conference. *The Times*, 14.6.23.   [3] 5.1.23.
[4] The terms of the Welsh Concordat were published in the *School Government Chronicle*, 10.12.21.

interest in the proposals. Less than twenty years before, the religious controversy had assumed its most virulent form in Wales, but now the discussions passed almost without notice. With only 10 per cent of Welsh children in Church schools, the Anglicans were in a weak bargaining position and were prepared to accept less favourable conditions than Fisher had suggested in his large-scale plan. By the terms of the concordat, all Church schools were to be surrendered and Cowper-Temple instruction was to be given universally. In the event, the churches agreed unanimously to the terms, which were also acceptable to the local authorities, but the last word lay with the Welsh teachers who, still ridden with the bogey of religious tests, rejected them.[1] Their veto was decisive and the proposals came to nothing.

In England, it was the local authorities which took the initiative by making their own arrangements with the churches. The lead was given in 1924 by Cambridgeshire where, in consultation with the representatives of the religious denominations, an agreed syllabus of religious instruction was devised for use in provided and in transferred schools. This was a new way of dealing with the religious problem, and the example of Cambridgeshire was followed in many other areas so that by 1930 eight counties had their own agreed syllabuses. The result was a general improvement in the quality of religious instruction in council schools. The Bible ceased to be, as it had so often been in the past, a sort of theological 'lucky bag' into which each teacher might dip and interpret his findings as he chose. There was now a detailed scheme for his help and guidance. As a direct consequence of the higher standards, there was, on the part of the Anglicans, a greater willingness to transfer their schools. One area, the West Riding, made in 1926 a special agreement with the local diocesan authorities. The West Riding Concordat, as it was called, permitted managers to transfer their schools to the local authority, which, in turn, allowed them to retain two periods a week for denominational teaching; on the remaining three days of the week agreed syllabus instruction was to be given.[2]

In a variety of ways the local authorities were endeavouring to

---

[1] Resolution of the Executive of the N.U.T. in Wales, 11.2.22. The *Times Educational Supplement*, 18.2.22. The scheme was revived in 1925 on a local county basis, e.g. the Denbighshire Concordat.

[2] The terms of the Concordat were published in October 1925. *Education*, 6.11.25.

reach working agreements with the managers of voluntary schools. The great need was for central schools which could draw on the senior pupils of an entire area. Some authorities, therefore, adopted the Anson Byelaw,[1] which permitted the withdrawal of children, where parents so desired, for purposes of denominational instruction. Thus senior children transferred under a programme of reorganisation might still receive denominational instruction elsewhere. A few authorities[2] treated such children as a separate group and arranged for denominational teaching to be given within the school by regular members of the staff. In Lancashire, where four-fifths of the public elementary schools were voluntary schools, the need for agreement was particularly acute and the local authority was anxious to raise with the Board of Education the question of public aid towards the cost of improving voluntary school buildings.[3]

The post-war years had brought a great change of atmosphere. Apart from ardent minorities, it was now clear that the general public no longer cared about the religious issue. Opinion was now much more concerned with opportunities for higher education and, in particular, with securing an increase in secondary school places. Politically also, the post-war scene had changed. The Nonconformist political militancy had vanished and the old Liberal Party, with its strong Nonconformist alliance, was rapidly disintegrating. The growing Labour Party, on the other hand, was not anxious to revive an issue which might divide its own ranks. Nevertheless, despite attempts at the national and local level, agreement on the religious problem still eluded educational administrators. No settlement was possible without the full co-operation of the five great bodies of opinion, the Church of England, the Nonconformist churches, the Roman Catholic community, the local administrators and the teachers, and these interests were still too diverse and conflicting to be reconciled. Yet the necessities of the time, trade difficulties and industrial unrest, demanded a thorough overhaul of the educational system, with the provision of more technical and higher education and the breaking down of old classifications based on social rather

[1] The Anson Byelaw of 1902 permitted the parent to withdraw, on written application, his child from the school during the period of religious instruction. *Report*, P.P. 1903 [Cd. 1763].
[2] E.g. Warwickshire.   [3] Lancashire Resolution quoted in *Education*, 21.8.25.

than educational distinctions. Implicit in the thinking of the 'twenties was the idea that education for the majority of children should be much more generous and enlightened than the existing elementary education.

In the middle years of the decade the Board of Education endeavoured to translate this idea into practice. Its Circulars encouraged local authorities to reduce the size of classes,[1] to plan new elementary schools[2] and to introduce advanced instruction.[3] Perhaps the official requirements were best summed up in Circular 1358, issued in March 1925, which urged local authorities 'to secure that children of compulsory school age are taught in decent surroundings, . . . that they are enabled by the provision of suitable instruction to derive the fullest benefit from the later years of their school life, and that opportunities for further education are open to them according to their needs and abilities'. From the denominational point of view the basic assumptions which underlay the 1902 compromise were crumbling. The educational advances of the post-war period combined with inflation had entirely upset the old balance of commitments, and it was becoming increasingly difficult for the denominations to bear their share of the financial burden.

Two further publications in the years 1925 and 1926 threatened to accentuate the difficulties of the voluntary schools. The first was the Board of Education's list of schools with defective premises, the 'black list'. It was significant, but hardly surprising, that in the 'blackest' category the non-provided schools were twice as numerous as the provided schools,[4] for the majority of church schools were in old buildings erected at a time when educational requirements were very different. The second publication, in 1926, was the Report of the Consultative Committee on the 'Education of the Adolescent', the Hadow Report, which laid down a policy for the reorganisation of elementary education. Reorganisation with a view to the better provision of advanced elementary education had been in the air for some time and had already been pressed by the Board, but the Hadow Report, by recommending separate schools for juniors and seniors, gave a new impetus to the movement and enlisted popular support. It

[1] Circular 1325, 1924.   [2] Circulars 1334 and 1339, 1924.   [3] Circular 1350, 1925.
[4] Figures given by the President of the Board of Education, 12th February, 1931. *Parl. Deb.*, Commons, 5th Ser., vol. ccxlviii, col. 580.

proposed, in fact, a complete remodelling of the old elementary system with the raising of the school-leaving age to fifteen so that the senior school course could be organised on a four-year basis. The report was an expression of the wider conception of education of the post-war years and made it clear that in the future it would not merely be a question of improving and modernising existing buildings; new schools would have to be built, secondary schools for the more gifted children and senior schools for the remaining children over eleven.

So far as the denominations were concerned, the financial basis of the 1902 settlement would be completely outmoded. The new burdens would be beyond them and some adjustment would be necessary before they could co-operate in the programme of reorganisation. This would involve additional grants of public money and, as a *quid pro quo,* some relaxation of denominational control. The entire pace of reform had quickened during the six years since Fisher's attempted concordat, and with the official acceptance of the Hadow Report in 1928 the need for a resettlement with the churches became even more pressing. The task of the local authorities was now to design their programmes of reorganisation, in the words of Selby-Bigge, former Permanent Secretary to the Board of Education, 'to work out a jigsaw puzzle, and not only fit the individual pieces as they exist into their places, but get the size and shape of a good many pieces altered and make new pieces to fill up the gap.'[1] Their chances of success depended, to a large extent, on the co-operation of the churches, and already there were signs of a growing spirit of accommodation. Fisher himself had been cheered by the response of the official Anglican representatives, but it was clear that there was considerable dissension within the Church and that a powerful section would be reluctant to co-operate in Hadow reorganisation if it entailed the decapitation of Church schools by the loss of the senior pupils.

The official acceptance of the Hadow proposals caused grave anxiety to Roman Catholics. In the post-war years they had remained aloof from negotiations since at the national level Fisher's scheme had offered no solution to their difficulties and at the local level discussions on the basis of 'facilities' and agreed syllabus instruction had been of no interest to them. Periodically their spokesmen had brought up the Scottish solution, which would,

[1] *The Nineteenth Century and After,* vol. cx, 9.

of course, have given them all they desired, schools staffed with teachers of their own faith and financed entirely by the local authorities.[1] The Hadow programme of reorganisation now brought new problems for, in contrast to the all-age parish school, the proposed senior school would have to cater for the pupils of several parishes. Hence, quite apart from the prohibitive cost, reorganisation would cut clean across the parochial basis on which their system of schools was based and would sever the intimate connection which the parish priest had with his children. It was only gradually and with extreme reluctance that the Roman Catholic community came round to accepting the Hadow proposals and then on the express condition that they should receive special grants towards the building of new schools.

Meanwhile, in the absence of a national settlement, the local authorities had continued to make their own arrangements with the churches. The local schemes had certain features in common; they were designed to give the authorities control of the management, organisation and grouping of schools, and they included provisions for compulsory religious instruction in all council schools as well as for the provision of denominational instruction for children transferred from church schools under schemes of reorganisation. Already in April 1925, the County Councils Association had approached the President of the Board of Education, Lord Eustace Percy, with a request for an Enabling Bill, a permissive measure which would strengthen the authorities' powers to make local arrangements.[2] It was intended that there should be two sections in the Bill, the first embodying conditions of transfer (which were to include the provision of denominational instruction) and the second empowering authorities to make a single grant on approved conditions to non-provided schools for the purpose of putting them into a state of repair, without requiring the transfer of premises. The request had been sympathetically received and negotiations were proceeding slowly when unexpected developments on the denominational front wrecked the entire project.

This time it was the Church Assembly which did the damage by

---

[1] T. P. O'Connor, seconded by Sidney Webb, had tabled a motion in favour of the Scottish solution in the House of Commons, *Parl. Deb.,* Commons, 5th Ser., vol. clxiii, col. 1552. Motion put and agreed to 2nd May, 1923.

[2] A Statement was issued to the Press to this effect, 24.6.26.

accepting the strongly denominational report of its Education Committee. The Anglicans had, in fact, continued their deliberations on the religious issue uninterruptedly between the years 1921 and 1926; the National Society after discussion had issued Memoranda in 1922 and 1923, there had been direct negotiations with the Nonconformists at the Memorial Hall Conferences from 1921 to 1923, and an investigating committee, specially appointed by the Church Assembly in 1921, had already issued two reports. Throughout, the Anglicans had accepted the principle of unity of administration and had seemed to favour the idea of an Enabling Bill, but with the publication of the final report of the investigating committee in the autumn of 1926 the whole aspect changed. The recommendations included right of entry into new council senior schools, the establishment of local Religious Education Committees to supervise the religious instruction in all council schools, and the provision of new denominational schools by the local authorities. The entire spirit of the recommendations was one of mistrust of the local authorities, yet, when the report came before the Church Assembly in November, it was adopted[1] and so became official Church policy. The acceptance of the report by the Church Assembly was such a shock to local administrators that they immediately dropped the idea of an Enabling Bill and instead of re-opening the religious issue on a national level resolved to concentrate instead on local arrangements.[2]

In the meantime a new committee under the chairmanship of Sir Henry Hadow had been appointed by the Archbishops of Canterbury and York in July 1924. In some ways it seemed that the decision of the Church Assembly had prejudged the work of the second committee, but it continued its investigations and in 1929 published its recommendations in two reports: a Majority and a Minority report.[3] The Majority put their trust in the training colleges and were prepared to transfer Church schools to the local authorities; the Minority declared in favour of the maintenance of denominational schools and asked for further assistance from special State grants. In the end the reports of both committees were shelved. Their real significance was the continued

---

[1] *Church Assembly Proceedings*, VII, No. 2, 414.
[2] County Councils' Association Official Gazette, February, 1927.
[3] The *Guardian*, 29.11.29.

evidence of the deep rift in Anglican opinion, which made the prospect of national agreement seem as remote as ever.

In 1927, however, the National Society had adopted a major change of policy by accepting the principle of Hadow reorganisation and advising managers, in return for the Anson Byelaw provision, to send their older children to the new council senior schools. Once again there seemed a chance of agreement; once again, the idea of an Enabling Bill was revived and by 1929 was well launched. The Bill which Lord Eustace Percy now had in mind was a simplified version of his earlier scheme, confined to black list schools and to an emergency period. He was still negotiating when Parliament was dissolved for a General Election.

Meanwhile, in the localities, the authorities continued to make working arrangements with the churches; Dorsetshire, for instance, permitted right of entry in some schools, but was uneasy on the legality of these arrangements and in the autumn of 1928 made enquiries at the Board of Education. In reply, it received from the Board a communication which became known as the 'Dorset Letter'. Referring to the council schools in Dorset where right of entry was permitted and denominational instruction was given, though not as part of the school curriculum, the Board stated that the matter did not come within the scope of its administration and that it had no authority to advise 'on the technical regularity of such arrangements'.[1] The vagueness of the reply caused general surprise and consternation but when, two months later, the West Riding tried to get a more precise statement, the Board explained that the arrangement was to be restricted to the more remote areas where children could not in practice be withdrawn from the school premises. The teachers, however, had been thoroughly aroused and were highly suspicious lest the Board should permit fresh evasions of the Cowper-Temple Clause.[2]

The religious issue came up again during the 1929 election campaign. By now the principle of reorganisation had been universally accepted and there was also considerable pressure to extend the school-leaving age to fifteen, but the great problem for the denominations was to obtain financial aid which would enable

---

[1] The application of the Dorset letter depended on vacant accommodation being available. It was also based on the assumption that the group of children under religious instruction was not under school discipline.

[2] *The Times*, 3.4.29. In June the Executive of the N.U.T. once again expressed their opposition to 'creed tests for teachers' and 'right of entry'. *Ibid.*, 13.6.29.

them to reorganise their schools. Roman Catholics, in particular, were most apprehensive about the financial aspect and as a result of an active campaign in the constituencies, were assured of a good deal of support from Members. In the new Labour Government the President of the Board of Education, Sir Charles Trevelyan, lost no time in introducing an Education Bill to raise the school-leaving age. His tactics were prompted by economic rather than educational motives, for the country was in the throes of depression and the raising of the school-leaving age would cut down the number of unemployed. Only when his measure had failed did he come to grips with the main problem by consulting the various interests and working out proposals for a give and take arrangement.[1] On the one hand, the local authorities were to be entitled to spend money on the repair of existing voluntary schools (as distinct from the building of new schools) and were, in return, to have the right of appointing all teachers; on the other hand, denominational interests were to be safeguarded in two ways, by consultation on the appointment of those teachers who were to give denominational instruction (the number of whom was to vary with the number of children belonging to the denomination), and by right of entry for children transferred under reorganisation programmes from church to council senior schools. The President's objective was to reduce the number of religious tests and to leave the appointment of teachers in denominational schools to the good sense of the local authorities and managers. The National Union of Teachers, however, were very suspicious of the proposed arrangements, objecting both to right of entry and to any suggestion of tests for teachers.[2] Thus, while the attitude of the denominations was still uncertain, that of the teachers was wholly negative.

With consultations still at an indeterminate stage, the preliminary proposals were published in the form of a White Paper and then incorporated in a Parliamentary Bill in May 1930. It soon appeared that the President had again acted too precipitately. In Parliament, both Nonconformists and Roman Catholics attacked the Bill, the former because their single-school area grievances would still remain,[3] and the latter because their future needs had

[1] Subsequently published in the *White Paper,* Cmd. 3551.
[2] N.U.T. Resolutions at the Easter Conference, 1930. The *Schoolmaster,* 25.4.30.
[3] *Parl. Deb.,* Commons, 5th Ser., vol. ccxxxviii, cols. 1587 *et seq.*

been completely ignored.[1] Indeed, the Roman Catholics lost no time in launching a public campaign against the Bill, and among their activities deluged members of Parliament with postcards of protest. (Their aggressive tactics, particularly in the Liverpool diocese, caused a corresponding stiffening among the Nonconformists.) Meanwhile, some Labour members themselves were in revolt against other sections of the Bill. In the end, therefore, the combined opposition proved so strong that the Government, already hampered by their minority position, decided to drop the Bill.

At the beginning of the next session, in October, a last attempt was made to end the impasse, Trevelyan on this occasion reverting to his original Bill, which dealt solely with the extension of the school age. During the debates it became clear that unless the Government pledged assistance to the voluntary schools a number of their own supporters would vote against them at the third reading, so the President started negotiations with members representative of the main interests. By now, however, the Cabinet had become thoroughly apprehensive and in a letter to Trevelyan the Prime Minister, Ramsay MacDonald, stressed the need for caution. 'We have been putting all sorts of peoples' backs up recently one way and another', he wrote, 'and I do not want a first class education row flaring up in this country. Should there be any hitch everybody will blame somebody else, but in the end we shall be left with the squalling infant in our arms.'

Trevelyan's new proposals differed in certain important respects from those of preceding years. Firstly, the local authorities were to be permitted to contribute not the whole, but a proportion, fixed at 50 per cent as a minimum and 75 per cent as a maximum, of the cost of reorganising church schools. Secondly, two alternative methods were suggested for the appointment of those teachers, to be called 'reserved' teachers, who were to give denominational instruction. Thirdly, undenominational teaching was to be secured in all single-school area schools and in all other schools to which children might be transferred under programmes of reorganisation. Lastly, instead of the right of entry, proposed in the earlier scheme, the Anson Byelaw was to be made universally applicable. The proposals were favourably received by all sections except the Nonconformists, who had reacted violently to the

---

[1] *Ibid.*, Commons, 5th Ser., vol. ccxxxix, cols. 1542 *et seq.*

K

Roman Catholic campaign of the preceding months. In retaliation they had organised monster meetings and even sent emissaries to consult with Lloyd George.[1] Their fear was that the denominationalists, particularly the Roman Catholics, would consolidate their ground and so be in a stronger bargaining position when the time came for a general settlement. They were adamant, therefore, that the head teachers of the newly reorganised church schools should not be denominationally reserved. It is clear that at root their objection was to anything which would infuse new life into the denominational schools. By the middle of January 1931, Anglicans, Roman Catholics and teachers had indicated their willingness to accept the proposals; only the Nonconformists remained implacable, and this despite the concessions which the new proposals had included. They had been less violently opposed to Trevelyan's earlier scheme because they had believed, quite mistakenly, that it was to be merely a temporary emergency measure. The new proposals made it quite clear that future improvements were to be the responsibility of the local authority. Roman Catholics, on the other hand, who had laboured under a similar misapprehension earlier in the year, now welcomed the categorical statement contained in the new scheme. After a month of intensive negotiations the Government published their proposals in a White Paper,[2] indicating in an introductory note that they were regarded as acceptable by all parties except the Nonconformists.

Meanwhile Trevelyan's third Bill had met disaster. In the Commons denominationalists had emphasised their opposition to any measure which ignored the needs of the voluntary schools, and had succeeded in incorporating an amendment to that effect from a Roman Catholic member, J. Scurr.[3] The Lords, however, were completely opposed to the main principles of the Bill, the raising of the school-leaving age and maintenance allowances, and rejected the measure by an overwhelming majority.[4] For a brief moment it looked like a major conflict between Lords and Commons. Trevelyan was all for defying the Lords[5] but, in the event, more moderate counsels prevailed and the President, deeply

---

[1] The *Manchester Guardian*, 22.1.31.   [2] Cmd. 3786.
[3] *Parl. Deb.*, Commons, 5th Ser., vol. ccxlvii, col. 256.
[4] *Ibid.*, Lords, 5th Ser., vol. lxxix, col. 1162. The voting was 168 to 22.
[5] In his letter of resignation to the Prime Minister, 19.2.31 (*The Times*, 3.3.31), Trevelyan indicated his feeling.

disappointed, resigned office on 2nd March. The Government were in sore straits. Their most valued measures, the Education Bill and the Trade Disputes Bill, had withered away and their strength had been dissipated by party strife. Humiliated by successive failures and impotent before the gathering financial storm, they had adopted a weak and vacillating policy and, at the critical moment, had evaded a constitutional conflict on the education issue.

All three Labour Education Bills had failed, and Trevelyan, who had embarked on his task in a fine burst of enthusiasm, had gone the way of so many before him. Throughout, he had been driven by the necessity of relieving the unemployment problem and dominated, therefore, by economic rather than educational considerations. He had attempted to avoid the difficulties inherent in the dual system by rushing through hastily-contrived measures and treating fundamental problems as side issues. Like his predecessors he had discovered too late the immense complexities involved and had failed to reconcile the widely different claims: of the Roman Catholics and Anglicans for maximum grants, of the Nonconformists for full public control, of the teachers for freedom from tests and of the local authorities for efficiency and economy. But the responsibility was as much the Government's as Trevelyan's. Once again there had been revealed a situation which could hardly be touched too tenderly, a situation full of delicate issues with which only enduring tact and patience could fitly deal.

As a result, reorganisation was everywhere held up. The children were the real victims. Though it was unthinkable that a problem which affected the common welfare so deeply should remain unsolved, no progress was possible during the prolonged financial crisis which first struck the country in the autumn of 1931. When the national emergency was at last over the Coalition Government prepared to reopen the issue. The Minister concerned, Lord Halifax, proceeded cautiously by patient exploration of the ground. Though the general situation seemed more promising, there was still the old difficulty of reconciling conflicting claims, of Nonconformists for a temporary emergency measure and of Roman Catholics for a permanent long-term settlement. By the spring of 1935, however, discussions were well under way, the President having worked out a balanced compromise whereby the gains for each sectional interest would outweigh the losses. He had taken as the basis of negotiations the Trevelyan proposals of 1931 and had adapted them to fit the contemporary situation. His successor, Mr Oliver Stanley, continued the discussions so that the new proposals should incorporate the minimum demands of both parties, of the Nonconformists for the limitation of subsidies to an emergency period (fixed at three years),[1] and of the Roman Catholics for assistance towards the building of new senior schools in return for giving up the right of appointment of teachers.[2] Politically, the provision of a time limit was expedient; educationally, it was important since it provided an incentive for the denominations to act promptly. Agreed syllabus instruction was to be available in single-school areas for the children of those parents who desired it, and, similarly, under the Anson Byelaw, which was now to become universal, denominational instruction was to be available for children transferred from church schools to council schools.

By the end of the year the President had secured agreement on all sides and was able to proceed to the Parliamentary stage. His Bill, introduced on the 19th December, had two main features, the raising of the school-leaving age to fifteen and, as a corollary, a temporary adjustment of voluntary school liabilities. The Bill, in fact, went much further than the Trevelyan proposals; for the first time it made Exchequer grants, in the form of building subsidies, available for voluntary schools, though it was true that the building subsidies were to depend on the goodwill of the local authorities, who were empowered to make grants of between 50 and 75 per cent towards the cost of new non-provided senior schools, that they were to be limited to an emergency period, and that the denominations were being asked in return to surrender, with certain reservations, the right to appoint teachers.

All parties now accepted the main proposals, the raising of the school-leaving age and building grants for reorganisation. Roman Catholics, though they would have preferred a large-scale national settlement, nevertheless welcomed the Bill as a step in the right direction.[3] They were interested only in building grants for reorganised schools, whereas the Anglicans wanted, in addition,

[1] The Joint Education Committee of the Federal Council of Evangelical Free Churches and the National Council of the Evangelical Churches had passed a resolution in favour of a three-year emergency grant, 19.10.34.
[2] They were to retain right of consultation before appointment.
[3] Speech of the Archbishop of Westminster. The Birmingham Post, 13.3.36.

to secure 'facilities' instruction for children transferred from
Church schools to new council senior schools. Indeed, Anglicans
would really have liked something more general than the Anson
Byelaw and harked back persistently to the famous Dorset Letter
of 1928, but they were not prepared to press their views to an
issue.[1] Nonconformists welcomed the increased measure of public
control, though they were deeply conscious of the sacrifices asked
of them. It was only with great difficulty that some of them had
been brought to accept the proposals; nothing more could
possibly be conceded.[2] The teachers and local authorities had also
been co-operative, the National Union of Teachers, in particular,
adopting a much more reasonable attitude than in previous years.
Teachers and Nonconformists alike, however, kept a vigilant
watch during the passing of the Bill lest there should be any
attempt to extend the number of reserved teachers.

Every party had conceded as much as it could and it was quite
clear that any serious alteration in the balance at the Parliamentary
stage would imperil the entire scheme. In fact, the Bill was
threatened twice and on both occasions saved only by the swift
and decisive action of the President. The first occasion was a fresh
outburst of Roman Catholic agitation in the north in the New Year
which, had it not been speedily checked, would have brought
Nonconformist reaction against the measure. The second was the
insertion by the Archbishop of Canterbury, Dr Lang, in June of
two vital amendments, the first designed to extend building
grants to junior schools affected by reorganisation, and the second
to permit, in certain cases, right of entry in the council senior
schools.[3] Teachers and Nonconformists were furious at the new
demands, which they regarded as a violation of the previous
gentleman's agreement,[4] and for a few anxious days the entire
settlement was in jeopardy. However, the Archbishop himself
withdrew his request for right of entry[5] and on the return of the
Bill to the Commons the Government promptly deleted his first

---

[1] The Archbishop of Canterbury's speech at the Annual Meeting of the National
Society, 6.5.36, N.S.

[2] This was clear from a meeting of the Joint Education Committee of the Federal
Council of Evangelical Free Churches and the National Council of Evangelical Free
Churches, 10.2.36.

[3] *Parl. Deb.*, Lords, 5th Ser., vol. ci, col. 319.

[4] The *Schoolmaster*, 9.7.36, the *British Weekly*, 9.7.36.

[5] *Parl. Deb.*, Lords, 5th Ser., vol. ci, col. 342.

amendment. In the words of the President, 'the addition (i.e. of grants for junior school buildings) would entirely destroy the basis upon which the whole of that part of the Bill rests.'[1] The Bill was saved and, its final form corresponding closely to the terms of the preliminary concordat, received the Royal Assent in July.

The 1936 Act was the first breach in the 1902 compromise and an attempt to adjust denominational commitments to contemporary conditions. Based on agreement between all interests, it was tangible proof that the old animosities were at last subsiding. In one area, however, sectarian controversy necessitated further legislation. This was in Liverpool, where the continual influx of Irish had caused acute overcrowding in the Roman Catholic schools of the dockside area. The gravity and scale of the problem required immediate action but, despite the fact that the 1936 Act offered an obvious solution and despite the willingness of the Roman Catholics to co-operate, the local authority made no attempt to fulfil its responsibilities. The real trouble was that the problem had become a major issue in the fiercely sectarian local politics, and what finally brought matters to a head in the spring of 1938 was the deliberate refusal of the newly elected City Council to apply the relevant clauses of the 1936 Act.[2] Thereafter events moved swiftly. The then President of the Board asked the local authority to submit an effective alternative plan for the provision of the necessary school accommodation and, when none was forthcoming, a substantial proportion of the Board's grant was withheld.[3] The final outcome was a special version of the 1936 Act, the Liverpool settlement of 1939, a Parliamentary measure empowering the authority to build the necessary schools, which were then to be leased to the denominational managers at rentals between 25 per cent and 50 per cent of the loan charges.[4]

The result of the 1936 Act was that 519 proposals for new senior schools were submitted in the three years which were allowed, 289 by the Roman Catholics and 230 by the Anglicans.[5] In addition, some 12,000 school places would be available for

---

[1] *Ibid.*, Commons, 5th Ser., vol. cccxv, col. 950.

[2] *Minutes of Proceedings of the Select Committee on the Senior Public Elementary Schools (Liverpool) Bill*, 359.

[3] £15,000 was to be withheld from each monthly instalment paid to the local authority.

[4] See Appendix B.   [5] White Paper, *'Education Reconstruction'*, Cmd. 6458, para. 49.

Roman Catholic children under the Liverpool settlement. In submitting so many schemes at a time when their community were deeply affected by trade depression and unemployment, Roman Catholics showed great foresight and determination and ensured that the majority of their senior pupils would be covered by their proposals. Anglicans, however, were concerned with far larger numbers. More than 300,000 of their senior children were in all-standard schools and only a small fraction of these were covered by the proposals they submitted; for the rest, they were apparently prepared to co-operate in the local authorities' general schemes of reorganisation.

As it happened, the outbreak of war in September 1939 prevented the great majority of proposals from materialising, but the denominations were assured that the Board would consider further legislation to cover proposals which had failed to materialise for causes beyond the control of the promoters.[1] The importance of the 1936 Act should not be over-estimated as it was, after all, an expedient to deal with an emergency situation. Nevertheless, it stands as the first clear encroachment on the compromise arrangement of 1902, and as a frank admission by all concerned that certain premises, on which that measure had been based, had now changed. Moreover, it was significant that the long line of failures had at last been broken and that some general spirit of accommodation had replaced the obstructionism of the past.

Before the outbreak of war in 1939 there was one further development of significance, the publication, in 1938, of the Consultative Committee's Report on Secondary Education, the Spens Report as it was called after the chairman, Sir Will Spens. The Committee expressed the opinion that existing arrangements for pupils over eleven had ceased to correspond with the actual structure of modern society and they were particularly concerned to remedy the previous neglect of the elementary schools in the matter of space and amenities. The Committee proposed, therefore, that for all children primary education should end and secondary education should begin at the age of eleven. There were to be different types of secondary school, grammar, technical and modern, all with 'parity of esteem'. The principle of equality of status, implicit in the Hadow Report, was now made explicit

[1] *Ibid.*, Lords, 5th Ser., vol. cxiv, col. 1213.

and in all types of secondary schools regulations were to be uniform for the size of classes, for the scale of salaries, for material conditions including the provision of gymnasia, handicrafts and housecraft rooms, and for a minimum school-leaving age.[1] In its recommendations the Spens Report was bold, generous and comprehensive. It condemned the distinct vertical division in education, the legacy of the nineteenth century, and advocated the principle of equality of opportunity. For the churches, however, the implications of the report were more ominous even than those of the Hadow Report and the provision of new types of schools covering a longer period of school life would be an impossible task for them.

Since the last great settlement, in 1902, the whole conception of education had changed. Then, it had been merely a question of elementary instruction; now, there was to be secondary education for all, and the churches must either provide the additional and vastly superior accommodation or confine themselves to the field of primary education. The combined effect of educational reform and declining money values had completely transformed their financial responsibilities. In 1902 the cost of a school place in an all-age school was £4 or £5; by the late 'thirties a junior school place was costing £50 and a senior school place £100 and this during a period when the possibility of obtaining help from voluntary sources had greatly diminished. Moreover, the expansion of the urban areas surrounding the great cities had placed on voluntary bodies the burden of providing additional schools. Altogether, the scale of their commitments had changed beyond recognition. Yet, despite the wider conception of education, despite the change in money values, despite the need for new schools, the financial principle behind the 1902 Act had remained unaltered. Throughout the 'twenties and the 'thirties there had been constant attempts at revision, but of all the schemes only the emergency measure of 1936 had materialised, and even this had become outmoded two years later with the publication of the Spens Report. In the circumstances only a radical reshaping of the previous settlement would enable the denominations to participate in the new developments.

[1] *Spens Report,* 298–302.

———————◆———————

Chapter 7

The Butler Act, 1944

The outbreak of the second world war in 1939 brought educational developments to a standstill. The building of new schools under the 1936 Act was impossible and the proposals of the Spens Committee remained stillborn. Nevertheless, the war impelled men to think about the needs of the future, since totalitarianism threatened more than mere physical existence and challenged the very idea of democracy. Despite the anxieties of the time a good deal of thought was therefore given to the purposes of society, and those who surveyed the domestic scene in a mood of self-examination and criticism were appalled by the glaring injustices which the war brought to light. Evacuation in particular revealed conditions of squalor and ignorance which few had dreamt existed, for the filth, malnutrition and indiscipline of many of the young evacuees came as a severe shock, a shameful reminder that even in the twentieth century Disraeli's 'two nations' still persisted. Clearly education had a vital part to play in the national campaign against ignorance, poverty and disease, but the entire educational system first needed overhauling so that inequalities and anomalies could be eliminated and full scope given to ability wherever it existed. By 1941 this movement for educational reconstruction was rousing keen interest and, with the 'total' character of the war welding the nation together as never before and emphasising the common interest of all in ensuring that the rising generations should be educated for their responsibilities, the general spirit of the time was favourable to reform. As for the sectarian and political controversies of the past, there was hope that the old bitterness had receded and that the nation could, in the words of Mr R. A. Butler, who became President of the Board of Education in July 1941, 'spread its wings and plane over many of the rugged crags which have hitherto held up the columns of advance.'[1]

It was clear that agreement on the religious issue must precede any measure of large-scale educational reform. Half the schools in the country were still church schools, but their organisation and amenities were far behind the standards of the council schools. For example, as a result of the Hadow scheme of reorganisation separate senior schools had now been provided for 62 per cent of the senior pupils in council schools, but for only 16 per cent of those in church schools.[2] Under the Spens recommendations there was to be equality of opportunity and higher standards of accommodation and amenities, but the fact remained that the non-provided schools could not afford to bring their buildings up to date. A great number of them were old and, erected at a time when ideas of educational method were rigid and narrow, were extremely difficult to adapt to modern requirements. Altogether, 90 per cent of the non-provided schools compared with 50 per cent of the provided schools had been built before 1900.[3] Similarly the Board of Education's black list, now very much out of date, included 541 voluntary schools, but only 212 council schools. Less than 2 per cent of the total number of council schools were on the list, compared with 4½ per cent of Church of England schools and more than 6 per cent of Roman Catholic schools. As regards premises and amenities there was, then, a clear and ever widening disparity between the provided and the non-provided schools.

During the 'twenties and 'thirties administrators had found the dual system increasingly cumbersome and wasteful. Not only were there large numbers of non-provided schools which were too small to be run efficiently and economically, there were also whole areas where reorganisation was held up for lack of co-operation between the two types of schools; on the one hand managers of church schools, though unable themselves to build new senior schools, were reluctant to part with their older children, while on the other the local authorities were unwilling to build small schools for their pupils alone. Moreover, on professional and religious as well as administrative grounds, there were many objections to the dual system. These were the problems

---

[1] *The Times*, 10.4.42.
[2] White Paper, '*Education Reconstruction*', Cmd. 6458, para. 47.   [3] *Ibid.*, para. 46.

which remained from the past; vast new problems would arise from the application of the principle of 'secondary education for all'. Hitherto, the dual system had not found its way into secondary schools, in all of which the right of entry was permissible, subject to the discretion of the local authority, though in practice parents had rarely availed themselves of the opportunity of having their children instructed in their own faith during school hours.

The previous decade had seen numerous attempts at piecemeal reform, but now something far more drastic was required, a complete revision in the existing relationship between the three great partners of the national system, the State, the local authorities and the voluntary bodies. The form which the revision was to take would need careful deliberation. Broadly speaking, the choice was between ending or mending the dual system. But there were different ways both of ending it and of mending it, and every possible solution had to be viewed against the historical background and in the light of the contemporary opinions of teachers, administrators, churchmen and the general public.

The general pattern of opinion had evolved gradually. Foremost among the opponents of the dual system in its existing form were the teachers and local administrators. The teachers, as represented in the powerful National Union of Teachers, had very definite views. They stood firmly by the Cowper-Temple Clause and regarded tests for teachers, right of entry, or any form of clerical supervision, as suggestive of subordination and degrading to their profession. Ideally, of course, they would have preferred the complete abolition of the dual system but, failing that, they wanted to see the powers of voluntary school managers severely curtailed.[1] Local administrators, too, would have welcomed the abolition of the dual system, but they were determined, in any case, to secure such extension of their powers as would enable them to enforce equal standards of building and organisation in all schools.[2]

Free Churchmen were likely to speak with some vehemence on the subject of the dual system, and despite the eclipse of Nonconformity of recent years their views commanded considerable respect. They had never ceased to resent the Anglican monopoly in the single-school areas, still some 4,000 in number, where

---

[1] *Educational Reconstruction,* published for the April conference of the N.U.T., 1942.

[2] *Education. A Plan for the Future,* published on behalf of the Association of Directors and Secretaries for Education, 1942.

the schools were social as well as educational centres.[1] Village memories were long, and those responsible for administering the 1936 Act had been astonished at the animosities which still survived. For many years Nonconformists had clamoured for the abolition of the dual system and the least they would now accept was the provision of council schools accessible to all children in the country and the abolition of religious tests for teachers. They had long venerated the Cowper-Temple Clause as the great bulwark of the undenominational system and they were anxious that Christian teaching should be given in all schools; but they maintained the traditional Nonconformist objection to denominational instruction being given at the public expense, believing that any distinctive teaching, which went beyond the common ground upon which all major Christian bodies were agreed, was an extra which must be provided not in the day school but in the home and Sunday school.[2] Nonconformists, then, looked forward to a unified system under complete public control, but a unified system could not do without the buildings of the voluntary schools and these would be expensive to buy or replace. To this problem the Free Churches could offer no immediate solution. As in the past, they hoped that the church schools would gradually disappear, either by closure or by transfer to the local authorities, but they had no contructive policy to suggest and, regardless of the educational fate of the children involved, they were prepared to wait until by process of attrition the Anglican, if not the Roman Catholic, schools were eliminated.

Anglicans were destined to play a decisive part in any future negotiations since they owned 85 per cent of the non-provided schools and could, as they had on previous occasions, wreck any scheme of reform. Clearly, therefore, the chances of a settlement would depend very largely on whether agreement could be reached with them. The difficulty, however, was to know what the Church as a whole really wanted, for it contained within itself a great variety of educational opinion. Divisions which were barely evident at the beginning of the century had deepened and broadened between the wars. In 1902 the great body of Anglicans

---

[1] Figures given by the Parliamentary Secretary. *Parl. Deb.*, 5th Ser., Commons, vol. cccxcviii, col. 1901.

[2] Views expressed for example, in the *Baptist Times*, 5.8.43; the *British Weekly*, 4.11.43.

had stood militant and determined in defence of their schools; now it seemed that increasing numbers were less anxious to preserve their own schools than to ensure sound Christian teaching for all children in all schools. They were appreciative of agreed syllabus instruction and urged that the Church should put its money not into its old and dilapidated schools but into the training of teachers who would set the tone of religious life in all types of school.[1] On the other hand, there were still Churchmen who believed that only a Church school could achieve a true Christian atmosphere. With Dean Inge they held that 'Religion is caught rather than taught; it is the religious teacher, not the religious lesson that helps the pupils to believe.'[2] They felt, as Lord Hugh Cecil had felt in the past, that the real value of the denominational school was the association of school and Church, so that the children could go quickly from one to the other without any waste of time and could be trained for membership of a worshipping community. Anglo-Catholics, the most vigorous and the most vocal section within the Church, held yet another point of view. They were anxious to retain their schools only so long as the existing system remained and were chiefly concerned to secure 'facilities' which would allow denominational teaching to be given in council schools.[3]

In the twentieth century the numbers of Anglican schools had fallen from 12,000 to 9,000 and the proportion of the nation's children they were educating from 40 per cent to 22 per cent. This decline had been due to a variety of causes, to movements of population, the amalgamation of small schools and the increasing confidence in the religious instruction given in council schools. In the twentieth century the Church had built very few schools; in fact, it had scarcely built at all between the wars and had made no attempt to keep pace with the expansion of the suburbs round London and the provincial cities. Even the offer of the 1936 Act had met with meagre response. A large number of Anglican schools were still rural single-school area schools, unreorganised and not infrequently black-listed. Survivals of that nineteenth-century village life dominated by squire and parson, they were

---

[1] Views expressed, for example, by Canon Braley, *A Policy in Religious Education*, 35 *et seq.*

[2] '*Speculum Animae*', 1911, 38.

[3] *A Statement of Educational Policy*, issued by the Oxford Diocesan Council of Education, October 1942.

almost the last vestige of the pre-democratic era, and did not represent the hopes and aspirations of a different social age. Already pre-war figures of black-listed and unreorganised schools presented a sombre picture for the Church of England. Post-war developments would necessitate new buildings as well as extensions and adaptations to existing buildings, and the total cost would be completely beyond the Church's resources.

It was significant that Anglicans and Free Churchmen had drawn closer together in recent years, for they had realised that to prolong former antagonisms would merely weaken the common cause for which they stood. Above all, the war-time challenge of a pagan totalitarian power had impelled them to unite in support of a system of education based on the Christian faith. However, neither the Church of England nor the Free Churches were able to command the strength and authority which had once been theirs. At the time of the Forster Act, even at the time of the Balfour Act, they had directly and overtly exercised political power, but in the 'post-Christian' era of the mid-twentieth century the climate of opinion was entirely different, and the distinction between Church and Chapel had become a negligible element in the modern political system. No longer could Nonconformity speak with its old force and vigour, no longer could the Church of England claim even the nominal allegiance of the masses. Never in English history had the voice of organised Christianity seemed less persuasive. However, although both the Church of England and the Free Churches had lost numerical strength, they had gained by the growing spirit of unity and co-operation. The traditional hostility and dislike had disappeared and disputes about Disestablishment were now memories of the past. Yet a revival of the education issue was not without danger for extremists on both sides still felt very deeply about the principle of church schools and, in the words of the veteran Nonconformist, Dr Scott Lidgett, there remained 'submerged rocks' which might imperil reform.

The other religious minority in the country was the Roman Catholic community. Since the last great settlement in 1902 Roman Catholics, too, had suffered politically by losing the Parliamentary support of the Irish Party as a result of Home Rule. In other ways, however, they had gained; numerically, in contrast to the other churches, they had grown steadily, and socially they were now accepted much more calmly in the life of the nation. Though still a small minority, they had a cohesion which could on occasion make them a powerful pressure group. The number of Roman Catholic schools had increased from 1,000 to 1,200 since the beginning of the century. They now formed 12 per cent of the voluntary schools and were educating 8 per cent of the total child population. In location, age and size there were striking differences between the Anglican and Roman Catholic schools for, while the Anglican schools were more often than not small village schools built in the nineteenth century, the Roman Catholic schools were urban schools, larger and generally newer.[1] In particular, the single-school area schools were almost entirely Anglican. On the occasions of both earlier settlements, in 1870 and 1902, the two communities had stood united in defence of their schools, but during the twentieth century their ways had parted; while Anglicans were now willing to consider some form of compromise, Roman Catholics insisted on retaining the full denominational character of their schools. Their determination sprang from their unchanging belief that religion should be the very essence of education, and that religion included not merely doctrinal instruction but the life and atmosphere of the school.[2] On the fundamental point of the control of education, that is on having Roman Catholic teachers for its children, the Church was absolutely rigid, but on such matters as the question of ownership of schools and the actual method of appointing teachers it was more flexible.

Roman Catholics had long claimed that they were paying twice for education: once for council schools, which they were unable to use, and again by bearing the cost of building and repairing their own schools. Their suggestion, however, that the rates they paid should be allocated to their own schools was hardly likely to find favour, for it was generally held that public funds represented the sum total collected for all the various public services, and that sectional groups were not entitled, unless they had majority backing, to demand that their contributions to public funds should be earmarked for specific purposes. What members of the Catholic community were particularly anxious about was the

---

[1] Many of their newly recognised schools, however, were in makeshift premises and a large number of them were on the black list.

[2] The Papal Encyclical of 1929, *Divini illius Magistri*, was the authoritative statement on Catholic Education.

extent of their future commitments. They would have to bring their black listed and unreorganised schools up to standard, provide new schools to meet the needs of their growing population, and be prepared to fulfil further requirements on the lines of the Spens recommendations. As Cardinal Bourne had foreseen in 1908, Anglican and Roman Catholic interests had completely diverged. Henceforth Roman Catholics stood alone, and their episcopal veterans, with vivid memories of the old contracting out schemes, were apprehensive lest any new plan should exclude their schools from the public system.

Why did the reformers feel it necessary to pay so much attention to the views of the religious minorities? There were several reasons. Firstly, it was a hard fact that half the schools in the country were still church schools. Secondly, churchmen had very clear convictions, and the views they expressed were positive and definite in contrast to the general attitude of apathy and indifference. Above all, the religious issue had its roots deep in the national life; it raised great questions of principle and could still, at moments of crisis, rouse feelings of passionate fervour and intensity. It was true that the majority of the English people, who were not teachers, administrators or definite members of any denomination, had little interest in the religious conflict. Their attitude towards religion generally has perhaps best been described as 'a combination of vague uncertainties, real sympathy and good feeling mingled with a large measure of indifference and ignorance'.[1] Religion rarely impinged on their everyday lives and although their unconscious assumptions were Christian the conscious profession of the Christian faith was completely alien to them. On the whole they probably preferred their children to receive some knowledge of the scriptures at school, though they would have been hard put to it to give their reasons.

Altogether, opinions had changed a good deal during the last few decades. The great majority of the English people had ceased to care about religion; former denominational antipathies had largely disappeared and the old passion and bitterness had passed. This new climate of feeling, combined with the wartime spirit of unity, encouraged educational reformers to think in terms of a new settlement. So it was that, despite the difficulties of administering the service during wartime and despite the hazards and

[1] Barker, *Character of England*, 83.

discomforts of their own evacuation quarters, senior officials of the Board of Education were inspired to plan for the future. Already in the spring of 1941 they had drawn up a provisional scheme for educational reform, the Green Book, which was circulated to educational associations and selected individuals in June. Entitled *Education after the War*, it was intended to serve as a basis for discussion on the content and methods of educational reform. Chapter IX of the book was concerned with the dual system and stated bluntly, 'If large numbers of children are not to be deprived of healthy and decent school conditions — to say nothing of good educational opportunities — there is no disguising the fact that, unless a considerable number of voluntary schools are to be brought to an end and replaced by new provided schools, some further assistance from public funds must be found towards the maintenance and improvement of the premises, where such improvement is possible.' The authors of the Green Book were well aware that although only the merging of all voluntary schools into the public system would remove the inherent defects of dual control, such drastic action would bring its own problems. Anglicans would demand the repeal of the Cowper-Temple Clause and Roman Catholics would insist on separate arrangements to ensure the denominational character of their schools. Therefore, despite the fact that a 'clean sweep' would appeal to administrators for the sake of educational efficiency, to the Free Churches for the sake of religious equality and to the teachers for the sake of professional freedom, the abolition of the dual system was not considered practical politics.

Instead the scheme suggested in the Green Book, intended simply as a try-out to test the reactions of those specially interested, was designed to modify the dual system and eliminate its worst features. Briefly, the denominations were to be relieved of certain financial responsibilities in return for submission 'to such extended public control as is necessary . . . to ensure the effective and economical organisation and development of both primary and secondary education'. The scheme differentiated between two stages of school life. In the non-provided primary schools responsibility for repairs, improvements and alterations was to pass to the local authority, which, in return, was to have sole right of appointing all teachers except those reserved teachers who were to take denominational instruction. In the secondary schools existing arrangements were to continue except where managers were unable to bear the cost of structural improvements; in such cases the local authority would bear financial responsibility in return for the right of appointing teachers, subject once again to the reservation of a proportion of teachers. Finally, the local authority was to be given overriding control of both primary and secondary education, so that it could determine the organisation and age-ranges of all schools and, with the Board's consent, close redundant schools.

Chapter IX also referred to the general provisions for religious instruction. Already in February 1941, Anglican and Free Church leaders had united in launching a public appeal for the firmer recognition of religion in the schools. Their joint recommendations, published in the form of the 'Archbishops' Five Points',[1] had included the universal provision of religious observance and instruction, and the inspection of that instruction by His Majesty's Inspectors. Obviously the Archbishops' recommendations were part of the larger problem of dual control, and the Green Book now integrated them into the general scheme of reform. Firstly, religious observance and instruction were to be enjoined by statute in all provided primary and secondary schools, such instruction to be given in the form of agreed syllabus instruction and to be inspected; secondly, in the non-provided schools, the agreed syllabus was to be available where parents required it; lastly, regulations for all types of secondary schools were to become uniform by the abolition of the Cowper-Temple Clause in provided modern schools. It was expected that the suggested interference with the Cowper-Temple Clause would provoke attack; nevertheless, it was deliberately included as part of the general balance and was intended to compensate the churches for the measure of public control over their schools.

The Green Book solution was highly complex. Designed to remove the most glaring defects of the dual system, the lack of control by the local authorities over the organisation of non-provided schools and the inability of denominational managers to bring their school premises up to modern standards, it would at the same time mitigate a further defect, which had prevented the most efficient use of staff in an area, namely, the appointment of teachers by denominational managers. Educationally, there was

[1] *The Times*, 13.2.41.

much to be said in favour of a scheme which, by giving complete responsibility to the local authorities ensured equality of opportunity for all children in publicly maintained schools. On the other hand, it would arouse criticism on several counts: the abolition of the limitation on the numbers of reserved teachers, the continuance of the single-school area grievance and the abolition of the Cowper-Temple Clause in secondary modern schools.

It was just after the circulation of the Green Book that Mr Butler took up his appointment as President of the Board. He was himself in keen sympathy with the movement for educational reconstruction and firmly convinced of the need for overhauling the educational system even at a time when the nation's vital energies were devoted to the war effort. In September he sent a record of his early impressions to the Prime Minister. He was insistent on the need for major reconstruction which must, as he pointed out, be preceded by a settlement with the churches. Mr Churchill, however, had lively memories of the 1902 controversy and made a cautious reply. 'We cannot have any Party politics in wartime', he wrote, 'the religious issue would raise these in the most acute and dangerous form.' Undeterred, Mr Butler continued to explore the problem and to examine the views of those specially concerned. Aware that any mishandling might easily revive old and bitter conflicts, he resolved to steep himself in the topic and master every aspect and detail. He began, therefore, with a study of its history, and discerned in the blunders and misfortunes of the past much that was relevant to the present. Only when he had a firm grasp of the background and of the complexities involved did he enter into discussion. Compared with some of his predecessors Mr Butler had unique personal qualities which augured well for success. The mingling in his own family background of Anglican and Nonconformist traditions endowed him with a depth of insight and understanding of the problem, while his sincerity of purpose, patience and diplomatic skill enabled him to treat it with the utmost delicacy and thoroughness. It was his deliberate policy to spend a long time over preliminary negotiations so that all the mistakes could be made in private and not before the public eye.

Anglicans regarded the Green Book much more favourably than did Nonconformists. The Archbishop of Canterbury, Dr Lang, strongly supported the proposals, which, he considered, had all the advantages and none of the disadvantages of the 1936 Act; they provided, he said, help towards secondary schools without asking the churches in return to contribute towards primary schools. Indeed, some Anglicans indicated their willingness to concede much more to public authority,[1] though at the other extreme there was a section, including the Bishops of Oxford and Gloucester, who wished to take almost as strong a line as the Roman Catholics about the preservation of the character of their schools. Nonconformists, on the other hand, were highly critical of the proposals for reservation of teachers and of the suggested abrogation of the Cowper-Temple Clause in the new modern schools, and the President was warned that the Green Book solution 'could not but lead to a head-on collision with the Free Churches'. Mr Butler did not find the Nonconformist attitude at this stage particularly helpful or constructive, but subsequent discussions made him deeply appreciative of the statesmanlike qualities of men like Dr Scott Lidgett, who took a broad view of the problem and used the weight of their influence to restrain the more extreme of their co-religionists.

Roman Catholics were keenly critical of the Green Book proposals, which did not, as they had hoped, pick up the threads of the 1936 Act nor offer them any assistance in the building of new schools. Instead, the hierarchy suggested the Scottish solution or the Liverpool settlement. It was the veteran Bishop Brown of Pella, formerly Monsignor Brown,[2] who was, as always, the most ardent champion of the Scottish solution, while other members of the hierarchy's negotiating committee preferred to concentrate on the Liverpool system as a basis for a general settlement. The Liverpool arrangement, however, had been deliberately designed to meet a special emergency and had never been intended to serve as a precedent. Moreover, Mr Butler considered it important to include Anglicans and Roman Catholics 'under the same umbrella' for it could look invidious if a special scheme were invented for Roman Catholics alone.[3] However, the President did not underestimate the importance of the community nor did he forget that it was a Roman Catholic amendment which had virtually destroyed the Trevelyan proposals in 1931. He was disappointed by the

---

[1] E.g. The Bishop of Liverpool in his *Religion and Education*, 1941.   [2] See p. 96.
[3] Mr Butler was to emphasise this point both privately and publicly, e.g. *Parl. Deb.* 5th Ser., Commons, vol. cccxcviii, col. 1912.

hierarchy's critical reception of the Green Book scheme which, as Bishop Brown later admitted, would have suited his community much better than the final solution.

Meanwhile both teachers and administrators had challenged the Green Book proposals.[1] They would have preferred a more drastic revision of the existing system, the restriction of denominational responsibilities to religious instruction and to the right of consultation on the appointment of reserved teachers. The Green Book also attracted comment from a wider public. The Trades Union Congress, for example, launched a spirited attack[2] and demanded the abolition of the dual system, the restriction of religious teaching to agreed syllabus instruction, and the withdrawal of State support from all church training colleges. Altogether it was clear that the Green Book proposals had aroused considerable opposition. Anglicans alone had given them a favourable though not an enthusiastic reception; other groups had come out strongly against them. In particular, opposition to the proposed modification of the Cowper-Temple Clause had been so powerful and so violent that Mr Butler concluded that it 'was still regarded as the ark of the covenant by sections of the public too strongly convinced to be persuaded or ignored'. The Green Book scheme was therefore quietly dropped and instead efforts were concentrated on devising a new solution. By the spring of 1942 fresh proposals had been worked out and it was these, rather than the earlier tentative solution, which were to be the basis of the final settlement.

★   ★   ★   ★   ★

The new scheme was in origin the combined work of Mr Chuter Ede, the Parliamentary Secretary, and one of the senior officials of the Board. In the form of a White Memorandum it was later sent to all who had received the Green Book. Its basis was an option which would be open to all denominational schools alike. The first alternative, which was to be compulsory in single-school areas, was for owners of non-provided schools to hand over their schools for use as council schools. In return, the local authorities

---

[1] See p. 139.
[2] *Comments on the Green Book*, subsequently published as *Memorandum on Education*, August 1942.

would undertake the entire financial responsibility, the denominations still being entitled to use the premises on Sundays and also on weekdays when they were not required for educational purposes. There was no provision for reserved teachers nor for denominational instruction in the school building; if parents wished their children to receive such instruction they were entitled to withdraw them during the first period of the morning session. The second alternative introduced the idea of a 50 per cent grant towards the capital cost of alterations and improvements but not towards the building of new schools. Managers who were willing and able to raise the other 50 per cent were to retain the right of appointing and dismissing the teachers and were to control the religious instruction. The Archbishops' Five Points were incorporated in the scheme, and finally, in order to place all secondary schools on the same footing, the Cowper-Temple Clause was extended to the grammar schools.

The second alternative, which in the Act became the basis of the option for 'aided' schools, was designed for those who insisted on retaining the fully denominational character of their schools. The first alternative, designed to extend the public system to the single-school areas, was in its original form very hard on the Anglicans and was to undergo considerable revision. The President himself was very critical of it in its early form and wrote to the Parliamentary Secretary, 'It would ease my mind were we to introduce a little less spirit of compulsion into the rather staccato terms of the present B5 (the paragraph concerning the single-school area schools).'[1]

Naturally Free Churchmen were delighted with the new scheme, which, by eliminating the denominational atmosphere in the single-school area schools, removed their chief grievance. Dr Scott Lidgett was very emphatic on this point and said that if the single-school area proposals went through the Free Churches would not object to the 50 per cent Exchequer grant to other voluntary schools. Many Anglicans, however, were aghast. Lord Selborne, as soon as he heard of the White Memorandum, telephoned the President and warned him that the National Society would put up strong resistance. 'The Church', he said,

[1] As he said publicly 'to apply compulsion for the sake of unification of administration would be neither equitable nor in accordance with our national tradition'. *The Times*, 10.4.42.

'had got only five mingy points and was being made to give up all her schools.' He was, however, prepared to consider the President's suggestion that some denominational teaching might be given within school hours and, possibly, within the school buildings of a school accepting the first alternative. Altogether, the Anglicans were very sorry to see the Green Book solution superseded by a less favourable scheme.

The White Memorandum was among the first correspondence to be received by the new Primate, Dr William Temple, who was at once confronted with a very delicate situation. However strong his inclination to co-operate in plans for educational reconstruction, he could not ignore the outraged feelings of a large section of his community who looked to him for a lead. Hence his first speech to the National Society, entitled 'Our Trust and Our Task', was a stalwart defence of Church schools. 'If we wish to avoid Totalitarianism,' he declared, 'there is merit in the very duality of the dual system.' He refuted the suggestion that in return for the acceptance of the Five Points, which were designed to strengthen religious training in all schools, the Church should be expected to cede control in the schools she had built and declared himself resolutely opposed to the 'wholesale surrender or transfer of Church schools'. Naturally the *Church Times* was enthusiastic about the tone of the speech and referred to it as 'Dr Temple's Trumpet Call'.[1] In the preparation of his speech, however, the Archbishop had obviously borne in mind the particular audience he would be addressing. He subsequently wrote to Canon Tatlow, 'I was doing a rather elaborate egg dance, and some of the eggs are such that it is most important not to break, because the smell would be awful!'[2]

At the Board of Education the Archbishop's speech was not considered particularly helpful. It was felt that some knowledge of the extent of future commitments might encourage him to take a more realistic view, and so on 5th June, on the occasion of the President's next meeting with Dr Temple and other representatives of the National Society, Mr Butler took the opportunity of reading out some very 'damaging statistics' concerning Church schools. This, in Mr Butler's opinion, was one of the most important interviews of the entire negotiations. He himself described it as the 'hot interview', firstly because the room itself with all the windows blacked out was extremely hot on that summer afternoon,

[1] 5.6.42.   [2] Iremonger, *William Temple*, 572.

secondly, because Dr Temple had brought with him the 'hottest' of his Bishops, the High Anglican Bishop of Oxford, Dr Kirk, and lastly, because he himself launched the offensive by revealing the full extent of the existing disparity between provided and non-provided schools. He quoted, for example, comparative figures of unreorganised schools, of black listed schools and of schools which had been built in the previous century. The President recorded in his personal memoranda, 'these statistics visibly impressed his Grace who has confirmed to me since that it was on this occasion that he realised that the Government were in earnest about educational reconstruction, and that he would have to do his best to wean his flock from their distaste at the White Memorandum and the alleged threat to their schools.'

The President's broadside had an immediate effect. Five weeks later, Dr Temple was able to give Mr Butler a preliminary draft of the National Society's Report which offered some hope of compromise. While resisting the wholesale transfer of Church schools in single-school areas, the draft report suggested that agreed syllabus instruction should be given not only in single-school area schools but also in other Church of England schools. Managers were to be free to supplement it by denominational teaching and, at such times, facilities were to be available on the school premises for further agreed syllabus instruction if this was desired. It was also proposed that the appointment of teachers in non-provided schools should pass to the local authorities with provision for consultation over the appointment of reserved teachers, including head teachers. Managers were to raise a 'proportionate contribution' towards repairs and improvements, the rest being paid by Exchequer grants. One section of the report was still incomplete; in an earlier draft the National Society had asked for the general right of entry for clergy, but the Archbishop had urged some form of modification, which was still under consideration. In discussing the draft with Dr Temple, the President immediately enquired whether the combination of agreed syllabus and denominational teaching would be met by a concession enabling the Church of England to give its own religious teaching on the premises on two days a week. The Archbishop indicated his approval of the suggestion which became the basis of the option for 'controlled' schools under the Bill.

Dr Temple stressed the confidential character of the report and was insistent that its contents should not become known. He indicated that by September he and his team would be ready to discuss details at the Board and that he would discuss the proposals in the meantime with Dr Scott Lidgett and try to obtain as much Free Church approval for them as possible. He was hopeful that the scheme, with perhaps some amendments, would be accepted by the Church Assembly in the late autumn. Publicly, the Archbishop used his influence to prepare Anglican opinion. At his first diocesan conference at Canterbury, for example, he stressed the need for a realistic approach to the education question. 'Our main task', he said, 'is not surely to be fighting a rearguard action in perpetual retreat until we are driven off the field by the competition of the resources of the State, but to take care that we are interpenetrating with our influence all that the State itself is doing.'[1] Meanwhile the draft report of the National Society was examined closely at the Board of Education and in the weeks that followed the President endeavoured to 'dovetail' official policy with the proposals of the National Society so that the latter could come forward publicly with a scheme which the Government could accept. His main concern was to modify the stringency of the first alternative of the White Memorandum, to eliminate the note of compulsion in order to make it more acceptable to Anglican opinion. The result was that in September, when the Anglican representatives came for official discussion before submitting their draft report to the Church Assembly, the President was able to lay before them the revised version of the White Memorandum. The first alternative had been substantially modified. Schools in this category were to retain their identity as non-provided schools, though obligation with regard to repairs, alterations and improvements was to pass to the local authorities, agreed syllabus instruction was to be compulsory, but denominational religious instruction was to be given on the school premises under arrangements made by the managers for a number of periods a week (later defined as two) to the children whose parents desired it; finally, the responsibility for the appointment and dismissal of teachers (with the exception of a defined proportion of reserved teachers) including the head teachers was to rest with the local authorities. In explaining the second alternative Mr Butler emphasised the heavy expenditure which future stan-

[1] *Ibid.*, 571.

dards of accommodation would entail. He had anticipated that most parishes would find the second alternative beyond their means and had therefore been at pains to amend the first alternative. However, Anglicans displayed some anxiety about ceding the right of appointment of head teachers to local authorities, and Mr Butler in subsequent discussion with Dr Temple endeavoured to devise some scheme of consultation.

Gradually, the outlines of the future settlement were taking shape. The President had, first of all, penetrated to the heart of the problem and had decided, after a careful scrutiny of all claims, that only a compromise solution was politically practicable. Now, his efforts were concentrated on securing its acceptance by all parties and he was concerned to move with the utmost care and vigilance lest he should arouse just the kind of dissension and difficulty which had proved fatal in the past. Since it was first of all imperative to secure acceptance by the Anglicans, the owners of the great majority of voluntary schools, he had already made it his business to present the new Primate with a realistic picture of future commitments and had, in consequence, been assured of Dr Temple's co-operation. There had been no question of a secret arrangement; the Archbishop had simply faced the facts.

In the autumn of 1942 the revised White Memorandum emerged as Plan III and was sent to the individuals and organisations which had received copies of the Green Book and White Memorandum. The basis of the first alternative was the agreed syllabus, on which there was already in the localities a measure of agreement between Anglicans and Nonconformists. The basis of the second alternative, designed for denominationalists who could not accept agreed syllabus instruction, was the 50 per cent grant towards structural improvements. Of the various proposals of the twentieth century, Plan III most closely resembled the Liberal Bill of 1906. Like Birrell, Mr Butler and his advisers had distinguished between the two types of church schools, the 'moderate' denominational schools and the 'extreme' denominational or 'atmosphere' schools. Their first option corresponded to Clause 3 of the 1906 Bill, and their second to Clause 4. Plan III, however, while it avoided the principle of compulsory transfer implicit in Birrell's Bill, and even in single-school areas allowed managers freedom of choice, was less considerate towards the 'extreme' denominational schools. It was based on an option offered to all alike and Mr Butler himself was responsible for the final form of the first alternative, the device of the controlled school as it was to be called. This was the single most important feature of the entire settlement for, by extending public control without at the same time impairing the historical continuity of the denominational foundation, it was generally acceptable both to the opponents of dual control and to the great body of Anglicans.

Nevertheless, the President was to meet a good deal of criticism during the coming months. In reply to critics of the first alternative, he was to point out that each sectional interest would gain something, Anglicans from the provisions for denominational instruction and the reservation of teachers, and Nonconformists, local authorities and teachers from the extension of public control and the diminution of professional and administrative dualism. Similarly, on the second alternative, he was to hold the balance between, at the one extreme, secularists and Free Churchmen, who considered the 50 per cent grant too lavish, and, at the other extreme, the Roman Catholics, who clamoured for more generous assistance; to the former he was to emphasise the high cost of bringing existing buildings up to standard, to the latter he was to stress the danger of popular reaction against undue pressure from a minority group.

In October the National Society published its statement on the future of Church schools.[1] The document had undergone considerable revision since the summer so that it might correspond more precisely with the Board's scheme. There was still, however, a vital and significant difference; the second alternative of the Board's plan appeared here as the first alternative, thus putting the emphasis of the document upon that choice. In the outline of the Society's second alternative, the section on headships contained a definite acknowledgement of the danger of imposing a religious test on some ten thousand teachers, but asked specifically for some measure of consultation. On the whole, the two schemes had blended well and Mr Butler recorded, 'This was probably the best bit of grafting of one stock on another which was done during the course of negotiations.'

The Times admired the realism of the National Society's report and estimated that seven out of every eight Church schools would cease to be fully denominational.[2] Among Anglicans, however, there was considerable misgiving and more than a suspicion that

[1] Entitled 'The Interim Report on the Dual System'.   [2] The Times, 29.10.42.

everything had been arranged by 'a back stage concordat'. The *Church Times* expressed astonishment that no attempt had been made to secure 'facilities' for denominational instruction in all schools.[1] Dr Temple foresaw heated discussion in the Church Assembly and took the precaution of obtaining from the President details of the 'damaging statistics' which had so impressed him in the summer. At the same time Sir Robert Martin, who was to move acceptance of the report in the Church Assembly, asked the Board to agree to a further concession, the application of the Dorset Letter in remote areas so that in exceptional circumstances children could receive denominational instruction by means of right of entry. At the critical stage of the Assembly debate in November the Archbishop himself took the lead. After denying that there had ever been 'anything in the nature of a bargain' between himself and the President of the Board, he quoted in full the discreditable statistics of black listed and unreorganised schools, and concluded with an appeal to members to support the motion as 'a wise adjustment to the situation in which we find ourselves'.[2] His intervention saved the day but it was quite clear that there was little enthusiasm for the report and more than a suspicion among some members that the National Society was 'selling the pass'. As Lord Selborne wrote to Mr Butler, 'After that debate I don't think Temple could possibly carry the Church in conceding anything else.'

Anglican acceptance of the report left the Roman Catholics completely isolated; a revival of the old denominational alliance was now out of the question. In September, Mr Butler had discussed Plan III with a deputation of the Roman Catholic hierarchy led by the two veterans, Archbishop Amigo of Southwark and Bishop Brown of Pella. The latter had immediately attacked the principle of the new scheme, saying that the choice was 'between taking over the schools or snuffing them out', and had expressed his preference for the Green Book proposals. In his reply, Mr Butler had emphasised the necessity of treating all denominations alike. He had revealed in confidence Dr Temple's willingness to concede a large measure of agreed syllabus teaching and to hand over the appointment of teachers, but he had also pointed out that some Anglican schools would adopt the second alternative and

[1] The *Church Times*, numerous articles from 30.10.42.
[2] *Church Assembly Proceedings*, vol. XXIX, No. 2, 296–9.

they would be treated in exactly the same way as the Roman Catholic schools. He had also taken the opportunity of reminding the deputation of the strong opposition towards denominational schools expressed by trade unionists and other sections in the community. Throughout his discussions with the Roman Catholics Mr Butler was concerned to prune their claims for public support. On the main financial principles he was adamant that any increase in the proposed grant would, by tempting the Anglicans to contract out, destroy the entire balance of the compromise; nevertheless, he was willing to consider such slight adjustments as would ease the burden.

The President found the process of negotiating with a committee of Bishops both slow and cumbersome and, at an early stage, he sought to quicken the pace by personal contact. In November, he visited the aged Archbishop Amigo of Southwark and, in January 1943, Cardinal Hinsley. On both occasions discussion centred on 'ways and means', and Mr Butler was clearly impressed by some of the Roman Catholic arguments. Both interviews were very friendly; indeed, the Cardinal expressed himself hopeful of a settlement, though he added, 'We shall never be able to stop a section of the Catholic community from shouting.' In the meantime there had emerged a new negotiating committee, including lay representatives, under the chairmanship of the Archbishop of Liverpool, Dr Downey.[1] Mr Butler did not find this change of tactics very encouraging and both the size of the new committee and the uncompromising character of its chairman brought new difficulties.

It was at this point that the Roman Catholic press, which had been giving increasing publicity to the education issue, began an intensive campaign in support of the Scottish solution. Simultaneously, Lenten Pastorals roused the laity to action, demonstrations and mass meetings were held, Parents' Associations sprang into being and Roman Catholic trade unionists organised resistance to the official policy of the Trades Union Congress. It was significant that throughout the discussions the Roman Catholics showed far less devotion to their school buildings than did the Anglicans. While many Anglicans regarded the transference of their schools as a betrayal of their trust deeds, Roman Catholics were not concerned about their possession of the school premises. From the Cardinal downwards they said, 'Take the buildings, take

[1] The appointment of the new Committee was announced in the *Tablet*, 6.2.43.

everything you want, but in the schools under the new management, every teacher must be a Catholic and the child must have all his education in a Catholic atmosphere.' They indicated that they would be prepared to cede the actual appointment of teachers to the local authority on condition that Roman Catholics were appointed. Above all, their concern was for the future, and the President's plan provided no assistance for the building of schools in new centres of population or for the provision of additional school places elsewhere. The Scottish solution alone would solve their problems and it was the Scottish solution which they now adopted and pressed with great vigour.

Like Fisher before him, Mr Butler had examined the Scottish solution very carefully, and in the New Year of 1943 he even visited Scotland in order to study it at close quarters.[1] He found that the system was working well there though in certain areas there was evidence of anti-Catholic reaction. He noted that 'when a community gets 200 per cent of what it wants, it is not in so healthy a position as one which faces up to and accepts a fair compromise'. His visit, however, confirmed his previous impression that the Scottish solution was quite unsuited to the conditions in England and Wales where the Cowper-Temple Clause had been in operation for over seventy years, where there were many different sects and where the number of church schools actually exceeded the number of local authority schools. Moreover, he felt that some of the supporters of the Scottish solution were ignorant of the dangers of public control. 'I am quite satisfied, and I am convinced that His Lordship of Cardiff, the Roman Catholic Bishop, would agree with me', he wrote, 'that this would be equal to the eventual destruction of the Catholic faith, at any rate, in certain parts of the Principality.'

Meanwhile there was the inevitable reaction against the Roman Catholic agitation by teachers and by Free Churchmen. The National Union of Teachers denounced the Scottish solution as likely to perpetuate denominational tests for teachers;[2] the Free Churches condemned the Roman Catholic demands as 'exorbitant and rigid'.[3] Once again the old fears and suspicions were reviving. The Roman Catholic hierarchy issued a solemn warning, 'If the need should arise it would be our distasteful duty, and we should

---

[1] His public reactions were described in *The Times*, 23.2.43.
[2] The *Catholic Herald*, 12.2.43.   [3] The *Methodist Recorder*, 20.5.43.

not shirk it, to protest with all our energy and to oppose by all lawful means any proposals which would threaten the existence of our schools.'[1] Free Churchmen for their part dwelt on the past, on the reputation of Roman Catholics for casuistry and on the danger of their using public money for propaganda purposes. Between the two extremes the President endeavoured to hold the balance. He urged the Roman Catholics to consider his offer in terms of practical politics, 'I am approaching it in the spirit that it is better to take what is possible to get through Parliament than attempt the impossible,' he said. He emphasised to Nonconformists the new powers of public control over the denominational schools. Both parties were reminded that any plan for reforming the dual system must be based on a give-and-take arrangement and that no sectional interest could expect complete satisfaction. He must, as he put it, 'hold the scales evenly between competing views.'

Free Church representatives, however, continued to be very uneasy about the future of the single-school area schools, and harked back longingly to the White Memorandum which had excluded such schools from a choice of options. It was Dr Scott Lidgett who played the decisive part of peacemaker in a statesmanlike intervention reminiscent of another occasion some forty years before when his wisdom and good counsel had prevailed against the strident extremists of passive resistance.[2] He had been deeply impressed by the patient consideration which the President had given to all claims and by his plea for a balanced settlement. At the spring conference of the Free Church Federal Council, therefore, he strongly supported the compromise which, he said, the Board had worked out. Without revealing its substance he indicated that it would go 'a very long way towards the subordination of the non-provided schools to the nation and the local authorities and so do away with denominational restrictions on head teachers and staff'.[3] By the spring of 1943 Anglican and Free Church leaders had indicated their willingness to accept the compromise. This was revealed in a letter sent to all members of Parliament in May, signed by the Archbishops of Canterbury and York, the Moderator of the Free Church Federal Council and representative Free Church leaders. It concluded with the hope that, 'if differences arise between the religious bodies they will be confined to a small area of

[1] The hierarchy's 'Statement on The Schools Question'. The *Tablet*, 15.5.43.
[2] See p. 87.   [3] *The Times*, 1.4.43.

the Bill and will not be such as to impede the educational advance so urgently needed in the general welfare.'[1] Some of their followers, however, remained highly critical, the *Church Times*, for example, continued to fulminate against the unrepentant defeatism' and 'cowardly obstinacy' of the Church Assembly's report,[2] but the opposition of the Anglican dissidents was never serious. So far as the Church of England was concerned, the outstanding problem to be settled was the proportion of reserved teachers under the first alternative, a delicate matter especially in the small rural schools where excessive Anglican claims might upset the entire balance. Indeed, the Parliamentary Secretary once found it necessary to issue a sharp warning to the Anglicans. 'We are walking', he said, 'on a knife edge with precipices on either side and some people seem to enjoy shaking the top.'

Meanwhile Mr Churchill had decided to give some public indication of the Government plans for educational reconstruction. In the early phase of negotiations he had been cautious, even unsympathetic. As head of the War Cabinet he could not risk any revival of domestic conflict which, by dividing the nation, might imperil the entire war effort, but he had been greatly impressed by the progress of discussions and was now convinced that the times were opportune. In March 1943, ten days before the Prime Minister was due to give one of his broadcasts to the nation, Mr Butler went down to Chequers for discussion. He recorded that after dinner one night Mr Churchill read the Home Affairs portion of his speech, 'at great length and with incredible gusto and asked me whether I thought he was lacking in force and vigour: I said I thought he was not.' It was Mr Churchill, therefore, who revealed to the public the Government plan for educational reconstruction. In his broadcast on 21st March, he looked to the future and embraced wholeheartedly a programme of social reform. He linked education with the great welfare services which should transform the life of the nation and emphasised the need for equality of educational opportunity. In particular, he touched on the importance of religion as the 'fundamental element in school life' and welcomed the progress made by all the religious bodies 'in freeing themselves from sectarian jealousies and feuds while preserving fervently the tenets of their own faith'.[3]

By the summer the religious settlement had been approved

---

[1] *The Times*, 10.5.43.   [2] The *Church Times*, 5.3.43.   [3] *The Times*, 22.3.43.

officially by Anglicans and Free Churchmen, and it had also been accepted by all the secular interests concerned, local authorities, teachers and educational associations. Roman Catholics alone were in opposition. The War Cabinet at this point decided not to present a Bill before the summer, but to bring out a White Paper in general terms and have a debate on it. This would enable them, in Mr Butler's words, 'to test the temperature of the water before taking the plunge'[1] and would give them the opportunity of making further adjustments before introducing the Bill. In the meantime, Mr Butler was to be engaged in arousing public interest and in ascertaining the views of those specially concerned. The White Paper, 'Educational Reconstruction',[2] published in July 1943, set out the Government's proposals for a complete recasting of the national service with the provision of education in three successive stages, primary, secondary and further. Chapter 3 was devoted to religious education and included the Archbishops' Five Points. Chapter 4 dealt with the voluntary schools and outlined the new proposals for dual control; the main features were the revival of agreements for those schools which were to have been built under the 1936 Act[3] and, for all other schools, the choice between the two alternatives of Plan III, the first to be called 'controlled' status, the second 'aided' status. The religious settlement now revealed to the public was a delicately balanced structure which had been built up with the utmost care over a period of two years. The President, having considered all interests and explored all possible solutions, had judged it impossible to ignore the complexities of the historical background and start afresh. He had therefore aimed not at an ideal solution but at one which was politically practicable and in which all partners could co-operate.

Both Anglicans and Roman Catholics would gain by the new Exchequer grants to those schools which chose aided status, and many Anglicans would welcome the provisions for controlled status which would preserve something of the historical continuity of their schools. On the other hand, both options would require considerable sacrifices, the controlled status because it would necessitate the surrender of the denominational atmosphere of the schools, and the aided status because it was accompanied by new official requirements, which would impose heavy financial burdens, particularly

---

[1] *Parl. Deb.,* Commons, 5th Ser., vol. cccxci, col. 1871.   [2] Cmd. 6458.
[3] To be called 'special agreement' schools.

for new schools. Critics of the old dual system would have much to be thankful for, the extension of public control, the improvement of the quality of religious instruction and the reduction of the number of tests for teachers. But at the same time they would be asked to agree to the expenditure of additional public money on denominational schools, possibly even on single-school area schools.

The White Paper was debated in the Commons at the end of July. In his introduction the President anticipated criticism from the Roman Catholic pressure group. By meeting all denominational claims, he said, 'we should have met one point out of a catalogue of many. We should have met the need of denominations . . . but . . . we should have alienated beyond recall certain partners in the field of education who are indispensable, namely the authorities, the Free Churches and the teachers.'[1] The debate which followed was remarkable for the complete absence of controversial atmosphere. In the Lords, however, the Archbishop of Canterbury, while welcoming the proposals, urged concessions on certain points, the reopening of the 1936 offer of 75 per cent grants and, in certain circumstances, the provision of new denominational schools.[2] His manoeuvre was unexpected, but it was apparent that it did not constitute a serious challenge, and was probably designed to forestall more extreme amendments from High Anglicans. In the months that followed Dr Temple sought to rouse enthusiastic support for the Government proposals. Speaking to the Canterbury Diocesan Conference in October, he referred to the 'glorious opportunity' which the White Paper presented to the Church, and expressed concern at the apathetic response to an offer which only a few years before would have seemed unbelievably generous.[3] Once again he urged Churchmen to consider the whole programme of educational reform, indicating that in his view, 'the raising of the school age will of itself do more to make permanent the religious influence of the school than anything that can be done with directly denominational purpose.' Some Anglicans, however, were violently opposed to the proposals; they felt, in the words of the *Church Times* that 'Temple and Cowper-Temple have kissed each other',[4] and in the autumn they proceeded to organise opposition within the Church.[5]

---

[1] *Parl. Deb.*, Commons, 5th Ser., vol. cccxci, col. 1836.
[2] *Ibid.*, Lords, 5th Ser., vol. cxxviii, cols. 1004–6.　　　　[3] *The Times*, 26.10.43.
[4] 23.7.43.　　　　[5] The Church Education League. The *Church Times*, 30.7.43.

In the meantime Free Churchmen were becoming uneasy and restive. It was only with difficulty that Dr Scott Lidgett managed to allay suspicion on the future of the single-school areas, and it was certain that the President could not obtain any further concessions from Free Church representatives. However, the most determined opposition to the proposed settlement came from the Roman Catholics; clergy and laity were united in their resistance to the financial arrangement since it offered no safeguards against rising costs. In the words of one of their Parliamentary spokesmen, 'If what used to cost £500 now costs £1,200, it is not much consolation to be told that we are to be allowed £600.' Moreover, long experience of 'the progressive nature of the demands of the Board of Education'[1] made them chary of new liabilities. Lastly and most important of all, they were concerned about future new schools which would have to be built entirely from voluntary funds.[2] Dr Downey, the extremist spokesman, accused Mr Butler of political expediency and of preferring the easy path of compromise to a more courageous course. Like others in the past, he argued that the Roman Catholic religion was accepted in national life, that various Government departments provided facilities for Roman Catholics equally with others. Why, then, should the Board of Education be the 'odd man out'?[3] With the publication of the White Paper Roman Catholics intensified their campaign for the Scottish solution. To them the Anglican landslide was now complete; resistance to the present proposals depended on their community alone and though they could hardly have hoped for the Scottish solution they must have felt that this was the best means of compelling new concessions. On all sides feeling was rising. Nonconformists and teachers denounced Roman Catholic propaganda. Sir Frederick Mander, the Secretary of the National Union of Teachers, for example, gave a stern warning when he said, 'Unless you Catholics are careful what you say, you will cause such a wave of feeling in this country that all your non-provided schools will be swept away altogether.'[4] The Times urged moderation on the parties concerned lest the Government should despair of reaching a solution. 'The time for a settlement', it declared, 'is now or never.'[5]

---

[1] Parl. Deb., Lords, 5th Ser., vol. cxxviii, col. 1025.
[2] Joint Advent Pastoral Letter. The Tablet, 4.12.43. [3] The Catholic Herald, 6.4.43.
[4] Ibid., 17.9.43. [5] 10.12.43.

Meanwhile the President was busy, probing and sifting the various anxieties. On the one hand, he endeavoured to mitigate the single-school area grievance of the Nonconformists by arranging that agreed syllabus instruction should be available on the school premises.[1] On the other hand, he sought to allay the financial fears of the denominations. He urged the Roman Catholic community to think of the building costs they would have to bear, not in terms of capital expenditure, but rather in terms of loan and redemption charges. Meanwhile, he continued discussions with members of the hierarchy both individually and as a body. On the main point at issue, the application of public funds towards the cost of completely new denominational schools, Mr Butler remained adamant. He was, however, prepared to consider means of easing the burden so long as the main balance of the plan remained undisturbed, and he devised the transfer concession for existing schools as a means of compensating the denominations for redundancy caused by the action of the Government or of a planning authority; in return for the surrender of a number of school places in a certain locality the Board's 50 per cent grant would be paid towards the cost of building a new school (intended for the same population) for a similar number of pupils in another locality.

On 15th December, the Education Bill was introduced in the Commons. It was a comprehensive measure, covering the entire field, educational, administrative and religious. In the main, the clauses dealing with the dual system and with religious instruction followed the lines of the White Paper. There was one minor modification of terminology. Church schools were now designated 'voluntary' schools and not, as in the White Paper, 'auxiliary' schools. (Local authority schools were to be known as 'county' schools.) There were also certain adjustments designed to alleviate the grievances of the various sectional interests. The transfer concession would in some degree meet the Roman Catholic objection, the availability of agreed syllabus instruction in single-school area aided schools would ease the single-school area difficulty, and the problem of the small controlled school would be met by allowing denominational teaching to be given by clergy or lay people approved by the foundation managers, or by any teacher on the staff who volunteered to do so.

[1] Incorporated in Clause 76.

Representatives of all interests welcomed the general programme of educational advance. The leaders of the Anglican and
Free Churches demonstrated their approval by appearing together
on the public platform in support of the Bill. It was true, as the
Archbishop of Canterbury admitted, that they 'did not see eye to
eye' in regard to the proposed reform of the dual system but he
was himself 'quite sure that continued teaching on the lines of a
good agreed syllabus, and some of them are very good indeed,
will do more for religious knowledge in later life than can be done
by the best Church school ending its work at fourteen'.[1] Roman
Catholics, though welcoming the general educational reforms,
were highly critical of the financial conditions. In January 1944,
the hierarchy published a statement in which they declared, 'we
have never accepted, do not accept and never shall accept the Bill
as it now stands'.[2] In January also Dr Griffin, on the occasion of
his enthronement as Archbishop of Westminster, denounced the
White Paper proposals,[3] while in the country as a whole the
Roman Catholic agitation continued unabated. From the Protes-
tant Truth Society came a counterblast, a warning to the Government not to appease the Roman Catholics, 'for the simple reason
that they could no more appease religious dictators than our
statesmen in 1938 could appease Hitler and Mussolini'.[4]

There were many smouldering embers and the President was
prepared for sharp conflict at the Parliamentary stage, but he was
well fitted to deal with all opposition. No other member of the
front bench, with the single exception of the Prime Minister
himself, had undergone a more exacting training for, both at the
India Office and at the Foreign Office, he had had long experience
of defending Government policy in the face of heavy and persistent attack. His superb piloting skill on this occasion was to be
acknowledged by spokesmen from all parts of the House. The
relatively calm passage of the Bill was due very largely to the
President's careful preliminary work and to his patience and
resourcefulness during the debates. He himself described his
position as 'very like being on the bridge of a big ship and
steering that ship, without respite, past pointed rocks and round

---

[1] The *Times Educational Supplement*, 27.1.44.
[2] Statement issued 4.1.44, and published in all organs of the R.C. press, e.g. The
Tablet, 8.1.44.
[3] The *Tablet*, 22.1.44.   [4] The *English Churchman and St. James' Chronicle*, 9.3.44.

submerged reefs'. Throughout the discussion he was prepared to consider adjustments which did not conflict with points of principle or antagonise other interests. Thus he accepted a Lord's amendment that local authorities should 'have regard to the general principle that, so far as is compatible with the provision of efficient instruction and training and the avoidance of unreasonable expense, pupils are to be educated in accordance with the wishes of their parents'.[1] This recognition of parental rights was naturally welcomed by the denominationalists, but Mr Butler's chief concern was to devise some means of easing their financial burden. He was, for example, prepared to consider denominational requests for long-term loans if he could be quite sure that such loans would not encourage large numbers of Anglican schools to contract out, but would be used to bring a smaller number of schools up to a high standard and to make 'a really worth while job of them'. Once he was assured on this point[2] he engaged in a detailed investigation of a scheme for loan provision. The subject of State loans was also a prominent feature of his early talks with Dr Griffin. Mr Butler had a very high regard for the youthful Archbishop, who had a long record of devoted social work in the midlands and was anxious that his community should share in the new proposals for educational reconstruction. In particular, Mr Butler appreciated the Archbishop's sense of realism, a quality which had not always distinguished the Roman Catholic spokesmen. In his early days at Westminster, Dr Griffin relied a good deal on the advice of the Bishop of Hexham and Newcastle. It was the latter who, in discussion with the Parliamentary Secretary, offered to cede the appointment of teachers in return for an assurance that only practising Roman Catholics should teach in the schools. He too, raised the question of loan provisions. Early in February, the President was able to outline to Dr Griffin his plan for long-term loans; they would be at 4½ per cent covering a period of thirty to forty years, but would not be available for the building of new schools. The Archbishop obviously welcomed the proposal and Mr Butler asked him to co-operate by discouraging the current agitation. Dr Griffin responded at once: speaking at the Cathedral Hall, Westminster, on 13th February,

[1] *Parl. Deb.,* Commons, 5th Ser., vol. cdii, col. 968.
[2] Mr Butler referred to the Bishop of London's assurance in the Church Assembly. *Ibid.,* Commons, 5th Ser., vol. cccxcviii, cols. 1916–17.

he indicated that the hierarchy was prepared to accept a compromise. 'If we cannot obtain full justice', he declared, 'at least it should be possible for us to enter into the national scheme of educational reconstruction.'[1] Within a very short time Mr Butler was able to acknowledge the 'handsome withdrawal of certain methods of propaganda' used by the Roman Catholics in preceding months.[2]

Meanwhile Mr Butler proceeded to work out the full details of loan provision. His consultations with members of Parliament had revealed a widespread desire to alleviate the financial burdens of the churches, and he had evidence that even the strongest opponents of denominational schools would accept a scheme of State loans provided the terms were comparable with those available to local authorities.[3] His intention was that provision should be on the lines of a business transaction, and to overcome the difficulty of security he suggested that the loans should be made through the diocese. Both diocese and managers, therefore, would be jointly responsible for repayment. In his address to the Committee of the House on 4th April, he explained the new provision for State loans. It was, he said, to be confined to existing aided and special agreement schools and was to be available only for 'initial expenses'. He was able to indicate that both Anglican and Roman Catholics approved of the scheme.[4] At the report stage the President introduced two more amendments designed to maintain the general balance. The first, providing safeguards against the abuse of loans in single-school areas, was intended to temper the Nonconformists' grievance;[5] the second, providing grants in respect of 'displaced pupils', embodied concessions already promised to the denominationalists.[6] During the concluding stages of the debate spokesmen of all interests expressed their approval of the religious settlement, though the Roman Catholics qualified their remarks by reference to the financial uncertainties of the future.[7] The Bill occupied the Lower House

[1] The *Tablet*, 19.2.44.

[2] *Parl. Deb.*, Commons, 5th Ser., vol. cccxcviii, col. 1911.

[3] *Ibid.*, Commons, 5th Ser., vol. cccxcviii, col. 1953.

[4] *Ibid.*, Commons, 5th Ser., vol. cccxcviii, cols. 1911–16.

[5] *Ibid.*, Commons, 5th Ser., vol. cccxcix, col. 1857. In such areas there was to be a conference of the interested religious denominations and, if necessary, a local inquiry, before loans were granted.

[6] *Ibid.*, Commons, 5th Ser., vol. cccxcix, col. 1782.

[7] *Ibid.*, Commons, 5th Ser., vol. cccxcix, col. 2236.

only 19 days, whereas the 1902 Bill had occupied it 59 days and the 1870 Bill 28 days. Remarkably enough, in view of past history, the House was left with a day or two to spare at the end of the discussion.

Many factors had contributed to the final success. In the first place, there was the perseverance, sincerity and diplomatic skill of the President himself. Despite their courage and good intentions, many of his predecessors had lacked the necessary patience and sense of realism. Mr Butler, on the other hand, had examined all aspects of the problem and had left nothing to chance; he had studied the historical background, and had consulted ecclesiastics, administrators, and representatives of the teachers, in fact, as he said, almost everybody except the children themselves; he had balanced all interests and gauged what was politically practicable; he had made every effort to meet criticisms and to allay anxieties. The partnership, also, of Mr Butler, the President, and Mr Chuter Ede, the Parliamentary Secretary, had been a singularly happy one, and the mingling of two quite different traditions had contributed very considerably to the strength and success of their endeavour. Indeed, the combination of two men, strikingly different in background and experience, yet complementary in their sympathies and understanding of the religious problem, was invaluable in the long period of planning and negotiation. There was no doubt also that circumstances had been peculiarly favourable. If some of his predecessors had been precipitate or tactless there were others who had been baulked by party conflict or sectarian strife. Mr Butler, however, had rightly judged the time opportune: politically, he was neither committed nor circumscribed by party pledges, and the powerful coalition Government of which he was a member was fortified by the wartime spirit of unity in the nation. Lastly, success had been due to what Mr Butler himself described as 'a strange interchange of personalities'. It was indeed fortunate that the main partners in negotiation had all displayed a sense of goodwill and moderation, that ecclesiastics had by their wisdom and statesmanship restrained the more irresponsible of their followers, and that administrators and teachers had had the prudence and foresight to put educational reform before private principle. The final compromise, of course, gave complete satisfaction to no one, but it gave everyone sufficient, so that in the general reckoning of gains and losses all would have been sorry to see the proposals dropped.

That a settlement was reached at all was itself a conspicuous and remarkable achievement. Approved by all interests, the 1944 compromise formed an integral and indispensable part of the education structure. It made possible a great forward movement in education, the expansion of the national system by the provision of varied types of educational activity, which by developing the talents of future generations should extend individual opportunities and enrich the life of the entire nation. The dual system remained, but the new settlement was deliberately designed to restrict the sphere of dual control and to simplify its problems. In the history of English education the 1944 compromise marks a vital stage in the adjustment of past to present; it was not a final solution, nor did its authors intend it to be.

Chapter 8

---·❋·---

Developments since 1944

In the immediate post-war years there were inevitably difficulties and frustrations before educational reform could be put into effect. Labour and materials were scarce and the development plans which local authorities were required to present took considerable time to prepare.[1] Nevertheless, the school-leaving age was raised to fifteen in April 1947, and in the emergency period temporary huts were provided to accommodate the extra age-group, as well as to cater for the increased numbers of infants entering primary schools. For some time the lag in building and the delay of local authorities in submitting their development plans combined to obscure the problems of the voluntary schools, but even the earliest plans revealed a disturbing and quite unexpected feature which impinged on the religious settlement, namely, the large number of village schools scheduled for closure because they were considered uneducational and uneconomic. The 'slaughter of the innocents', as Mr Butler called it,[2] was something which had never been contemplated in the negotiations preceding the Act, and it threatened to deprive many Anglican managers of their right of option. As early as 1947, therefore, the Ministry[3] took steps to check the process of erosion by urging local authorities to consider village schools 'individually on their merits'[4] and by scrutinising all the circumstances very carefully before approving proposals for closure. The Ministry's concern was again revealed in the report for 1953, which referred sympathetically to village schools, pointing out that at their best they 'help pupils to understand their neighbourhood and strengthen

---

[1] 126 (out of 146) development plans had been submitted by the end of 1947. *Report*, P.P. 1947, Cmd. 7426, 2. The majority were not approved until 1951. *Report*, P.P. 1951, Cmd. 8554, 9.
[2] *Parl. Deb.*, Commons, 5th Ser., vol. cdlxxiv, col. 1913.
[3] The Ministry was created by the 1944 Act.
[4] *Circular 90.*

their roots in the community to which they belong'.[1] Nevertheless, within a decade of the passing of the Act over a thousand village schools, the majority of them Anglican, had disappeared completely.

As far as aided schools were concerned, shortage of labour and materials delayed building programmes considerably, but quite soon estimates of financial commitments began to look uncomfortably large. Many of the requirements of the Building Regulations issued in March 1945 went beyond anything the churches had contemplated. Everywhere existing schools fell far short of the high standards demanded, so that school managers had to study the realities of the situation closely before deciding the status of their schools; in many urban areas, for example, where it was impossible to extend school sites, they had to think in terms of 'transferred' schools, while in the villages it was the cost of the necessary structural alterations, including the provision of assembly halls in even two-roomed schools, which was the crucial factor in determining their choice. As for new schools, the early estimates became increasingly unreal and showed wide divergence in different areas. By 1949 the most gloomy of the prognostications made by churchmen at the time of the Act seemed likely to be fulfilled. During the previous two years the school population had risen by half a million,[2] and greater increases were certain to occur in the following decade. Moreover, this spectacular expansion, together with the large-scale movement of population to new housing areas, had coincided with a period of acute inflation in which building costs had more than trebled those of pre-war years. Clearly the churches had little hope of keeping pace with events under the existing settlement, and in December 1949 the Roman Catholic community, which had accepted the financial basis of the 1944 Act only with the greatest reluctance and had foreseen some of the present perils, opened a campaign for additional State aid. The agitation was premature and met with little direct response, though a year later the Ministry's economy measure, which reduced the allowable cost of school places by $12\frac{1}{2}$ per cent, was of indirect assistance.[3]

The problems of voluntary schools were discussed at some

---

[1] *Report,* P.P. 1953, Cmd. 9155, 9.
[2] *Report,* 1947, *op. cit., Report,* P.P. 1949, Cmd. 7957, Tables of statistics.
[3] *Circular 209,* issued in October 1949, came into force in 1950.

length in Parliament in May 1950. During the debates it was most noticeable that all sections of opinion, including even spokesmen of the Roman Catholic community, were anxious to avoid reopening the religious issue.[1] Nevertheless, there was genuine concern at the scale of voluntary school commitments and a desire on the part of both political parties to ease financial burdens. Accordingly the Government, which had already been tempering the wind by generous interpretation and favourable administration of the Act, now set to work to alleviate denominational hardships by legislation within the framework of the existing settlement. A new measure, the 1953 Act, widened the definition of displaced pupils and made grants available for building aided schools in new housing areas; at the same time, in order to maintain the balance of the original settlement, local authorities were empowered to build new controlled schools.[2]

Ten years after the 1944 Act there was considerable disquiet at the slow progress in carrying its provisions into effect. There was, in particular, widespread disappointment that one of the main purposes of the Act, the extension of secondary education to all children was far from being realised, since many senior children were gaining little from an extra year spent in schools which were too cramped and out-of-date to be able to offer them an adequate range of activities. Despite the fact that 2,000 new schools had been built and $1\frac{1}{4}$ million school places brought into use, the rate of school building was hardly sufficient to keep pace with the rapidly increasing school population. Church building programmes were barely under way and, with over 200,000 senior children in all-age schools, reorganisation remained a major problem, particularly in rural districts. In 1954, therefore, the Government determined to intervene in these areas and pressure was put on county authorities, and indirectly on the Anglicans as owners of large numbers of village schools, to complete reorganisation within a fixed time.[3]

Concentration on rural reorganisation during the next few years obscured the difficulties of urban schools, but in December 1958 a Government White Paper[4] focused attention on secondary

---

[1] *Parl. Deb.,* Commons, 5th Ser., vol. cdlxxiv, col. 2036.

[2] Educationally and economically it was often sensible in rural areas to replace a number of existing controlled schools by a single new school. *Report,* 1953, *op. cit.,* 13.

[3] *Circular 283.*   [4] Cmd. 604. 'Secondary Education for All: A New Drive.'

education as a whole and launched a five-year building plan to include urban as well as rural reorganisation. Recognising that a high proportion of all-age schools were voluntary schools, the Government indicated that it was willing to consider further financial aid to the churches. Already in 1957 Roman Catholics, who were particularly involved in urban reorganisation, had stressed the urgency of additional assistance and had asked specifically for a 75 per cent grant to cover new schools as well as existing aided schools.[1] In the New Year of 1959 they took steps to secure wide publicity in an effort to rally support. They pointed out that the original estimate of £9 millions as the cost of re-organisation of Roman Catholic schools had been revised in 1951 to £28 millions, a figure which had now become quite unrealistic, and that in addition their current estimates for new buildings now ran to £60 millions. Anglicans, in the meantime, had presented their demands to the Government.[2] Unlike the Roman Catholics they were anxious to preserve the basis of the original settlement and confined their request for a 75 per cent grant to existing or transferred schools. There was thus a significant distinction between the claims of the two communities; the Roman Catholic Church was anxious to extend its school system in order to provide for the children of its increasing population, the Established Church was concerned to maintain an adequate aided stake in the national system and was prepared only in exceptional circumstances to build new schools. Some Anglicans were even as vehemently opposed as the Nonconformists to the Roman Catholic request for the extension of a 75 per cent grant to completely new schools.[3] After the publication of the White Paper negotiations proceeded with new intensity. The Minister of Education, Sir Geoffrey Lloyd, had like his predecessors to pick his way carefully amid conflicting interests, but in the event both private and Parliamentary discussions proceeded relatively smoothly. There were murmurs of disapproval from members of the old guard of Nonconformity,[4] though by this time it was clear that they had become quite unrepresentative of Free Church opinion and completely divorced from their younger co-religionists.[5] Anglicans,

---

[1] *Catholic Education*, No. 7, December 1959, 1 *et seq*. ('Background to the Education Act 1959', by Rt. Rev. Andrew Beck, Bishop of Salford.)

[2] *Ibid.*, 14.   [3] *The Times*, 23.1.59.   [4] *Ibid.*, 19.6.59.

[5] E.g. views expressed by Rev. J. Huxtable, Principal of New College, in a pamphlet, *Church, State and Education*, 14–15.

by suggesting Free Church representation on the governing bodies, offered a very practical remedy for the problem of the single-school areas,[1] but perhaps the most striking feature of the entire negotiations was the statesmanship and restraint of the Roman Catholic leaders. In contrast to the years before 1944 the hierarchy had a simple, coherent policy which was pursued firmly and consistently. There was no noisy press campaign and there were no violent clamours for the Scottish settlement, such as had jeopardised discussions in the past. Indeed the leading Roman Catholic spokesman, Bishop Beck, frankly admitted that members of his community expected to bear some additional cost in return for teaching their own faith.[2]

In the end the solution, presented as an agreed measure to Parliament, was based on the analogy of the 1936 Act. The earlier measure had subsidised new senior schools if they were built to match existing junior schools. The 1959 Act extended a 75 per cent grant to all aided secondary schools, whether in existence or projected, which were built to cater for children at existing primary schools. As in 1936, primary schools were deliberately excluded, but a new and significant feature was that all types of secondary schools, grammar, technical and modern, now qualified for the grant.[3] The arrangement was simple and practical; based on past precedent it involved no new principle, though it went far towards meeting maximum demands. Nevertheless, there was, in the words of The Times, 'a certain impermanence'[4] about the new legislation, which merely filled in the gaps and left the primary base untouched. Coming fifteen years after the previous revision of the dual system, the 1959 Act was no more than an interim measure designed to give the denominational system that fair chance of survival which the original settlement had intended.

By 1959 it was possible to discern the new pattern of the dual system which had emerged since the war, a pattern in which the total number of voluntary schools had declined and the various proportions changed.[5] The Church of England, for example, had lost more than 10 per cent of its schools and now retained fewer than 8,000, of which approximately two-fifths were aided; the

[1] Report, P.P. 1959, Cmnd. 1088, 21.
[2] The Times Educational Supplement, 15.7.57.
[3] The old dual system had been limited to elementary education and the effect of the 1944 Act was to extend it to a single type of secondary school, the modern school.
[4] 12.6.59.   [5] See Appendix C.

Roman Catholic Church, in contrast, had increased its schools by about 25 per cent, in fact by over 300.[1] Of all the nation's children 13 per cent were now in Anglican schools and 8 per cent in Roman Catholic schools. Naturally, it had been assumed in 1944 that Roman Catholics would be interested only in aided status; it had, however, been expected that Anglicans would find controlled status the more practicable alternative and Mr Butler himself had envisaged only exceptional Anglican schools becoming aided. The most surprising feature of the new pattern, therefore, was the fact that over 3,000 Anglican schools had chosen aided status. The larger number had been a consequence of the business acumen of Churchmen in spreading costs over a number of years by a Church operated loan system, the Barchester Scheme.[2] It had also been the result of encouragement and assistance from the Church of England Council for Education, which since 1948 had been officially responsible for school policy, as well as the shrewdness of Churchmen in the localities, who had sold valuable urban sites in order to rebuilt elsewhere. Naturally, policy had varied from diocese to diocese. In Lancashire and London where Churchmen had been particularly keen to preserve a fully denominational atmosphere the proportion of aided schools was larger. Other dioceses, particularly those covering rural areas, had by deliberate design chosen to go over almost entirely to controlled status, so that by 1959 some 4,500 schools, three-fifths of the total number, were in this category. Controlled schools were able, of course, to supplement, at the parents' request, agreed syllabus instruction with denominational teaching on two days a week, and in some areas controlled schools seemed hardly to have been affected by their change in status, whereas in other places they had become indistinguishable from county schools. Their character depended essentially on the vigour of the local clergyman, the loyalties of the teachers and the extent of Anglican influence over new appointments.

Despite the closing of many of the smaller schools, the Anglican pattern of schools had remained essentially rural, and the typical school was still the village school with fewer than a hundred

---

[1] It is difficult to give precise figures because of the difference in structure between pre-war and post-war official tables. About 40 R.C. schools had been closed and 341 new schools built since 1945.

[2] The *Times Educational Supplement*, 30.4.55.

pupils.[1] In contrast, with 90 per cent of their schools classed as urban schools (and of comparable size to county schools) the strength of the Roman Catholic community lay in the towns, and therefore the problems which confronted them were quite different from those of the Church of England. The vigour and vitality of the community were reflected in the scale of their endeavour, which was some three times greater than that of the Anglicans; in fact by 1959 they had provided 100,000 new places over their pre-war total of fewer than 400,000 and had projects for another 150,000.[2]

A feature of the balanced settlement of the 1944 Act had been compulsory teaching of agreed syllabus instruction in both controlled and county schools. By 1959 there was plenty of evidence to suggest that undenominational instruction had improved both in content and in character. Already in 1954 the Institute of Christian Education had reported that 'religious knowledge is not an optional extra. Nor is it marginal. Educationally the subject has been put on a level at least no lower than that of others in the curriculum.'[3] Parents had seldom objected to their children receiving agreed syllabus instruction though few had expressed any positive feelings. What was clear was that many children, probably the great majority, who had no connection at all with a church, met religion only as a subject of the school curriculum. The future alone would show whether any significant proportion would receive from agreed syllabus instruction that vital seed which leads to membership of a believing Christian congregation or whether it would be to all an institutional study remote from the purpose of life.

In the new picture of the dual system which had evolved fifteen years after the Act, the total number of voluntary schools had diminished by a tenth, while, more significantly, that of fully denominational schools had shrunk by about a half. The problems of the dual system, though far from being solved, had been greatly simplified; only a seventh of the school population, fewer than a million out of a total of seven million children, now attended aided schools, and the proportion of single-school area

---

[1] The average size of a Church of England school was 111, that of a Roman Catholic school 261 and that of a county school 283. Almost 4,000 Anglican schools had fewer than 100 pupils. *Report,* 1959. *op. cit.,* Table 10.

[2] See Appendix C.   [3] *Religious Education in Schools,* para. 65.

schools had been drastically reduced. It had been expected that aided status would place a great burden on voluntary resources and prove a searching test of the devotion of religious congregations to their schools. Indeed it had been deliberately intended that conviction and self-sacrifice rather than past benevolence should be the criteria of their existence. In the event the strain had exceeded all wartime estimates and had necessitated a measure of alleviation.

✶   ✶   ✶   ✶   ✶

More than ninety years have elapsed since the formal establishment of the dual system in this country. In the intervening years since 1870 the entire aspect of education has changed; in the nineteenth century the State was concerned merely with elementary education and money was spent grudgingly in order to establish a bare minimum standard. The leading statesmen of the age were hardly interested in the educational needs of the country. Their passions lay elsewhere and education was a tiresome aspect of domestic legislation which they supported without zeal or enthusiasm. In contrast, education in the mid-twentieth century is recognised as a national investment, and on grounds of expediency alone the State must develop all available talent. Education has a prominent place in the pronouncements of party leaders and in the pledges of Parliamentary candidates; it touches the hopes and aspirations of large numbers of parents, it is a constant topic of discussion in the press and on sound and television broadcasting. Education has become news.

In the past the great spring of popular education was voluntary enterprise and the system of national education still draws strength and vigour from the variety of traditions within it. For our own age, which is struggling to preserve and uphold moral standards, no tradition is so vital as that of the church schools which link faith and practice. The churches are still, as they have been since 1870, partners in the national system of education, and the principle of the financial 'void' which Gladstone required of them has persisted to our own day. But circumstances have changed; local authority schools now predominate and the church school is the exception, although all publicly provided schools are required to give undenominational religious instruction. There is a sense, therefore, in which justice requires that

N

those for whom undenominational instruction is no substitute, either for the dogmatic content of their religion or for the religious atmosphere of their schools, should not be penalised for their beliefs. Abstract justice, however, is one thing, practical politics are another, and as yet a reopening of the whole issue would be premature. The principle of the 'void' therefore remains, and supporters of voluntary schools must bear a financial burden over and above their general contribution to education in the form of rates and taxes. But it is a burden which is no longer crushing and unbearable, and many churchmen are wise enough to value the status of their schools and to appreciate that independence is a privilege worth paying for.

The problem as yet remains unresolved. In the past it was confused by political and sectarian issues, but today public opinion is indifferent to religious feuds, and the political parties are no longer divided on a matter which can now be debated calmly and rationally. What lies ahead? In the foreseeable future there are certain to be further alleviations and adjustments to enable the churches to keep up with current requirements in education; in the more distant future the whole question is bound to come up again. At that point, perhaps a generation hence, the assumptions on which the dual system was based can be re-examined and considered in the light of the contemporary situation. Fisher and Butler both in their day judged the time and circumstances inopportune for the introduction of the Scottish settlement. But even since 1944 significant changes have taken place: opinion has softened; numerically, the fully denominational schools have shrunk to a small, though a vital, proportion of the whole. It may well be that some future Minister will be able to merge the two systems on terms which will ensure the distinctive character of denominational schools. Indeed such a unification may seem to him a necessary practical expedient, the only way of securing equality of opportunity for all the nation's children. Native empiricism may in the end find a permanent 'English solution' to reconcile the claims of Church and State.

Bibliography

A. PRIMARY SOURCES

Reference to archival material is made in the notes. Board of Education files for the period 1900–8 are now in the Public Record Office, but at the time of writing were still in process of being classified.

The following sources have also been used:

1. *On the voluntary Societies*
   (*a*) Manuscript records.
   Minutes of the Standing Committees and sub-committees of the Catholic Poor School Committee and the Catholic Education Council.
   Minutes of the Standing Committee and of sub-committees of the National Society.
   (*b*) Printed records.
   Annual Reports of the following: the British and Foreign School Society, the Catholic Poor School Committee, the Catholic Education Council, the National Society, the Wesleyan Education Committee.

2. *On the School Boards*
   (*a*) Manuscript records.
   Minutes of the School Boards of Birmingham, Leeds, London and Manchester.
   (*b*) Printed records.
   Reports of the School Boards of Birmingham, London, Leeds and Manchester. Addresses and miscellaneous school board publications.

3. *Government publications*
   Parliamentary Debates (Hansard).
   Parliamentary Papers.

4. *Proceedings of Church Assembly*

5. *Letters*
   In British Museum, Additional Manuscripts.

6. *Periodicals*, etc.
   Journals, organs of the national, religious and educational press. Pamphlets published by the following: Education Settlement Committee, Fabian Society, Liberal Publication Department,

Liberation Society, National Conference on Education, National Free Church Council, National Education League, National Education Union, National Society, National Union of Teachers, Nuffield Committee, Primrose League, Sword of the Spirit, Trades Union Congress.

B. SECONDARY SOURCES

Adams, F., *A History of the Elementary School Contest in England*, 1882.

Allen, B. M., *Sir Robert Morant*, 1930.

Amery, J., *Life of Joseph Chamberlain*, vol. IV, 1951.

Armytage, W. H. G., *A. J. Mundella 1825–1897*, 1951.

——, 'A. J. Mundella, Vice-President of the Council and the Schools' Question 1880–85', in *English Historical Review*, vol. 63, 1948.

Armstrong, R. A., *H. W. Crosskey, His Life and Work*, Birmingham, 1895.

Bateman, C. T., *John Clifford*, 1904.

Beck, G. A. (ed.), *The English Catholics 1850–1950*, 1950.

Bell, G. K. A., *Randall Davidson*, 2 vols., Oxford, 1938.

——, *The English Church*, 1942.

Bingham, J. H., *Education under the local authority in Sheffield. The Period of the School Board, 1870–1903*. Sheffield, 1949.

Binns, H. B., *A Century of Education*, 1908.

Birrell, A., *Things Past Redress*, 1937.

Braley, E. F., *A Policy in Religious Education*, 1941.

Brown, C. K. F., *The Church's Part in Education: 1833–1944*, 1944.

Brown, W. F., *Through the Windows of Memory*, 1946.

Burgess, H. G., *Enterprise in Education*, 1958.

Carr, J. A., *Life and Work of Archbishop Benson*, 1898.

Connell, W. F., *The Educational Thought and Influence of Matthew Arnold*, 1950.

Cornish, F. Warre, *A History of the Church of England in the Nineteenth Century*, 2 vols., 1910.

Cox, J. G. Snead, *Life of Cardinal Vaughan*, 2 vols., 1910.

Craik, H., *The State in its Relation to Education*, 1884.

Dale, A. W., *Life of R. W. Dale of Birmingham*, 1898.

Dale, R. W., *The History of Congregationalism*, 1907.

Davies, R. E. (ed.), *John Scott Lidgett: a Symposium*, 1957.

Denison, G. A., *Notes of My Life*, Oxford, 1878.

Denison, L. E. (ed.), *Fifty Years at East Brent*, 1901.

Dugdale, B. E. C., *Arthur James Balfour*, 2 vols., 1936.

Edmonds, E. L., *A Critical Investigation into the History, Function and Status of Local Inspection of Schools*. Ph.D. Thesis of the University of Leeds, 1960.

Educational Yearbook of the International Institute of Teachers, Columbia, 1932.

Evans, W. and Claridge, W., *James Hirst Hollowell and the Movement for Civic Control in Education*, Manchester, 1911.

Evennett, H. O., *The Catholic Schools of England and Wales*, Oxford, 1944.

Edwards, J. Hugh, *David Lloyd George, the Man and the Statesman*, 2 vols., 1930.

Fisher, H. A. L., *An Unfinished Autobiography*, Oxford, 1940.

Garbett, C., *The Claims of the Church of England*, 1947.

Gardiner, A. G., *Life of Sir William Harcourt*, 1923.

Garvin, J. L., *Life of Joseph Chamberlain*, 3 vols., 1933.

Gautrey, Y., *School Board Memories*, 1937.

Green, J. L., *Life of Jesse Collings*, 1920.

Grier, L., *Achievement in Education: the Work of Michael Sadler, 1885–1935*, 1951.

Gregory, R., *Elementary Education*, 1905.

Grove, R. B., *An Investigation into Public Opinion and the Passing of the Education Act of 1870*, M.A. Thesis of the University of London, 1949.

Halévy, E., *History of the English People in the Nineteenth Century*, 6 vols., 1951.

Heenan, J. C., *Cardinal Hinsley*, 1944.

Henson, H. H., *Sir William Anson, 1843–1914*, 1929.

——, *The Church of England, its Nature and its Future*, Cambridge, 1939.

Hodder, E., *Life and Work of the Seventh Earl of Shaftesbury*, 3 vols., 1886–7.

——, *Life of Samuel Morley*, 1889.

Holland, B., *Life of Spencer Compton, Eighth Duke of Devonshire*, 1911.

Howard, C. H. D., *Lord Randolph Churchill*. History, vol. 25, 1940.

——, 'The Parnell Manifesto of 21st November 1885 and the Schools' Question', *English Historical Review*, vol. 62, 1947.

Hughes, D. Price, *Life of Hugh Price Hughes*, 2 vols., 1907.

Iremonger, F. A., *William Temple, Archbishop of Canterbury, his Life and Letters*, 1948.

Jenkins, R. H., *Mr. Balfour's Poodle*, 1954.

——, *Sir Charles Dilke*, 1958.

Kekewich, G., *The Education Department and After*, 1920.

Kirk Smith, H., *William Thomson, Archbishop of York*, 1958.

Knox, E. A., *The Tractarian Movement*, 1933.

Leese, J., *Personalities and Power in English Education*, Leeds, 195

Leeson, S. E. Spencer, *Christian Education*, 1947.

Lidgett, J. Scott, *My Guided Life*, 1935.

Maccoby, S., *English Radicalism, 1853–86*, 1938.

——, *English Radicalism, 1886–1914*, 1953.

Macdonnell, J. C., *Life and Correspondence of William Connor Magee, Archbishop of York*, 2 vols., 1891.

Marchant, J., *Dr. John Clifford*, 1924.

Martin, A. P., *Life and Letters of Robert Lowe, Viscount Sherbrooke*, 2 vols., 1893.

Mathews, H. F., *Methodism and the Education of the People, 1791–1851*, 1949.

McKenna, S., *Reginald McKenna, 1863–1943*, 1948.

Miall, A., *Life of Edward Miall*, 1884.

Montmorency, J. E. G. de, *National Education and National Life*, 1906.

——, *State Intervention in English Education*, Cambridge, 1902.

Morley, J., *Life of Gladstone*, 3 vols., 1905.

Ogg, D., *Herbert Fisher, 1865–1940*, 1947.

Oldmeadow, E. J., *Francis, Cardinal Bourne*, 2 vols., 1940–4.

Purcell, E. S., *Life of Cardinal Manning*, 2 vols., 1895.

Reid, T. Wemyss, *Life of the Rt. Hon. William Edward Forster*, 2 vols., 1888.

Religious Education in Schools, Report of an Inquiry by the Institute of Christian Education, 1954.

Rigg, J. H., *National Education and Public Elementary Schools*, 1873.

——, *Essays for the Times*, 1866.

Sacks, B., *The Religious Issue in the State Schools of England and Wales, 1902–14*, New Mexico, 1961.

Sandford, E. G., *Frederick Temple, Archbishop of Canterbury*, 2 vols., 1906.

Shewell M., E. J., *An Historical Investigation of the Development of a Local System of Education in the City of Birmingham, from 1870 to 1924*, M.A. Thesis of the University of London, 1952.

Smith, W. O. Lester, *To whom do Schools Belong?*, Oxford, 1943.

Spalding, T. A., *The Work of the London School Board*, 1900.

Spender, J. A. and Asquith, C., *Life of H. H. Asquith, Lord Oxford and Asquith*, 2 vols., 1932.

Spender, J. A., *Life of the Rt. Hon. Sir Henry Campbell-Bannerman*, 2 vols., 1926.

Telford, J., *Life of James Harrison Rigg*, 1909.

Temple, W., *Life of Bishop Percival*, 1921.

Townsend, H., *The Claims of the Free Churches*, 1949.

Trevelyan, G. O., *Sir George Otto Trevelyan*, 1932.

Webb, S., *London Education*, 1904.

Wilson, J. M., *Autobiography, 1836–1931*, 1932.

Wolf, L., *Life of the First Marquess of Ripon*, 2 vols., 1921.

Yearbooks of Education, 1933, 1940 and 1951.

Other secondary sources, when briefly used,
are quoted in full in the notes.

Appendix A

MINISTERS AND SECRETARIES

Vice-Presidents of the
Committee of Council on Education   *Secretaries*

1870–1874	W. E. Forster	
1874–1878	Lord Sandon	
1878–1880	Lord George Hamilton	Sir Francis Sandford, 1870–84
1880–1885	A. J. Mundella	
1885–1886	Hon. E. Stanhope	
1886	Sir Henry Holland	Patrick Cumin, 1884–90
1886	Sir Lyon Playfair	
1886–1887	Sir Henry Holland	
1887–1892	Sir William Hart Dyke	
1892–1895	A. H. D. Acland	Sir George Kekewick, 1890–1902
1895–1900	Sir J. E. Gorst	

Presidents of the
Board of Education

1900–1902	Duke of Devonshire	
1902–1905	Marquess of Londonderry	
1905–1907	Augustine Birrell	Sir Robert Morant, 1903–11
1907–1908	R. McKenna	
1908–1911	W. Runciman	
1911–1915	J. A. Pease	
1915–1916	A. Henderson	Sir Lewis Amherst Selby-Bigge, 1911–25
1916	Lord Crewe	
1916–1922	H. A. L. Fisher	
1922–1924	E. F. L. Wood[1]	
1924	C. P. Trevelyan	
1924–1929	Lord Eustace Percy	Sir Aubrey Symonds, 1925–31
1929–1931	Sir Charles Trevelyan	
1931	H. B. Lees-Smith	Sir Edward Pelham, 1931–7
1931–1932	Sir Donald Maclean	
1932–1935	Lord Irwin[1]	
	(Viscount Halifax)	

[1] E. F. L. Wood became Lord Irwin in 1925 and Viscount Halifax in 1933.

1935–1937   Oliver Stanley
1937–1938   Earl Stanhope   Sir Maurice Holmes, 1937–45
1938–1940   Earl De La Warr
1940–1941   Harold Ramsbotham
1941–1944   R. A. Butler

Ministers of Education

1944–1945   R. A. Butler   Sir John Maud, 1945–52
1945   Richard Law
1945–1947   Ellen Wilkinson
1947–1951   George Tomlinson
1951–1954   Florence Horsburgh
1954–1957   Sir David Eccles   Sir Gilbert Flemming, 1952–9
1957   Viscount Hailsham
1957–1959   Geoffrey Lloyd
1959–1962   Sir David Eccles   Dame Mary Smieton, 1959–
1962–   Sir Edward Boyle

Appendix B

LEGISLATION AFFECTING
VOLUNTARY SCHOOLS

*A summary of relevant legislation 1870 to the present day
(attempted legislation is in italics)*

1870   33 and 34 Vic. c. 75. Elementary Education Act. (Forster Act.)

School boards were to be formed to supply deficiencies of school accommodation (Clause 6) and to have absolute discretion to supply additional accommodation. (Clause 18.)

A Conscience Clause was to apply in all schools (Clause 7) and board schools were forbidden to teach any religious catechism or formulary 'distinctive of any particular denomination'. (Clause 14 (2).)

School boards were permitted to pay school fees of poor children at any public elementary school (Clause 25) and given power to set up free schools. (Clause 26.)

At school board elections every voter was to have as many votes as there were members of the school board. (Clause 29.)

Parliamentary grants were not to be made in respect of religious instruction and were not to exceed in any year the school's income derived from other sources. (Clause 97 (1) and (2).)

1876   39 and 40 Vic. c. 79. Elementary Education Act. (Sandon Act.)

School boards and, in districts where there were no school boards, school attendance committees (appointed by councils in boroughs and Guardians in parishes) were to enforce attendance. (Clause 7.)

Poor parents of children attending voluntary schools were to apply to Guardians for payment of school fees. (Clause 10 which repealed Clause 25, 33 and 34 Vic. c. 75.)

Schools could earn up to 17s. 6d. per child and more where the extra was matched by income from other sources. (Clause 19 (1) which replaced Clause 97 (2) Vic. c. 75.)

1891   54 and 55 Vic. c. 56. Elementary Education Act. (Free Education Act.)

A Parliamentary fee grant of 10s. a year was to be payable for each child in a public elementary school and fees were to be reduced by that amount or abolished entirely. (Clauses 1 and 2.) Voluntary schools might pay their fee grants into a common fund and so help each other. (Clause 6.)

1896   59 *Vic. Education Bill. Bill 172.*

Provided for the establishment of county and county boroughs as authorities for education with powers over secondary and technical education and the duty of distributing a special aid grant to necessitous schools. (Clauses 1–4.)

The 17s. 6d. limit was to be abolished (repeal of Clause 19 (1), 39 and 40 Vic. c. 79), and voluntary schools were to be exempt from the rates.

Denominational teaching was to be permitted in board schools. (Clause 27.)

1897   60 Vic. c. 5. Voluntary Schools Act.

Aid grant of 5s. per scholar was to be paid to necessitous schools and voluntary schools were enjoined to form associations. (Clauses 1 and 3.)

The 17s. 6d. limit was abolished by repeal of Clause 19 (1), 39 and 40 Vic. c. 79 (Clause 2), and voluntary schools were to be exempt from the rates. (Clause 3.)

1902   2 Ed. 7. c. 42. Education Act. (Balfour Act.)

New local education authorities (councils of counties and county boroughs) were to take over the work of the school boards and also to control secular instruction in public elementary schools not provided by them. (Clause 5.)

Managers of non-provided schools were to include representatives (usually one third) appointed by L.E.A. (Clause 7 (1) (d).)

Managers of non-provided schools were to appoint teachers, subject to the consent of the L.E.A., and to control religious instruction. (Clause 7 (1) (c) and (6).)

1904   4 Ed. 7. c. 18. Education (Local Authority Default) Act.

Empowered the Board of Education, in case of default by an L.E.A., to pay money direct to managers of schools and deduct the amount from the grant payable to the L.E.A. (Clause 1.)

1906   6. Ed. 7. *Education (England and Wales) Bill. Bill 160. (Birrell Bill.)*

All non-provided schools were to be transferred to L.E.A.s. Ordinary 'facilities' for special religious instruction (on two mornings a week) were to apply in the majority of transferred schools. (Clause 3.) Extended 'facilities' to apply to those schools in urban areas where four-fifths of the parents voted for them. (Clause 4.)

1907 7 Ed. 7. *Special Religious Instruction Bill. Bill 73. (1st McKenna Bill.)*

A one clause measure designed to transfer from the L.E.A. to managers the cost of denominational instruction (estimated at one fifteenth of teachers' salaries) in non-provided schools.

1908 8. Ed. 7. *Elementary Education (England and Wales) Bill. Bill 112. (2nd McKenna Bill.)*

All rate aided schools were to be under the control of the L.E.A.s. (Clause 1.) Non-provided schools in single-school areas must be transferred to L.E.A.s and in these schools denominational instruction might be given out of school hours; remaining non-provided schools were to be given the option of becoming contracting out schools. (Clause 2.)

1908 8. Ed. 7. *Elementary Education (England and Wales) Bill. Bill 376. (Runciman Bill.)*

All rate aided schools were to be under the control of L.E.A.s. In transferred schools denominational instruction might be given on two mornings a week if paid for by the denominations themselves. Non-provided schools in single-school areas must be transferred to L.E.A.s; remaining non-provided schools were given the option of becoming contracting out schools.

1930 21 Geo. 5. *Education Bill. Bill 203. Trevelyan Bill.*

L.E.A.s were empowered to give financial aid to managers of non-provided schools to enable them to make enlargements or alterations for purposes of reorganisation. (Clause 2.) L.E.A.s were also empowered to make arrangements for children transferred from non-provided schools under programmes of reorganisation to receive denominational instruction. (Clause 3.)

1936 26 Geo. 5 and 1 Ed. 8. c. 41. Education Act.

L.E.A.s were empowered to make grants of up to 75 per cent for the building of new schools for senior pupils. (Clause 8.) Teachers in these schools were to be appointed by L.E.A.s but managers were to be consulted before the appointment of any 'reserved' teachers who were to give denominational instruction. (Clause 10.)

Religious instruction in accordance with the syllabus used by the L.E.A. was to be available in non-provided schools. (Clause 12.)

1939   2 and 3 Geo. 6. c. 60. Senior Public Elementary Schools (Liverpool) Act.

In order to supply accommodation for senior children in nonprovided schools the local authority was empowered to build schools and charge rent for them. (Clause 1.)

1944   7 and 8 Geo. 6. c. 31. Education Act. (Butler Act.)

Schools established by L.E.A.s were to be known as county schools, schools otherwise established were to be known as voluntary schools. (Clause 9 (2).) In those voluntary schools which were aided and special agreement, two-thirds of the managers were to be foundation managers, in those which were controlled, one-third of the managers were to be foundation managers. (Clause 18(a).)

In all county and voluntary schools the day must begin with collective worship and religious instruction must be given, subject to a Conscience Clause. (Clause 25 (1) (2) and (3).)

In county schools religious instruction was to be in accordance with an agreed syllabus. (Clause 26.)

In controlled schools at parents' request religious instruction in accordance with the trust deed might be given by 'reserved' teachers twice a week; otherwise religious instruction was to be in accordance with an agreed syllabus. (Clause 27.)

In aided or special agreement schools religious instruction was to be under the control of managers and in accordance with the trust deed. (Clause 28.)

The Minister and local authorities were to have regard to the general principle that, 'so far as is compatible with the provision of efficient instruction and training and the avoidance of unreasonable public expenditure, pupils are to be educated in accordance with the wishes of their parents.' (Clause 76.)

Ministry grants of 50 per cent towards alterations and repairs were to be available to aided and special agreement schools. (Clause 102.) Similar grants were to be payable to schools transferred to new sites and to schools accommodating 'displaced pupils.' (Clauses 103 and 104.)

1946   9 and 10 Geo. 6. c. 50. Education Act.

L.E.A.s were permitted to enlarge controlled schools when enlargement did not amount to the establishment of a new school. (Clause 1.)

1953   1 and 2 Eliz. 2. c. 33. Education (Miscellaneous Provisions) Act.

Widened the definition of 'displaced pupils' in Clause 104, 7 and 8 Geo. 6. c. 31. (Clause 1.) L.E.A.s were permitted to establish new voluntary controlled schools. (Clause 2.)

1959 7 and 8 Eliz. 2. c. 60. Education Act.

75 per cent was to be substituted for 50 per cent as the amount of the grant payable in respect of aided and special agreement schools under 7 and 8 Geo. 6. c. 31. (Clause 1 (i).)

The Minister was also enabled to make a grant of 75 per cent towards the cost of new aided schools to provide accommodation for pupils who had already attended aided primary schools. The grant was to be available only for work subsequent to programmes notified to L.E.A.s for the twelve months beginning April 1959. (Clause 1 (2) and (3).)

Appendix C

SCHOOL STATISTICS

I. *Board and Voluntary Schools, 1870–1900*

	No. of schools	*Average attendance*	*Expenditure**			*Annual grant**		*Fees**		*Voluntary contributions or rates**		
			£	s.	d.	s.	d.	s.	d.	£	s.	d.
1870												
C. of E.	6,382	844,334	1	5	7½	8	9	7	11¾	0	7	5¾
R.C.	350	66,066	1	0	6	8	10	4	10¾	0	6	3
British and Wesleyan	1,549	241,989	1	6	1½	8	11¼	10	8½	0	5	4½
All Voluntary	8,281	1,152,389	1	5	5	9	9¼	8	4¼	0	6	11¾
1880												
C. of E.	11,416	1,471,615	1	14	10¼	15	3¾	10	3½	0	7	9¾
R.C.	758	145,629	1	10	6	15	3½	8	4¾	0	7	4¼
British	1,438	243,012	1	16	0¼	15	9¾	13	1¼	0	6	3
Wesleyan	569	121,408	1	14	7	16	0½	15	6¾	0	2	7
All Voluntary	14,181	1,981,664	1	14	7¾	15	5	10	9¾	0	7	3
Board	3,433	769,252	2	1	11¾	15	7¾	9	0	0	18	7
1890												
C. of E.	11,922	1,682,167	1	16	10½	17	5¼	10	8	0	6	11½
R.C.	946	193,838	1	14	6½	17	4¼	9	6¾	0	7	2¾
British	1,365	255,496	1	19	3¼	17	11	13	7½	0	6	0¼
Wesleyan	551	131,934	1	17	4	18	0¾	16	1¾	0	2	7
All Voluntary	14,784	2,263,435	1	16	11½	17	6¼	11	2¾	0	6	7½
Board	4,714	1,468,892	2	5	11½	18	5¾	9	1	0	18	0½
1900												
C. of E.	11,777	1,885,802	2	6	3	20	8	1	4	0	6	7
R.C.	1,045	255,036	2	4	4	20	0	0	7	0	6	2
British	1,079	220,032	2	9	5	20	9	2	11	0	7	1
Wesleyan	458	125,727	2	6	8	20	7	4	10	0	3	2
All Voluntary	14,359	2,486,597	2	6	4½	20	7	1	5¼	0	6	4¾
Board	5,758	2,201,049	2	17	7½	21	3	0	4½	1	5	6¼

* For each child in average attendance.

Taken from the *Reports of the Education Department*.

II. Council and Voluntary Schools, 1903 and 1938

Year	Council schools		C. of E. schools		R.C. schools		Methodist		Others	
	Number	Pupils	Number	Pupils	Number	Pupils	Number	Pupils	Number	Pupils
1903	6,003	2,870,213	11,687	2,338,602	1,058	337,295	452	157,519	1,042	263,651
1938	10,363	3,540,512	8,979	1,125,497	1,266	377,073	119	17,235	189*	27,168
Increase or Decrease	+4,360	+670,299	−2,708	−1,213,105	+208	+39,778	−333	−140,282	−853	−236,484

* The number of Jewish schools was given in 1938 as 13. The other *Reports* quoted in this Appendix do not list Jewish schools separately.
Taken from the *Reports of the Board of Education.*

III. County and Voluntary Schools, 1959

	County		Aided		Controlled		Special agreement		Total	
	Schools or depts	Pupils	Schools or depts	Pupils	Schools or depts	Pupils	Schools or depts	Pupils	Schools or depts	Pupils
County	18,861	5,337,481							18,861	5,337,481
Church of England			3,378	411,555	4,519	463,138	25	8,405	7,976	889,692
Roman Catholic			1,960	500,743	2	179	66	27,072	2,033	529,972
Others			148	51,676	307	89,453			460	144,042

Taken from *Education in 1959*, Table 3.
[Note. The status of 64 voluntary schools with 11,485 pupils was still undetermined.]

IV. *New Voluntary Schools, 1945–59*

	Aided		Controlled		Special agreement		Total	
	Schools or depts	Pupils	Schools or depts	Pupils	Schools or depts	Pupils	Schools or depts	Pupils
Church of England	71	15,780	87	16,290	10	3,555	168	35,625
Roman Catholic	273	70,605			68	25,870	341	96,475
Others	24	4,825	33	4,835	1	360	58	10,020

Taken from *Education in 1959*, 18.

V. *New Voluntary Schools, 1945–61*

	Aided		Controlled		Special Agreement		Total	
	Schools or depts	Pupils	Schools or depts	Pupils	Schools or depts	Pupils	Schools or depts	Pupils
Church of England	98	22,140	89	16,670	19	6,420	206	45,230
Roman Catholic	374	101,275			96	36,610	470	137,885
Others	31	5,925	36	5,625	2	810	69	12,360

Taken from *Education in 1961*, 13.

Appendix D

SCOTTISH EDUCATION ACTS

Legislation relevant to church schools

1872 35 and 36 Vic. c. 62. Education (Scotland) Act.

The preamble said that managers of public schools could, as in the past, give religious instruction to children whose parents did not object.

(School boards, therefore, acted according to 'use and wont'. In the words of one of Her Majesty's Inspectors in 1878, 'The public schools are to all intents and purposes denominational schools. Public and Presbyterian are practically interchangeable terms.')

1918 8 and 9 Geo. 5. c. 48. Education (Scotland) Act.

Clause 18 outlined the conditions of transfer of voluntary schools to local authorities and also the conditions on which new schools might be built.

All teachers appointed to the staff of any transferred school by the education authorities 'shall in every case be teachers who . . . are approved as regards their religious belief and character by representatives of the church or denominational body in whose interests the school has been conducted'. (Subsection 3 ii.)

'the education authority shall appoint as supervisor without renumeration of religious instruction for each such school, a person approved as regards religious belief and character and it shall be the duty of the supervisor so appointed to report to the education authority as to the efficiency of the religious instruction given in such school. The supervisor shall have right of entry to the school at all times set apart for religious instruction or observance. The education authority shall give facilities for the holding of religious examinations in every such school'. (Subsection 3 iii.)

All voluntary schools had to be transferred within two years of the passing of the Act or lose the Government grant. (Subsection 5.)

If it was established 'after such enquiry as the Department deem necessary that a new (voluntary) school is required . . . it shall be lawful for the education authority of that area to provide a new school to be held, maintained and managed by them. . . .' (Subsection 8.)

[Within two years of the passing of the Act 301 voluntary schools were transferred (of which 226 were Roman Catholic).

Between 1918 and 1943 36 new Roman Catholic schools and 1 new Episcopalian school were built by the local authorities. (*White Paper*, 1943, Cmd. 6426.)]

Index

PRINTED IN GREAT BRITAIN BY ROBERT MACLEHOSE AND CO. LTD
THE UNIVERSITY PRESS, GLASGOW